BEHIND CLOSED DOORS

Also by Seth Alexander Thévoz

Club Government: How the Early Victorian World was Ruled from London Clubs

BEHIND CLOSED DOORS

THE
SECRET LIFE OF
LONDON PRIVATE
MEMBERS' CLUBS

SETH ALEXANDER THÉVOZ

ROBINSON

ROBINSON

First published in Great Britain in 2022 by Robinson

5 7 9 10 8 6 4

A CIP catalogue record for this book
is available from the British Library.

ISBN: 978-1-47214-646-5 (hardback)
ISBN: 978-1-47214-647-2 (trade paperback)

Typeset in Adobe Garamond Pro by SX Composing DTP, Rayleigh, Essex

Printed and bound in Great Britain by Clays Ltd, Elcograf S.p.A.

Papers used by Robinson are from well-managed forests
and other responsible sources.

Robinson
An imprint of
Little, Brown Book Group
Carmelite House
50 Victoria Embankment
London EC4Y 0DZ

An Hachette UK Company

www.hachette.co.uk

www.littlebrown.co.uk

For H. B. H.,

to whom I owe so much.

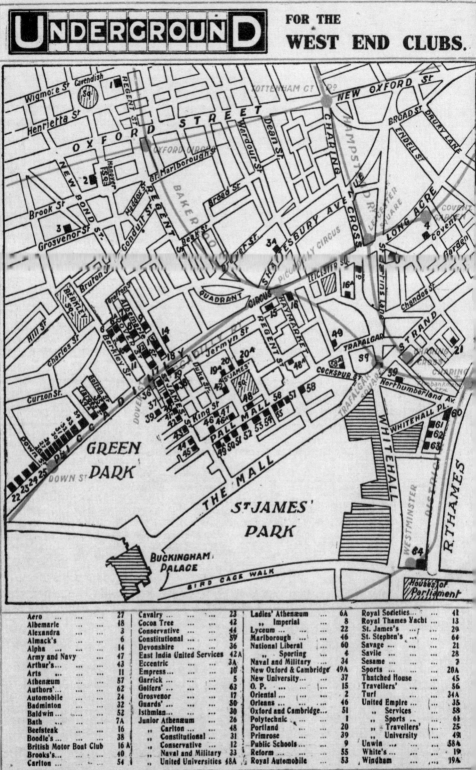

London Clubland at its height, before the First World War. Source: *Clubland* journal (1910). Picture reproduced by permission of the British Library.

Contents

Introduction

'Yes, but . . . what do people *do* in these clubs?'

I was at Buckingham Palace, working a summer job as a tour guide at the age of nineteen, and amid the gossip of the servants' canteen I'd let slip that I'd just been elected to a club for the first time. Even though I'd made it perfectly clear that this club was basically just a very convivial lounge, and even though the palace's footmen were no strangers to the idea that, far from Olympian debauchery, closed doors usually bred quiet domesticity, they were still obsessed by the idea that . . . *something* dwelt behind these closed doors. As the conversation went further, and was brought up time and again, it became obvious that a number of assumptions were made about the kind of place I had joined.

It had to be entirely male, white, affluent, Protestant (and Anglican to boot), not to mention elderly, with nary a member under seventy. Moreover, its politics were expected to be reactionary bordering on fascist, and the Club's main feature being a roaring fireplace surrounded by snoozing elderly members.

All of these assumptions are wrong. They could also have been entirely right.

How we think of London private members' clubs is dominated by the image they presented in the late twentieth century – when they were trapped in a cycle of decline. The above is an accurate pen-portrait of what a club looks like when it is on its last legs; my last book referred, in what David Palfreyman called 'rather un-academic language',[1] to 'clapped-out old farts sat by a roaring fire, sunk in deep leather armchairs, hiding behind newspapers and passing out from a surfeit of port'.[2]

But it was not always that way. And it is very unrepresentative of the buzzing, thriving, wheeler-dealer places these clubs were at their peak. It often comes as a complete surprise to tell people, for instance, that not only did women's clubs exist in prime Central London hotspots as early as the 1860s, but that more than fifty of these clubs once flourished in the capital. Only one of those survives today, barely hinting at the entire world which once existed. Nor do people fully believe that women frequently visited men's clubs (successive film and TV adaptations of *Around the World in 80 Days*, complete with the invariable 'Great Caesar's ghost! A woman, in the club!' scenes, have a lot to answer for); nor that there were already mixed-sex clubs in London by the 1870s. Nor that Victorian club memberships were rather more diverse – ethnically, socially, religiously – than people give them credit for. Nor that clubs served as the template for a wide variety of popular institutions, from sports clubs to sex clubs.

Behind Closed Doors tells the story of London's hidden world of private members' clubs, from their seventeenth-century beginnings to the present. In telling this story, a clear theme emerges: everything we instinctively think we knew about clubs is wrong. Yes, they may have started out as white, male, aristocratic watering holes – but that's only part of the story. The book looks at how all sections of society built their own clubs and lived their lives there, highbrow and lowbrow, women and men, black and white, working, middle as well as upper class, international as well as British. It shows how

2

the club was central to the British doing leisure in a distinctive way through the centuries.

This is a history, but it is not a *strictly* chronological one. The chapters are themed and roughly chronological; and while they also have dates signposting when these themes were most obvious, there is also some flitting back and forth to show when things started, and where they would end.

If you are one of the tedious people who come up to me with striking regularity to ask variations on 'What is the best/most exclusive club?', or 'Which club should I join?', or even more explicitly, 'Which club keeps out the riff-raff, and how can I get in?', then this book is not for you. Nor is it for the man in North America who wrote to me, claiming already to be a member of a well-known European club (although I didn't believe him), asking to be introduced to a dozen American-based members so that they could help 'a friend' secure election to that club, promising me 'to compensate you for your time. Consider this an "introduction service" to gentlemen in clubland.'

On the other hand, if you are curious to understand a private world, hidden in plain sight, which has provided a sort of running thread alongside the last few centuries of history, then this book is very much written with you in mind.

It is tempting to walk into many a club, imagining that they must be dripping with history. Surprisingly, club members are not necessarily good sources of information. Today's historic London clubs inherited grand buildings, but not necessarily paperwork or archives. In reality, the most ornate features can be modern pastiches; and many of the tallest tales told of 'the good old days' are apocryphal anecdotes someone once heard about someone else's club and pinched for their own; or else garbled on the third retelling.

This is particularly true given the turnover in club committees. It is tempting to think of the 'glorious committee', benevolent and omniscient, gently administering the club for the benefit of future members. In reality, club committees are often as ignorant, bitchy and backbiting as the most Machiavellian nest of politicians, with a high turnover of differing regimes seeking to undo the 'dangerous innovations' of the last group, lending an irregular, 'stop-go' quality. Club servants – themselves just as prone to sport a sharp pair of fangs, if only to survive the whims of ever-changing committees – are often at the mercy of these changing administrations. The result is that there is nowhere near the continuity of records that club members like to pretend exists; and the truth is often a casualty of clubs shuttling back and forth between different regimes. This means that until a surge of interest among academics and architectural historians in the last thirty years, club history was often consigned to self-congratulatory back-slapping. Typically, most club histories would give you 'the story' (of doubtful provenance) about how the club was set up way back when, plus a dash of first-hand stories about the last decade or so of recent memory – and almost nothing in between. It was usually padded out with something about people getting drunk. The main appetite for club history was something in short, bite-sized chunks that could be understood in the bar after a heavy meal, and wasn't too taxing on the brain.

And Clubland legends and myths are rife – Davy, the elderly hall porter at Boodle's in the Second World War, who had spent his whole life working at the Club, showed actor David Niven around in 1939. He confidently insisted, 'Of course, the Scarlet Pimpernel, he was a member, sir, and all his gang, too.'[3] Naturally, the Scarlet Pimpernel was as fictional as Sherlock Holmes.

Much has been said about exclusivity in clubs – whole tracts have been written on the subject.[4] Yet it is a concept which many club members and club managers themselves do not understand. Clubs can often be held up as marvellous examples of exclusivity, citing their half-empty dining rooms and libraries, confusing exclusivity with simply being a failing business. And failed they have. I never tire of pointing out the statistic that nine out of ten traditional London clubs have gone bankrupt. Whereas there were once 400 of these establishments, there are now around forty. Nor has the process of decay stopped; the last decade has seen half a dozen historic London clubs close, while some others remain in serious financial trouble, especially after the Covid-19 pandemic stopped club members from exercising the one core purpose which their club serves: socialising.

Exclusivity – literally, the quality of defining a club based on excluding others – has had a chequered history with clubs. For one thing, it has not been a constant feature. London clubs in their original form had disreputable, even plebeian origins. They then went through an 'aristocratic phase' lasting barely fifty years, from the 1760s to the 1810s, before the defining feature of London clubs for over a century was *inclusivity*, as they successively sought to open their doors to more members, and ever more clubs were set up to meet a growing demand. Only in the half-century or so after the Second World War did they revert to being 'exclusive', and then as a symptom of decline rather than through any well-thought-through strategy. Where clubs have been dying out, it has been when the more ignorant, modern-day younger members have eagerly set about trying to cosplay around their imagined fantasy caricatures of what they *think* clubs once looked like, rather than finding out more about the truth – which is endlessly more fascinating.

So, I urge you to settle back with an aged tawny port and enjoy *Behind Closed Doors*. It may not be quite the story you were expecting.

Prologue

What a club looks like

'What does a club looks like?' It might seem like a superfluous question, but there is no agreed answer to this. Members of single-room establishments like Pratt's or the Beefsteak consider luxuries like a Smoking Room to be entirely redundant and are happy to cling to their solitary long table for just a couple of dozen guests; while members of the labyrinthian Royal Automobile Club are astonished that anywhere else could ever make do *without* multiple bars and dining rooms, over a hundred bedrooms, an Italianate marble swimming pool, a Turkish bath and a second clubhouse in the country. Clubs come in all shapes and sizes, from the grandest to the dingiest.

It is essential to have some idea of what lies in store for you behind those 'gloomy portals'. They almost inevitably come without any kind of brass plaque, because clubs tend not to advertise their presence. Given the degree to which angry mobs have occasionally vented onto them, this is perhaps wise. Yet once you get to know what lies behind those closed doors, they exercise considerably less awe and mystique, and the similarities between them become apparent.

It is a cliché that clubs are often not welcoming to visitors. What is often overlooked is that they are not always terribly welcoming to their own members either – especially new members. The actor

Donald Sinden had never set foot in the fêted Garrick Club before he was elected in 1960, and recalled his first visit, acceptance letter in hand, and how he showed it to the porter. 'I am a new member,' he said. 'Oh, yes. I will inform Commander Satterthwaite. You will find the bar at the top of the stairs' was the full extent of his greeting.[1] Given this aloofness, it is a wonder anyone joins any clubs at all.

If you set foot in a club, the first thing you are likely to encounter is the fearsome Porter's Lodge. There, someone in a uniform, who has typically worked there for decades, will ask you for your business, trying to stand vigilant against intruders. And there are a surprising number of would-be intruders every day: all manner of inquisitive journalists, curious tourists, students on a spree, not to mention a fairly regular smattering of Walter Mitty fantasists, drawn to private members' clubs like flies to a light bulb. Throughout history, one of the many secrets of Clubland has been the prevalence of gatecrashers.

A long-standing myth of Clubland is that the mighty Porter has an encyclopaedic memory of thousands of members, kept up to date with rolling updates on deaths, resignations and newly elected members. In reality, the beleaguered Porter has a near-impossible job, rarely knows more than a handful of regulars (some of whom fell behind with their fees years ago, and are still being genially waved in, years after they last paid a subscription). The beleaguered Porter cordially does their best to bluff their way through the day. Amiable familiarity or haughty frigidity are called upon, depending on whether they think a visitor has any real business there. As most clubs are far too polite to ask for anything as gauche as a membership card (there are rare exceptions),* 'club-crashing' is a lot more common

---

* The Carlton Club has had a strict card-access system, a necessity given its historic targeting by terrorists; and the Royal Automobile Club is so large with its 17,000 members, that no one ever seems to know anyone else, and so membership cards have to be produced at every transaction.

than you might think – perpetrators tend to get caught, but several steps inside, rather than on the front door.

The doyen of club-crashers notes his favourite method of blagging his way into their hallowed doors: 'Members' clubs have a soft spot for those who owe them money. Arrive in the morning with $250 in cash and demand entry to pay your bill from last night. There is no bill. You then insist, it's at the bar upstairs.'[2] He then elaborates on how one-off gatecrashers can become habitués of the club: 'Leave a scarf in the cloakroom permanently. Use the cloakroom ticket to get in the following day. Now you're pretty much a member.'[3] Of course, after the clubs have all read this, they will have refined their security arrangements; yet throughout the ages, the plucky intruder had regularly persisted.

Less successful than the pushy gatecrasher is the genuine visitor, trying to visit a friend who is a member. If the member has forgotten to leave word on the front desk, then the visitor will be ushered into a small, discreet waiting room opposite the Porter's Lodge. The visitor may think the room is located there for their own benefit. Actually, it is for the Club's. Shunting unknown visitors into a side room allows the Porter to make discreet enquiries as to whether the newcomer is as welcome as they claim to be. If it turns out their visit is unwelcome or unexpected, then the positioning of the side room allows the member they are trying to visit to be discreetly smuggled out, without ever meeting their would-be guest.[4]

Once you have negotiated your way past the Porter's Lodge, and found somewhere to put your coat, you will almost certainly find yourself in the Club's Main Hall, probably facing a Grand Staircase. This is where clubs love to show off. It is the architectural equivalent of being taken into somebody's seldom-used front room, which is normally out of bounds for the children, but is there to showcase to visitors, with all the porcelain and silverware on display. In clubs, there is usually fine art on display. Or failing that, there is mediocre art. If you recognise the pictures, it will be because they portray some of the Club's most famous members. If you have no idea who these anonymous paintings represent, they probably capture the Club's biggest donors and benefactors. There may also be a display cabinet or two. Relatively little actually tends to go on in the Main Hall, although there are exceptions to this, too, as it can be quite the busy interchange. None of the historical clubs were designed with bars, and so the Reform Club set up their bar in the central, pillared quadrangle, which was a stroke of genius: the whole point of a Main Hall (apart from making a favourable impression on visitors) is to serve as a people-watching space. As the very earliest prints of Clubland showed, the onlooker who sits in on the lobby, watching those coming and going, knows everything. Indeed, the term 'lobbyist' originated from this practice. Club-spotting around the front lobby was a keen practice of Victorian journalists; and while there were strict rules in place regulating what you could and couldn't divulge within a club, these rules rarely covered ground *just outside* a club. There was therefore a whole cottage industry in gossip that had been shared on the footsteps in front of a club, just outside its jurisdiction, yet holding the fresh, salacious promise of insights gleaned within, from one who watched the comings and goings of the lobby.

Where you visit within a club depends upon its layout. The most iconic room is usually the Salon, or Smoking Room. Eighteenth-century clubs called them Salons to reflect the fashionable court sensibilities which aped French aristocratic manners and affectations; although after the French Revolution, the popularity of the term declined. As the nineteenth century wore on, smoking grew as a pastime, especially after the Crimean War, when soldiers returned with Turkish cigarettes which exploded in popularity.

Intriguingly, smoking did not immediately catch on – many members harrumphed that they went to their clubs to *get away from* smoking. And before smoking had caught on, members snorted snuff in their clubs, not least as it exercised a similar social function, in much the same way that asking for a cigarette light served as a conversation opener (or pick-up line, should the members be that way inclined); members often laid down their own blends of snuff, the comparison of which could trigger off a whole conversation. Nevertheless, once smoking tobacco was introduced, the appetite for smoking grew exponentially – 'A man should always have an occupation', Oscar Wilde's Lady Bracknell wryly told us – and so almost all but the smallest clubs grew to have their own Smoking Room. Later clubs even employed extra technology to accommodate smoking, such as the extensive use of tiles to minimise the smell of tobacco soaking into a room's wallpaper and furniture. Of course, if you step into any Smoking Room now, the first thing you will be told is that smoking is forbidden, as a result of the UK's 2005 smoking ban. Today, it largely serves as a quiet room in which to read the day's papers.

The next 'essential' room in most clubs is the Dining Room, although the older clubs persist in calling this the Coffee Room, in recognition of the roots of the earliest clubs as purveyors of coffee, when it had the cachet of a luxury item. Most clubs have a 'Club Table', a large, long table where strangers are seated and can introduce themselves to one another, a holdover from the sociable long benches of Oxbridge colleges and the Inns of Court. Often invoked, though long gone, are the days when clubs insisted on boiling all loose change for cleanliness, and on ensuring that all newspapers were ironed with a hot iron to guarantee crispness.[5] Besides which, this seems to have only ever occurred in a tiny minority of clubs – although the iconic image endures.

11

Clubs operate their own dining culture, which can include elaborate theatrical ceremonies as the main course is carved, and the dessert trolley brought out for your delectation. Many clubs have banned tipping outright, on the slightly strained grounds that 'A club is an extension of the member's home, and the member wouldn't tip servants in their own home.' This hasn't stopped the practice of tipping from carrying on uninterrupted, but it happens discreetly, 'underground' even. A member giving staff gratuities can be disciplined or even expelled, while the staff member can face the back the niceties of twenty first century employment law have not always percolated through to every London club.

Generally speaking, good food in these Dining Rooms is a rarity. Club members tend to dine at their clubs in search of good company, rather than because the food is anything to write home about. Clubs *have* been known to be at the forefront of gastronomic creativity, particularly in the nineteenth century. Yet today's club Dining Rooms are often sad shadows of their former selves, and the members' strong emotional attachments to their clubs and particularly their friends there, often makes them defensive bordering on blind to the many shortcomings of Clubland cuisine.

Asking a member what they make of their own club is often singularly unilluminating. If they haven't resigned out of either apathy or disgust, then they are likely to see their club through rose-tinted spectacles. It is almost an extension of their home; often considerably nicer than the rather modest home they go back to. You might as well ask an acquaintance what they make of their marriage: unless they are in the middle of a bitter divorce, they are unlikely to give much away, beyond a few pleasantries. So there is little point in asking a member 'What is the best club?' (They will always answer, 'Mine, of course', unless they're trying to toady their way into another club.) Similarly, asking a member what the food is like is rarely going to produce a candid answer. Many members see an admission of poor food as a personal slight, reflecting badly on their taste. Everything is 'Fine'.

The 'school dinners' phase of post-war slop being doled out is (mostly) a thing of the past, but Clubland meals often fare poorly compared to today's high street restaurants. What keeps them going is regular custom, with devoted members. Furthermore, members cherish having the mere right to be *there*, without being shooed away. No one will berate a club member for nursing a single pint throughout the whole evening. They've paid their dues, and so they have as much right to be in the place as in their living room.

The heart of most clubs is their Bar. This is often relatively modest. Alcohol flowed freely in even the earliest clubs, yet it would have been considered vulgar to have a whole room dedicated solely to vending alcohol. Added to which, the refreshment facilities could be sufficiently primitive that bringing one's own bottle was the norm. Accordingly, most club bars were not built until well into the twentieth century, and they often have the look of a pop-up island sitting uneasily amid a grand, historic art gallery. To this day, some are actually rather flimsy plywood structures.

Club bars are also conveniently priced. Not only do the bars and dining rooms tend to be well below West End prices (whether by accident or design), but they are rather more generous with credit than most commercial venues. 'Put it on my tab!' is a well-worn refrain, and while modern clubs keep detailed electronic accounts tallying up colossal tabs, the image remains of the permanently unpaid club bar tab. This need not be deliberate or malicious – even the most diligent member might stagger out in a state of such intoxication that they have forgotten their own name, much less that there is a bill to pay. Clubs can be quite understanding about that sort of thing. After all, if the member is a 'regular', they'll be back, and the bill will be waiting for them. If they don't come back, then the club already has their name and address.

For all its architectural modesty, a club's bar is where the members mingle. Space works differently within the Bar from everywhere else in a club. While the 'Club Table' exists in the Dining Room, relatively few people use it. (I can well remember a forlorn club Chairman recounting his nights spent 'on duty' at the Club Table, waiting to welcome nervous new members, only to nibble at his supper in isolation for hours on end, as nobody dared to approach.) Most members prefer to stick to their own tables, especially if they are bringing in outside guests with the intention of impressing them. The last thing they want is a stranger pushily barging in and delivering a monologue on the Worshipful Company of Fishmongers for the rest of the evening. By contrast, at the Bar that is exactly what members expect; and at least with the Bar being a more explicitly sociable space, it is far more acceptable to move on from one conversation to the next. Seated in the Dining Room, you face the peril of being stuck next to a bore for three (or more) courses of a meal. The Bar can be located anywhere from the corner of the Salon, to a little cubby-hole beneath the underground space below the staircase. It is not unusual for even the grandest of clubs to have their Bar somewhere like a converted corridor. There is a method to this madness, as it forces people to be close together and actually to speak to one another rather than vanishing off into their own corners.

Then there are a range of club function rooms. These are usually terribly impressive, and lined with grand paintings, yet they lie empty and unused most of the time. They are a testament to when clubs were built on a bigger scale in past centuries, with a surplus of rooms and facilities. Clubs now make the most of them by hiring them out for private events, but they do so very begrudgingly, with the result that they are often left idle for much of the day. Clubs tend to be highly mistrustful of outside functions: they only started hiring out their luxurious rooms for film and TV location shoots from the 1960s and 1970s, when they were teetering most closely to bankruptcy. Many clubs are institutionally ill-prepared for the normal background checks routinely made by other organisations, and so clubs are often left traumatised by the inevitable publicity fiascos if, say, a fringe political group discreetly holds a fundraising event without the Club's members even realising it. To this day the Reform Club still shudders at the memory of when they agreed to rent out the premises for a fashion shoot for a few hours in 1978. The following year, they were rather astonished to find that a string of nude photographs featuring a nineteen-year-old Paula Yates made the front cover, centrefold and main feature of *Penthouse* magazine, all making extensive use of the Reform Club's furniture, architecture and statues. A member at the time later complained to me, 'She turned up in a fur coat, we had no idea what was going on.' Clubs live in perennial fear of this kind of all-too-easy embarrassment and can adopt a wariness towards external functions.

The more extensive clubs may well be blessed with sports facilities. Like the Bar, these were seldom purpose-built, but are usually a fairly recent addition, making the most of some reclaimed space around the back, or underground. The sporting facilities of London clubs tend to be minimal. In this respect, they are very different from the much more extensive clubs found overseas, including the Athletic Clubs that are so common in major North and South American cities, and the huge Gymkhana Clubs found across India, Pakistan and the USA.

Most London clubs have a Billiard Room or Snooker Room, mainly out of a sense of obligation that it's the kind of thing they *ought* to have. It's often the least used room in the Club, a thick layer of dust building up on the green baize cloth of the table. More extensive clubs like the Oxford and Cambridge Club have found the space for larger facilities like squash courts and viewing galleries to watch matches. Few London clubs have a swimming pool, and none can quite compete with the lush Italianate marble pool in the basement of the Royal Automobile Club, accompanied by a neighbouring in-house Turkish bath. Few Central London clubs have the space for tennis courts, apart from more suburban ones like the Hurlingham Club in Fulham or the Queen's Club in West Kensington. Several clubs do, however, host gymnasiums, especially as today's gym membership comes at a very similar cost to club membership, and as we shall see, the modern gym's business model actually flowed out of the club business model. For that reason, it is perhaps surprising that more clubs do not host a gym; but the main thing it has to contend with is the widespread view of many members that a club is a place where they tend to go to put on weight, rather than to shed it.

Among the most sought-after facilities of clubs are their bedrooms. These are a godsend to members who live out of town, and want somewhere safe, friendly, reputable and affordable to stay. Servicing the bedrooms is also a huge drain on a club's finances, and for that reason quite a few clubs don't have them at all. Clubs are not hotels, and they cannot accommodate the public at large. Their total *potential* clientele is tiny. For this reason, they cannot operate on the basis of any profitable hotel, of filling 70 per cent of the rooms 90 per cent of the time, or 90 per cent of the rooms 70 per cent of the time. The earliest London clubs lacked bedrooms, but there was a soaring demand for them, and clubs did everything they could to acquire overnight sleeping space, including purchasing next-door annexes, adding extra storeys, or even wholesale demolition and reconstruction of clubhouses to add bedrooms.

Until the Savoy and the Ritz revolutionised London hotels in the 1880s and 1890s, hotels were seen as rather disreputable places, synonymous with brothels, and no one wanted to admit to staying in one. The idea of 'lodging at my club' when in town therefore grew in popularity, as a reputable way for out-of-towners to find a room for the night if they lacked family connections in town. If you visit a club's bedroom today, you are still likely to be surprised at how modest it can be: barely enough space for a single bed, a small wardrobe, and perhaps a square metre of floor space. Clubs did not want members permanently residing in the building – there were such sumptuous facilities on offer on their doorstep that moving in full-time was always a temptation – and so there was a conscious decision to go for 'hair shirt treatment' in providing the most basic overnight rooms. And naturally, the watchful Porter on the front door tended to ensure that no outside guests ever stayed overnight with a member, although this did little to stem sexual liaisons between members and guests within the clubs; it merely made it more likely that encounters would be limited to between members, staff, or members and staff.

Private members' clubs are often thought of as, by definition, being rather shy and retiring places that want to avoid scrutiny; yet many have seen themselves as having a public role to play. For this reason, many have had what might be called 'performing spaces'. Indeed, several of the now-defunct clubs, like the New Players Theatre Club and the Arts Theatre Club were explicitly private members' clubs based around a theatre, with the pick of the seats reserved for members, and a members-only clubroom attached.* Even the earliest clubs like Brooks's tended to have a grand room like the Subscription Room, for hosting gaming tournaments (although they might seem rather crowded now). Today, clubs have gradually

---

* Both the New Players Theatre Club and the Arts Theatre Club still exist as theatres, but have long since ceased to provide the club facilities which used to define them.

begun to rediscover the need for this flexibility, turning that never-used third Drawing Room into the kinds of function rooms described above, hiring them out to host lucrative conferences. Yet unless you are looking at a theatrical club, the chances are that the performing spaces were not purpose-built; and so they frequently have poor acoustics and odd shapes.

Then there are the corridors. Lots and lots of corridors. Clubhouses are often decades (even centuries) old, and far from having been immaculately preserved, everything is likely to have been redeveloped and knocked through and rearranged several times over through the years. This can leave a baffling maze of corridors for the unwary traveller. The corridors are usually the lowest priority for refurbishment, and so they can show you a clubhouse at its shabbiest.

These, then, are how the clubs' premises *physically* appear. Yet how do people behave? The casual gatecrasher can all too easily blag their way past the Porter, but it is usually their mannerisms that give them away; a certain befuddlement on where to put their coat, or where to find the Bar, or how to pay their bill. And people behave differently in clubs. There is a sort of familiarity, mixed with an understated way of showing off. People dress to impress, but they also dress to relax – how they choose to combine this balance often says a lot about them. (The British are notorious for having never quite got the hang of 'smart casual'; think Alan Partridge in green or mauve blazers.)

Clubs do not, despite the impression given in Sherlock Holmes stories, generally encourage silence. True, the now-defunct United Service Club had a 'Silence Room'. That is partly why it is now defunct. The odd club library has a silence rule, but many clubs have long since disposed of their libraries or relegated them to standard function rooms with only a sprinkling of shelves of books for decoration. Yet clubs are not particularly loud places, either – if you shout, you will immediately draw attention to yourself, and there is an almost permanent sense of being 'on display', even if it is just a passer-by thinking, 'That's what's-her-name who's always in on a Tuesday, I haven't seen her talking to him before.' Conversation is usually murmured quietly, unless somebody's had a few drinks too many.

Club members broadly fall into two categories: 'regulars' and 'show-offs'. The 'regulars', as the name suggests, spend a considerable portion of their lives in their club. It's often a place to stop off after work, for a drink or dinner on the way home, several times a week – if indeed they have places to call work or home at all. Some even try to snooze overnight in an armchair, tolerated by the night Porter, and even gently encouraged with a warm blanket. Most of the regulars' social engagements are with 'insiders', or other regular members of their club. They make up around 10 per cent of every club's members, but they are the people you are most likely to meet. 'Show-offs' make up the remaining 90 per cent of members. They are occasional visitors, perhaps only two or three times a year, who see a visit to their club as a rare treat. Their visits are so rare, they seldom know many other members when they turn up. Instead, they will bring their own company, in the form of guests to whom they wish to showcase the Club's premises. There can be a certain heavy-handed invocation to 'Look at my massive club', almost as if it were a virility symbol, inviting and expecting compliments. Their guests may be friends or lovers (male or female), but they are more typically family or work colleagues.

As clubs are places of leisure, members do not necessarily always bring their working lives or their home lives with them through the door. Ever keen to live their best lives within their clubs, they can be downright unrevealing about themselves. One Clubland historian wrote over a century ago:

We may know little of a man's private affairs, what his income is exactly, or even approximately, or how he earns it; what he does, indeed, 'by daylight,' as the saying goes; whether he is married, or has been, or separated, or lives *maritalement*; whether he owns a palatial mansion, or is satisfied with a modest bedroom in some shady corner of Clubland.[6]

Indeed, the reason why so many club members draw a discreet veil over such things is that their fellow members may be surprised at the sheer modesty of their home. Living so much of their lives in such grand surroundings obviates the need to get into such inconvenient intimacies.

Of course, club members do have a reputation for being eccentric, or downright odd. At best, these 'characters' can give clubs a unique atmosphere, at worst, they can be downright unpleasant. Every club has its 'bores', and the saying goes 'If you can't name the Club Bore, it's because you're the Club Bore yourself.' My own particular cross to bear is a man resembling a hard-boiled egg who frequents half of Clubland and combines ignorant, reactionary views, an overconfidence that everything he says is riveting and must go unchallenged, and a peculiarly squeaky voice that projects across several rooms.

And the sad reality is that clubs are not – and never have been – budding with a thousand Oscar Wildes, but are usually made up of perfectly ordinary people, and many of them are quite boring. Something in the grandness of the surroundings can often bring out a Walter Mitty tendency in the dullest businessmen, suddenly thrust into a dramatic setting, acting out their fantasy lifestyle. This is why so many members spend so much time in their clubs instead of their homes. Compared to the commute back home to Coleridge Close in Surrey, Clubland has infinitely more glamour.

Club members are renowned for their wit, yet the reality often falls short of the myth. For instance, former Conservative prime minister Stanley Baldwin and his wife went for tea in the Ladies' Drawing Room of his club, while Baldwin puffed on his trademark pipe. A servant cautiously approached him: 'Sir, would you please put your pipe out, you're not allowed to smoke in the Ladies' Drawing Room!' Baldwin answered, 'Bugger off!'[7] Scarcely the height of repartee.

Nevertheless, club members have often had their own, well-earned reputation for the amusingly understated. When the Naval and Military Club reported sightings of a ghost in 1994, it was believed to be that of Major 'Perky' Braddell, a member who had been killed in the Blitz. The Club refused to contemplate an exorcism, however, on the grounds that Major Braddell had never formally resigned his membership.[8] Presumably, they were waiting to present him with the bill for the outstanding five decades of subscriptions.

Then there was the case of Percival Osborne, who joined the Travellers Club in 1889, and spent sixteen years as an overseas member, resident in Japan. Feeling suicidal while 'temporarily insane', he journeyed to London, and at noon on Saturday 15 May 1905, he promptly shot himself in the Billiard Room (now the Castlereagh Room) of the Club. The shot was angled in such a way so that after passing through his skull, the bullet damaged the baize of the billiard table. The Chairman of the Club was unimpressed: 'A gentleman commits suicide in the lavatory. We shall make sure he never becomes a member of another club.'[9]

Osborne was far from the only Clubland suicide. Another club member killed himself by taking an overdose in his bedroom, yet despite being discovered lying on the floor by a servant leaving out his morning tea, was left there – the staffer simply assumed that he was drunk. Tragically, the member's life might have been saved if the servant had called an ambulance in time. Even more tragic was that the mourning family asked to see the room he expired in, only to then rob the body of all jewellery, and strip the room of valuables.[10] Clubland manners may be genteel, but the behaviour is capable of being just as outrageous as anywhere else.

Certainly, for an insight into 'Clubland' at its oddest and most parochial, look no further than the Annual General Meeting. These are forbidding occasions, rigorously sticking to a minimal agenda. ('I'm sorry, I cannot answer that. All questions must be put in writing at least fourteen clear days in advance, and the copy you sent me was only received thirteen days ago, due to my being away on holiday at the time.') They also seem to bring out a range of eccentric 'backwoodsmen' who are never otherwise seen, but apparently maintain their club membership solely for the privilege of competing in a sort of informal annual competition, to ask the most outrageous question at the AGM. It makes for quite the spectator sport.

Indeed, scrupulously sticking to the agenda seems to be very much a necessity, in fending off a flurry of irrelevant queries. There are always gripes about subscriptions – country members piping up that members living in town really should pay more, while town members bemoan how cheap the membership is for those living in the country, even though they are seen in the Club more frequently than anyone else. Assorted tax exiles try to argue that their main home in Jersey or the Isle of Man really should count as 'overseas' and that the Chelsea address is 'just a pied-à-terre'. Members get up to decry the Club stocking a particular newspaper, observing that the waiters seem to be the only people who ever read it, or bemoaning that they once chipped a tooth on some veal on the bone. I can remember one elderly member, well into his eighties, whose annual intervention was always an event, as much for a series of dramatic, ten-second, mid-sentence pauses as the content of his questions. One AGM saw a member rise to announce that the previous March, a fly had dropped into his rice pudding, and that it was now June. 'Why?' he asked, 'Why?'[11]

All this is further complicated by clubs maintaining the gentle fiction that all members are known to the staff by sight. At an AGM, this creates a recipe for chaos, as staff with furrowed brows struggle to identify each intervention being transcribed for the minutes. The hapless Chairman of the meeting is left mumbling, 'You, madam, Ms [unintelligible murmuring]', and feigning familiarity in a room often filled with strangers.

Clubs have always made good copy for journalists. For centuries, gossip columns have lapped up anecdotes from Clubland. The clichéd figure of the clapped-out reactionary, men-only club is a well-worn staple of many anecdotes. For instance, there is the notorious (possibly apocryphal) tale of the men-only club which notionally only permitted women to visit if they were the wives of members. Rumour spread that the flurry of attractive young women accompanying elderly members to dinner were – horror of horrors – not all married to their hosts, and a sign sprang up:

MEMBERS ARE ASKED NOT TO BRING THEIR
MISTRESSES TO DINE AT THE CLUB, UNLESS THEY
ARE THE WIVES OF OTHER MEMBERS.

And, of course, a rich vein of humorous Clubland literature sprang up, most notably by that indefatigably prolific satiriser of clubs, P. G. Wodehouse. From the 'Jeeves' stories to the 'Blandings Castle' novels, Wodehouse's world was filled with clubmen and clubwomen, from aristocrats at White's to servants at the Junior Ganymede Club. Yet the Club which epitomises Wodehouse's world is the fictional Drones Club on Dover Street. This was a composite of many different clubs, from Wodehouse's invocation of the raucous old Bachelors' Club to the swimming pool found in Dover Street's Bath Club. Yet above all, the key to Wodehouse was the importance of anachronism. By the time of his heyday in the 1920s and 1930s, nobody spoke like his characters anymore – they captured a series of manners and slang Wodehouse remembered from his youth in the 1890s and 1900s, which grew ever more anachronistic. As with Wodehouse's Clubland, the Clubland which we tend to think of is a caricature of a world that no longer exists, if it ever existed at all.

There is a tendency to look on clubs as a sort of immovable object, forever stuck in the past. To today's observer, the oldest, snootiest establishments seem ancient, as if stuck in a time warp, and so it is easy to assume that everything has been perfectly preserved for centuries. In reality, *every* club has frequently been reinvented every few decades, including in membership, décor, food and atmosphere. This book seeks to set out how and why clubs have changed so much over the years.

Chapter One

Early beginnings – scandal, coffee and chocolate

(1690–1774)

In the beginning, there was White's – or so we are usually told. If you read most histories of London's Clubland, they will confidently declare that it all began in 1693 with White's, that bastion of aristocratic Toryism, often called 'the oldest club in the world'. Even 130 years ago, with White's already being nearly two centuries old, there was an idea that it had always been stuck in a time warp, the template of all London clubs that followed, with an almost religious ritual: 'Dinner at White's is a ceremonial business, wax-candles, stately waiters, carefully decanted wine, courses that come on with procession-like solemnity, a long sitting over the wine, and with the older men a "whitewash" of sherry before your coffee and cigar.'[1] These images live on: the misanthropic old Duke (whose name changes with each fresh retelling), sitting in the bow window. The reckless bet for an astronomical sum of money over which raindrop would fall down the window first. The ambience of a Duke's house, with the Duke lying dead upstairs. These are all part of the mythology.

Sixty years ago, Charles Graves repeated the conventional wisdom that 'Clubland is a purely English invention', and that the great clubs of Paris, Savannah, New York, Montreal and Johannesburg 'would never have seen the light of day if Francesco Bianco had not started White's, and if two Coldstream Guards officers had not invented the first members' clubs in St James's'.[2] Almost every word of this is wrong.

The *real* story of London Clubland begins in two overseas locations. One is nearly 800 miles away from London in Italy, the other over 3,600 miles away in the Americas.

The first recognisable club was in North America: the South River Club, in the then colony of Maryland. We still do not know precisely when it was founded. Surviving press coverage merely confirms that it was already up and running by 1690. In the late seventeenth century, the South River Club had all the familiar trappings that we would later recognise in a club, including a clubhouse, members, servants, a balloting process for electing new members and a set of rules and regulations. The clubhouse was modest by today's standards – little more than a large shed. Its membership was tiny: thirty men (and no women). Yet within the South River Club lay the embryo of so much that followed. It is also quite possible, indeed probable, that other clubs flourished in North America around this time. So much of what we know of clubs is dominated by what has survived; as we shall see, the clubs of the past formed a now-vanished world, far wider than is often realised.

While the English colonist members of the South River Club were busily balloting for new members, across the Atlantic the members of what would one day become White's club in London had not even conceived of a club. So what did they have in London?

For centuries, London drew much of its power from its status as a port. It traded the world over, including with the 'New World' – particularly through the 'triangular trade' around the slave trade between England's North African trading posts and North American

26

colonies; and from the early seventeenth century, the growing English commercial monopoly in India through the East India Company. All this made London one of the busiest commercial ports on earth.

'Real' London, around the walled ancient Roman city that is today's financial district, was close to the docks. What was to become 'Clubland' was in the West End of Central London, long considered the capital's pleasure district. The West End's proximity to the homes of wealthy aristocrats gave it a sense of respectability. Yet as with so much of London, it remained a district of two halves – disreputable gambling dens, slums, bordellos and debtors' prisons existed side by side with aristocratic houses, theatres and fashionable shops which sold luxury imports such as coffee and chocolate.

Against this background, certain customs had developed around how people socialised in the public houses (or 'pubs') and taverns that were such popular drinking venues. Over centuries, patrons would become 'regulars' in their local tavern. What could be more natural than for these regulars to cluster together in a huddle? In itself, there was nothing distinctively English about this; the habit could be found over the centuries in watering holes the world over, from Mexico to Japan. Yet the language around it started to evolve in a peculiarly English way. The word 'club' first popped up to describe this in English in the mid-seventeenth century.

The first recorded use of the word 'club' in a social sense, the very birth of the idea, was in the word 'unclubbable' in 1633, and would grow in use against the backdrop of the English Civil War, so that it had become quite widespread by the 1650s. To be 'unclubbable' was to be the kind of selfish individual who would always find some excuse to not pay their bill.

From being 'unclubbable' evolved the notion of being 'clubbable', and part of a 'club'. This was rooted in a group of tavern regulars clubbing together, to defray costs. In an ideal club, the bills were split, and the whole culture of socialising was less expensive, and more equitable, than turning up in dread of being the one person who would be lumbered with the entire bill.

Clubs were therefore a radical idea from the start – I have (perhaps pretentiously) used the phrase 'aristocratic protosocialism' to describe these early clubs. Like their seventeenth-century contemporaries the Diggers and the Levellers (who wielded so much influence on ensuing progressive thought), the earliest 'clubs' had no intention of forging a better world, or of providing a template for others to follow. They were simply trying to run their own private community, in their own way. They redistributed, not because of any grandiose political dogma, but because it seemed the most affordable way of doing things. However, their tastes and sensibilities were very much informed by the aristocratic norms of the time – they wanted to enjoy the finer things in life, and by sharing their costs, they found they were able to enjoy good wine and good company in nice rooms, at a fraction of the price.

The language of these customs was not peculiar to London: many were found across England, from small villages to large cities. However, London had a particular combination of size, wealth and poverty, and a large transient international population around the port that provided the City of London with so much of its riches. London's wealthy – both 'old' and 'new' money – wanted fashionable places in which to socialise. And one enterprising Italian immigrant had an idea, heavily influenced by the clubs of America and the *Circoli* of Italy.

There is much that is unknown about Francesco Bianco (or Francesco Bianchi, according to some accounts), but he was an Italian immigrant who anglicised his name as Francis White. Joining seventeenth-century London's frenzy for luxury goods, he set up White's Chocolate Shop, selling both coffee and hot drinking chocolate (or cocoa). Instead of locating the business alongside rivals in the City of London itself, he opted for the up-and-coming neighbourhood of St James's. This was a risky venture: the area was fairly peripheral to London at the time, then still recovering from the Great Fire of 1666, while St James's still overlooked wide-open pig fields to the north, bound by the street Pigadillo – now called Piccadilly. Nevertheless, Bianco correctly guessed that locating his business right by the London residences of some of the grandest aristocrats of the day would guarantee a high-end clientele who would provide his chocolate shop with social cachet or 'snob appeal'. Naturally, there was an 'inner club' within the chocolate shop, for the regular patrons, as was the custom with so many other coffee houses.

The concept of the 'inner club' within a tavern, coffee shop of chocolate shop had an obvious advantage. It made it almost impossible for the local authorities to raid the establishment. In the centuries before a Metropolitan Police was founded in the 1820s, there was no one unified authority to keep the peace. A combination of militiamen, magistrates, sheriffs and other semi-judicial officials all kept order as best they could – no mean feat. Presenting them with the challenge that this was 'a private members' club' immediately threw doubt on any claims of oversight. This added serious legal obstacles to any attempt to raid the premises. What better way to create a haven for illegal gambling? And gambling remained both heavily illegal and immensely fashionable.

It also lent itself to other activities which were either illegal or frowned upon. In their earliest form based on informal arrangements in back rooms, clubs proved a popular homosexual meeting spot, known by the early seventeenth century as 'molly houses' or 'molly clubs'. Fern Riddell notes how 'These clubs offered their members the opportunity to meet, love and be themselves in an environment supposedly out of reach of the law.'[3] This legal 'outsider' status of the early clubs allowed a variety of subcultures to flourish.

White's is important with hindsight; but at the time, it did not seem terribly different from a great many other trendy coffee houses and taverns nearby, including the Star and Garter, the Cocoa Tree, the King's Head, the Cock Tavern, or the Bunch of Grapes. Nor would it be fair to describe White's in its first incarnation as a 'club' in the modern sense. It is simply that, of London's surviving clubs today, it was the one with the earliest roots. In much the same way that England is awash with taverns claiming to be 'the oldest pub in the country', so Clubland is awash with clubs vying for the 'snob value' of being able to claim to have got under the wire first. Most of these claims are relatively far-fetched. Even the United Service Club, not founded until 1815, still made the 'oldest club in London' claim.[4] For its first few decades, White's was a spectacularly successful coffee shop with a gambling room around the back; nothing more, nothing less.

That it *was* successful can be evidenced from several things, ranging from its rapid move to bigger and more expensive premises across the street, to the £2,750 legacy left by Francesco Bianco upon his death – then a huge sum.

Bianco died in 1711, whereupon his wife Elisabetta succeeded him in running the shop. She continued to do so until her own death in 1729. Judging by her entries in the local rate books, she grew ever more prosperous and came into her own – she is first shown after his death as 'Widow White', then 'Mrs White', and finally, 'Madam White'.[5]

After Elisabetta Bianco's death, the shop was taken over by one John Arthur, who had long been a friend and neighbour of the Biancos, and had worked as a servant and assistant manager at White's as early as 1702. In the interim, Arthur had also founded his own rival social venue on St James's Street in 1711, which he imaginatively called Arthur's. White's therefore retained something of the feel of a small, intimate family business for its first few decades.

Francesco Bianco himself remains an enigma. Few hard facts are known about him, beyond the contents of his will. The widespread assumption that he was Italian stems from the will, in which all of his beneficiaries and relatives had obviously Italian names. We do not even know where he originated from within Italy – Stephen Hoare speculates he was Venetian, but based only on Venice having been a centre of the coffee trade that was then popular with Englishmen on a Grand Tour, admittedly a rather tenuous connection.

While the presence of aristocrats' houses in St James's gave the area a social cachet, the district was far more diverse in the reign of Queen Anne than is often remembered. Seventeenth- and eighteenth-century St James's followed the classic pattern of early urbanisation, with extreme wealth and poverty living cheek by jowl. Early Hogarth prints satirised aristocrats wading through bailiffs, beggars and excrement to get to even the wealthiest venues. St James's Street itself was dominated by a large pillory, to which assorted criminals were chained and humiliated by passing crowds. The early members of White's would have looked out across this far from genteel scene, only a few metres away.

A common question of this era, which deserves answering, is why clubs started excluding women. There is no easy answer to this. Even the very first surviving set of club rules is – unusually for the time – written in gender-neutral language, referring to members as 'no one . . . nobody . . . members . . . any person . . . every person . . . every member'. In fact, it is noticeable how these rules went out of their way to use gender-neutral language, rather than ever describing members as 'a man'.[6] Restricting the club to men may well have come to be a convention, but we should not rule out the distinct possibility of women members during the first forty years of White's, in much the same way that historians have come to realise that women voters existed in public elections prior to

1832, before the 'Great Reform Act' first formally defined a voter as being a man. Similarly, some nineteenth-century club rulebooks would come to define members as men – but the significance of early rulebooks referring to a member as a 'person' should not be ignored. As with early women's voting rights, the main obstacle would have been financial, and so only a small number of wealthy women would have had the means to overcome this. No members' list survives for the first forty years of White's (although the first surviving list, from 1733, refers to a handful of elderly pre-existing members, all of them male).

Indeed, it must be stressed that any early club basking in the proximity to St James's Palace would scarcely have been able to claim many royal connections by excluding women. When White's opened its doors in 1693, Mary II still reigned as co-monarch. For most of the 1700s, during the reign of Queen Anne, much of the court revolved around the Queen's friend and intimate Sarah, Duchess of Marlborough. White's was, therefore, very much a product of late Stuart aristocratic femininity.

If we are to find a reason for the male dominance of clubs until the mid-nineteenth century, a better explanation is perhaps offered through the wider trends of socialising at the time. It was by no means unusual for 'separate spheres' to evolve in other forms of socialising, especially informal gatherings in pubs and taverns (although, even then, it was far from unknown for women to break bread with groups of men).[7] It is also worth noting that in the seventeenth and eighteenth centuries, the district of St James's in particular was what Percy Colson called, 'a whole quarter . . . devoted entirely to man and his various needs at their most expensive'.[8] The area boasted such innovations as men's hatters (one of which, Lock & Co, has existed since 1676, and has been at its present St James's Street location since 1765), tailors, barbers and cobblers. Therefore, when we think of a particular type of 'London' Clubland which has been so influential on other clubs worldwide, we tend to think of a business that emerged from this particularly masculine corner of London. This cottage industry in St James's masculinity fed into wider ideas of 'gentlemanliness', and the aspirations which arose around that.

A further likely reason for early clubs being centred around men is the example set by the Italian *Circoli*. As noted, the fully-fledged institutions like the South River Club of North America were but one obvious direct forebear of the London club. The other was found in Italy.

Historians have long searched for some ancient precursor to the London club, occasionally settling on some far-fetched invocation of classical Greek and Roman men socialising in bathhouses. There is little evidence of a direct link, but it sounds eminently respectable, with a frisson of implied homoeroticism.

A far more plausible precursor was in the Italian *Circoli*. They had their own language, culture and traditions which placed them apart from the private clubs of London. They owed much to the continental trend towards institutionalisation, especially in the wake of the Reformation and Counter-Reformation, and they reflected academic institutions going back to the Middle Ages.[9]

The very earliest *Circoli* predated even White's chocolate shop: the first, the *Circolo degli Uniti* (Union Circle) of Siena in Tuscany dates to 1657, originally under the full name of the *Nobile Conversazione de' Signori Uniti nel Casino di Siena*, or *Casin de' Nobili* for short, translating as Casino of Nobles. Peter Clark asks how great their influence was, and concludes 'Not much, it would seem', being restricted to 'some of the trappings', and noting 'sparse' evidence for direct emulation.[10] Like the Pall Mall clubs, they were centred around physical premises, with a sharply defined membership.

However, the most obvious echo was around their masculinity; like the earliest Pall Mall clubs, they reflected the *macho* tradition of excluding women from membership.

Much of what we do know of the earliest London clubs is around their choice of food and drink. From the very start, the earliest clubs were built around imported beverages from all over the world, although these were by no means limited to alcohol. Some of the highest demands for fashionable clubs and coteries were among coffee houses, with coffee having been in circulation since the early seventeenth century. Pasqua Rosée was an ethnically Greek immigrant from Ragusa, centred around Dubrovnik, who had met an English merchant named Edwards. Edwards had returned home, bringing Rosée as his servant, tasked with presenting guests with the coffee of which Edwards was such a devotee. Rosée spied a business opportunity, and in 1651 he opened England's first ever coffee house in Oxford. With the Puritan backdrop of the Interregnum, the coffee house was a very welcome alternative to alcohol. The following year, Rosée opened London's first coffee house: 'Pasqua Rosée's Coffee House in St Michael's Alley in Cornhill'. It was a runaway success, which prompted countless copycats. By the start of the eighteenth century, there were over 500 coffee houses in London alone.[11]

French wine, which would become such a status symbol in the nineteenth century, most notably the eponymous sparkling wines from Champagne, was still relatively obscure. Trading relations with France oscillated from variable at the best of times, to non-existent in times of war. In particular, war from 1667 severed the supply of previously popular French claret wine. In its place, there was a great appetite for the fortified port wines provided by Portugal. Port, as it became known, had a number of advantages. It was an exceptionally sturdy wine, so that once opened it would not go off for months – as a wine, it had been perfected in the seventeenth century for long, transatlantic voyages, as sailors noticed that their wine would be better preserved if a splash of brandy was added in advance; and it had the advantage of soaking in the oak taste of the wooden barrels, too, for improved flavour. Being fortified by brandy, it was also far stronger than regular wine, and so provided a relatively inexpensive way of getting drunk. And with Portugal having enjoyed an uninterrupted alliance with England that went back to the Treaty of Windsor in 1386, there was a reliable, well-established trading route for supplies to be shipped into the port of London. Indeed, as the port wine industry grew in the eighteenth century, much of it came to be dominated by expatriate English and Scottish anglophone families, such as the Burmesters, Butlers, Crofts, Grahams, Newmans, Sandemans, Taylors and Warres.[12] Early club illustrations vividly depict port as the tipple of choice.

Food was no less important, but was more noted for its large portions than for any haute cuisine. Service was just as important as substance, and the late seventeenth century saw a growing 'quest for informality', a backlash against the elaborate rituals and crockery of the French *ancien régime*.[13] This emphasis on casual, easy, informal dining at informal hours was to be a perfect foment for clubs.

Disaster struck White's when a fire broke out at about four o'clock in the morning on 26 April 1733. The blaze was considerable, even drawing in as spectators King George II and Frederick, Prince of Wales. A week later, Mr Arthur took up a temporary residence in Gaunt's Coffee House, further down the street, where he remained for the next three years.[14]

When White's was rebuilt, Arthur had it reconstituted as a club. It is from this 1736 re-establishment that the first London club rules survive – although they were far from being the first club rules in the world. It was a simple list of ten rules, stipulating the conditions for election, including a minimum quorum of twelve members needed to elect a new member, spelling out a guinea a year's subscription and expecting the swift settlement of bills by midnight.[15]

Perhaps the most revealing of these ten rules was the last: that new members could only be proposed and elected 'during the sitting of Parliament' – a recognition not only of the Club's aspirations to political importance, but also an acknowledgement that so much of London society revolved around the sitting of Parliament.[16] Alongside these rules was a list of eighty-two founder members of the newly constituted Club (although several of the more elderly members were habitués of the old White's). These included the prime minister, Sir Robert Walpole.[17]

While the new club was filled with political figures, it did not have the political prominence that would characterise later clubs. It was primarily a social venue, and informality was its defining feature. It had no clear set of politics, for many of the members, from William Pulteney to George Bubb Dodington (later 1st Baron Melcombe), cordially despised Walpole. This was a place for 'men on the make' to flaunt their wealth, and to unwind.

The early members of White's tended to be the wealthy and the fashionable, and they included self-made men as well as landed aristocrats. Conspicuous among them was Robert Clive, colonial pathfinder and genocidal psychopath, elected in 1762. Much of his adult life was spent abroad, as an official of the East India Company, so his use of White's would have been irregular and intermittent. In 1774, he slit his own throat with a blunt paperknife after a game of whist at his Berkeley Square home, a short walk from White's. Samuel Johnson summarised the widespread view of Clive's motives for his death: he 'had acquired his fortune by such crimes that his consciousness of them impelled him to cut his own throat'.[18]

The early White's was still a halfway house to being a recognisable club in the modern sense. In some ways it still resembled some of the informal 'club' gatherings in the backrooms of taverns that had elaborate rules and election rituals of their own. Where clubs would distinctly evolve in the mid-eighteenth century was in the professionalisation of club services, and club servants. Evolving research from Brendan Mackie shows how clubs adopted the codified practices, paperwork and customs of wider eighteenth-century administration, as shown in Mackie's pioneering research on a 'combination of paperwork and amity'.[19]

Early clubs, including White's, often specified that only members could dine there – the idea of club guests was a nineteenth-century innovation. For a members-only gathering, setting up a clubhouse with dedicated servants was a great extravagance. It was this kind of extravagance which the aristocratic clubs of the second half of the eighteenth century contributed.

In 1759, the entrepreneur William Almack set up a tavern at 49 Pall Mall, popularly known as Almack's. As with many taverns, regular gatherings took to meeting in the backroom, and in 1762 Almack began hosting and servicing a society at the house next door, 51 Pall Mall. This gathering was serviced for its first decade by a head waiter named Edwin Boodle, and came to be known as Boodle's club.[20] The success of the public tavern allowed private services for the Club next door to be subsidised. It also raised the stakes significantly, in the kind of facilities that could be offered to members.

Today, Boodle's is the 'second-oldest' club in London – or at least, the second-oldest of the surviving clubs, since Arthur's own club, having peeled off from White's eventually went bankrupt in 1940. Yet there are hints in the surviving Boodle's rules that even more clubs were already proliferating by the 1760s. One of the rules went through some rewriting. Though blotted out in ink, its original form can still be read:

> No person can be a member of this Society who is a member of any Club or Society in London whose meetings are supposed to be daily and whose numbers reach fifty, and of what is at present called Arthur's or by whatever name that Society or Club may be afterwards called, whether new or old club or any other belonging to it.[21]

The finalised rule simply stated that members of Boodle's could not simultaneously be members of Arthur's. The original version is intriguing – it implies both the existence of a number of existing clubs, and the expectation that more would soon be launched.

The Boodle's rule was ratified in 1763. The following year, a major club duly followed: Brooks's was founded by one of Almack's more enterprising waiters, William Brook, who left Almack's to found his own establishment.[22] A small number of businesses, used to catering to the demanding whims of their aristocratic clientele, were providing the skills and template for the growth of clubs.

These early clubs were immensely different from most of their later counterparts in one respect: the members did not own them. They were all operated by private landlords, as for-profit enterprises. Certainly, they catered to the demands of the wealthy. They were there to fleece the rich and the gullible, at a considerable markup. In this earliest form, their modern-day analogy is not the private members' club, but the elite concierge service for the super-wealthy. It was not until the nineteenth century that the member-owned club would evolve; and it would take the idea of a club in very different directions. Nonetheless, along a thin strip of houses dotted along the 'L' shape of St James's Street and Pall Mall, London's Clubland had been born.

Chapter Two

The Georgian clubs – the 'aristocratic phase' and the arrival of the middle classes

(1774–1820)

E ighteenth-century clubs are iconic. When writers have fawned over the exclusivity of clubs it is usually the world of the late eighteenth century that has come to mind. Yet it was also a very short-lived era, occupying a tiny world of only a few streets, with a handful of small, informal clubs, containing a few hundred members. Anthony Lejeune, the archetypal writer of 'safe', self-congratulatory Clubland histories, recognised, 'The temptation to which most clubland historians have succumbed is to let the Regency period bulk so large that it overwhelms the rest of the story.'[1] Clubland histories tend to be filled with gambling anecdotes relating to this period, often told with barely concealed envy at how much was lost on a hand of cards or a roll of the dice.

Trends moved fast during this era, because the late eighteenth century saw abundant social change, across all levels of society. Many of the eighty-two founder members of White's new club in 1736 had been very elderly. By the late eighteenth century, those in power were getting younger – George III acceded to the throne aged twenty-two, and Pitt the Younger became prime minister at twenty-four.[2] This filtered through to the fashionable clubs; perceptions changed from Hogarth's condescending view of the fashionable young 'rake' being an idle and dissolute object of mockery in a gambling hell, to the trendy phenomenon of the dandy.[3] The immense power wielded by a small concentration of fashionable aristocratic families projected the illusion of permanence. In reality, their flourishing may have been glamorous, but it was also very brief.

Clubs sought to differentiate themselves from their competitors, which were many: the informal gambling rooms, the coffee houses, the salons. They did this through a combination of reticence and excess. The reticence could be seen in a new-found degree of secrecy around clubs, adding lustre and mystique. The excess was found in a conspicuous level of consumption, touching upon everything: alcohol, food, architecture and gambling. For each club to stand out, it had to offer its members excellence in all spheres.

This level of excess was not unusual for the time. Lucy Inglis shows how the evolving reckless behaviour in London's more fashionable clubs reflected a wider trend:

> Gambling among the upper classes rose throughout the eighteenth century; by the 1780s, it had reached a near epidemic level. Pamphlets protesting against it appeared regularly. Popular feeling was that the ruling class, who theoretically held a moral authority, should know better.[4]

Indeed, this was part of a wider European phenomenon – revulsion at aristocratic excess accompanied the French Revolution. This had helped drive the fashion for more informal dining. Yet the scope to show off during this dash to informality was considerable, because the wealthy of the eighteenth century 'were far richer than they had been in the seventeenth century'.[5] There were various reasons for this, from the growth in banks offering credit and mortgage facilities, to Britain's highly profitable slave trade creating a new moneyed class, and multiplying the profits of rich investors. All this meant there was serious money to be made in clubs, especially if they catered for reckless gambling. Furthermore, as John Joliffe argues, the early club managers like William Brook found that running Brooks's 'was not only a plum job in itself, but it put him in touch with patrons who later gave him enormous commissions'.[6] Clubs were rapidly finding themselves the pre-eminent social networks of their day. It was, to coin a phrase, the opportunity to be in 'the room where it happens'. Even in their most 'aristocratic' phase, London clubs were a haven for 'fixers' who depended on patronage, including architects, bankers and politicians. Inglis further notes:

> Gaming itself was also changing: sociable partnership games, such as whist, were giving way to high-stakes, antisocial, player-versus-banker games, such as faro. What had been a luxurious pastime for people with money to spare was suddenly becoming an addiction.[7]

This captures the split personality to be found in these Georgian clubs. Most accounts wax lyrical about the camaraderie and the conviviality about such gatherings, yet the reality was that a good deal of time was given over to deeply antisocial practices. Days-long, around-the-clock gambling fuelled by port and laudanum was not conducive to witty conversation. One early twentieth-century historian of clubs reflected, 'Nowhere did bacchanal self-indulgence find greater and more deplorable scope than in the clubs. Roués came there to boast of their conquests, to waste their substance in riotous living, to drink to deepest excess. To be overcome in liquor called for no shocked comment.'[8] The notion that clubs were synonymous with good behaviour would be a later, nineteenth-century development, when rules were drawn up in response to too many incidents in the 'hell' of Georgian clubs.

Heavy drinking reflected the conspicuous consumption of alcohol in these early clubs. The Tory prime minister Pitt the Younger may have reached the premiership at just twenty-four, but he was dead at forty-six, owing in no small part to his fondness for the bottle. An oft-told tale maintained that his doctor recommended that in future he should 'limit his alcohol intake to no more than five bottles of port a day'. If the story is apocryphal, the alcohol consumption was by no means unusual for the time; and clubs were some of the most eager purveyors of exotic, marked-up alcohol for the aristocracy, making extensive use of well-connected wine merchants such as Berry Brothers on St James's Street.

Club food in the late eighteenth century was not particularly ostentatious. It often centred around a single joint of roasted meat by the fireplace, which the members would pick at, around the clock, for days on end until it was exhausted.[9] Nevertheless, the mere availability of food at all hours was in itself a considerable luxury, when most taverns served up meals at times convenient to their proprietor rather than their patrons.

Clubs further set themselves apart from rival establishments by investing in bricks and mortar. The modern idea of a clubhouse began to take shape. This would come to define what is meant by the idea of a club – particularly a London club. Any group or society can call themselves a 'club'; but when one thinks of a London club, it is a permanent set of premises that give it its name, rendering its ideas and social habits with a sense of permanence.

The earliest clubs had already been located close to the aristocracy in St James's. Aristocratic mansions began to appear in the area, commissioned from the most fashionable architects of the day, such as Matthew Brettingham's Cambridge House in 1756, and Robert Adam's Lansdowne House in 1762. Part of their prestige came from being located so close to nearby St James's Palace. These houses were essentially country mansions, complete with vast gardens, which just happened to have been built in the middle of London's growing West End. They were also to be an obvious influence on the clubs which cropped up nearby. The clubhouses of the period reflected the same inconspicuous design – elegant façades and understated, intimate halls which looked more like the private home of a wealthy aristocrat. Clubs were not (yet) built to impress on the outside.

Clubs also sought other ways to cultivate a sense of mystique. One means was to create an almost sectarian feeling of *belonging* – you belonged to your club, and to that club only. With this in mind, several clubs like White's and Boodle's stipulated that members could belong to no other club. It was to be a short-lived if momentarily powerful idea, for by the end of the eighteenth century London's most connected members sought to defy the rules and collect a range of club memberships anyway. It tends to be assumed, for instance, that the Tory politician Pitt the Younger was a member of White's, and his Whig nemesis Charles James Fox a member of Brooks's.[10] In reality, both men were active members of both clubs. The provisions banning multiple club memberships were wholly unenforceable. Instead, multiple club memberships were considered the hottest ticket in town, keenly flaunted by a lucky few, and those fellow members who were in a position to take action seldom wanted to jeopardise their own chances of joining and maintaining a second (or third) club.

All this made for an 'aristocratic phase' in clubs. They had come from informal, even plebeian, beginnings in the taverns of the seventeenth century. By the 1760s, London's premier, trend-setting clubs were almost obnoxiously elitist. Within half a century, clubs started to gravitate back to the middle classes, where they would remain.

It was in this 'aristocratic phase' of clubs that the notion of the eccentric member evolved. If you were poor, then you were simply mad; but if you were unorthodox and wealthy, then you were an eccentric. St James's clubs were a closed world, and behaviours which might seem odd (or even certifiable) in the outside world were humoured with good grace. One of the more quarrelsome Georgian members of White's was the 5th Viscount Allen, who 'hated leaving London even for a night and during his latter years his only exercise consisted in walking from White's to Crockford's just across the street'.[11] Similarly, excursions between clubs could be just as odd – an eighteenth-century Clubland bet had it that 'Mr P undertook to hit golf balls from St James's Street to Parliament Square in less than 80 strokes with a mashie iron.'[12] Some of these behaviours were less eccentric, and simply downright unpleasant. An early nineteenth-century Duke – reputedly Wellington – was recounted to frequently spend his day sitting in the bay window of his club, enjoying 'Watching the damned people get wet.'

The lasting, long-term legacy of the 'aristocratic phase' of clubs was in blackballing. The system of electing members by a secret ballot was nothing new, being rooted in the ancient Athenian practice of casting votes with different-coloured pebbles. Clubs simply updated this practice with colour-coded balls, white for 'Yes', black for 'No'.

The votes were cast in an ornate wooden ballot box, typically with two drawers for the different balls, which ordained a sense of occasion. It was also fairly redundant, since it failed to maintain much secrecy in the ballot. Ballotters had to furtively pick their colour-coded ball of choice, carry it in the closed palm of the hand and place it in the box. Inside the box it would have to be placed in the colour-coded tray that was either to the left or the right. All an onlooker needed to do to know how a vote had been cast was to watch a voter plunge their hand into the box, and see whether they twisted their wrist to the left or the right. It was pure flummery, but made for spectacular, secretive theatre, often conducted by candlelight approaching midnight.

What was peculiar about blackballing was its anti-democratic nature. Candidates to join a club were not put up to a popular vote of all the members. Instead, a right of veto was given to a certain *proportion* of voters.

Fictional portrayals of clubs often dramatise the process by having a single member wielding a single blackball being enough to block an applicant from joining. The reality was not so simple.

Eighteenth-century club rules did indeed allow a single blackball to block an applicant. Yet this needs to be understood in the context of only around ten members voting, either because of the limited number of members expected on the premises on any one evening, or because the decision had been delegated to a sub-committee of the Club. As the practice of blackballing was exported, so did this practice of having a *proportion* of blackballs being enough to exclude an applicant. One in ten balls was considered onerous, leading to too many blocked candidates; over time, the 'blackballing' threshold would be raised to one in four, or even one in three. Most London clubs today still operate on this principle.

Of course, blackballing could descend into farce: one unpopular applicant heard that eleven blackballs had been cast, when there were only ten voters. (It later emerged that a club servant had been so alarmed by the applicant that he had stealthily slipped in a black ball himself.)

One of the curious features of blackballing was the contrast between its Athenian democratic roots and it being avowedly anti-democratic. It awarded a right of veto to a certain number of existing members, even when a candidate was wildly popular. No good reason needed to be provided for a blackball. It enabled a club to maintain its unique character, and to keep out a number of bores, crackpots and controversialists. However, it also allowed vendettas, jealousies and bigotries to flourish – this was particularly the case when only one blackball in ten was required to keep candidates out. When the bar was higher (as with one-in-three balls), there would usually need to be some level of active campaigning and open discussion to trigger a blackballing, and so at the very least a more rational, assertable reason was required.

The previous chapter asked how (or even if) women came to be excluded from clubs so early on in their history. It is worth asking here how clubs came to exclude in general; for this undoubtedly happened in the 'aristocratic phase' of clubs, and blackballing played a key part in it, restricting admission to those familiar with a small social milieu. As clubs went on to reach their height in the late nineteenth century, it would be in the form of upper-middle-class clubs, and eventually lower-middle-class clubs that inspired a wave of copycat working-class clubs. How, then, did 'club' come to mean 'exclusive'? This is not a new question. Alexis de Tocqueville asked:

> I cannot completely understand how 'the spirit of association' and the 'spirit of exclusion' both came to be so highly developed in the same people, and often to be so intimately combined. Example a club; what better example of association than the union of individuals who form the club? What more exclusive than the corporate personality represented by the club?[13]

Clubland historian Amy Milne-Smith has suggested one answer, around the evolution of the idea of 'clubbability'. In the seventeenth century, the focus had been on *unclubbability*; simply keeping out those who were objectionable, mainly because they could not be relied upon to pay their bills when drinking. By default, anyone else was welcome. In the late eighteenth century, this morphed into a particular idea of 'clubbability', with:

> this fantastic ineffable term that they came up with to describe 'the right sort' of fellow . . . The great thing about exclusivity is that you define it how you want, and that's kind of the purpose; it should be a little mercurial. They would define a 'clubbable' man as who they want to spend an evening with, but who we want to spend an evening with is different, from person to person.[14]

This scarcely made for a coherent ideology – if anything, it invited eccentricity. Many clubs formed themselves as unincorporated associations, and one landmark judicial ruling described these organisations as 'the most anomalous group of human beings that is known to the law'.[15]

Clubs were to become more 'anomalous' in the nineteenth century, for two reasons.

The first reason was the founding of a new type of club: the member-owned club. The first of these was the Union Club, founded in 1799 and then reconstituted in 1821 on what would eventually become Trafalgar Square.[16] It was named after the union of Britain (the future of the Union was under active discussion at the time), and was the first member-owned club. Gone was the idea of an exploitative landlord, hiking up food and beverage prices to enrich themselves. Instead, the members were all joint shareholders, who collectively owned the Club.

This change in ownership counted for a great deal, for, as Bernard Darwin wrote, 'there is an immense difference between enjoying these things on sufferance as a guest or owning some minute fraction of them as a member'.[17] Members began to treat their clubs very differently once they were the owners, rather than the temporary guests of a proprietor. Codes of honour, both formal and informal, started to be much more strictly observed.

The importance of the Union Club cannot be stressed enough, because it became a template for the clubs that followed. Throughout the nineteenth century, when new clubs were being set up, they would literally convene their first meeting with a copy of the Union Club's rulebook, and vote clause by clause on whether to adopt each paragraph, or to adopt an amended version of it.[18]

Gradually, the member-owned club became the favoured model. Even the existing, aristocratic, proprietor-owned clubs would each stage their own management buyout from the membership in the nineteenth century. Brooks's in 1880, White's in 1891 and Boodle's in 1896 all eventually became member-owned clubs, copying these later clubs, despite having started out as proprietary clubs.[19]

The other huge shift in clubs of the early nineteenth century was the move towards middle-class clubs.

The first of the middle-class clubs centred around the professions was the United Service Club. For its first eight decades, it catered for senior army and navy officers above the rank of major or commander. While there *were* military clubs beforehand, these were either informal coteries in coffee houses and taverns, or else the elite Guards Club founded on St James's Street in 1810 for officers of the socially exclusive Coldstream, Grenadier and Scots Guards regiments.[20] The United Service Club dealt with the growing demand for officers to have somewhere to stage reunions, in the wake of mass demobilisations after Waterloo, and it was no coincidence that it was founded only a few months after the battle in 1815.

Although the United Service Club was intended to challenge the aristocracy's stranglehold over early Clubland, it was never intended to be a progressive institution. Not only did it remain reserved for senior military officers until 1894, but it must be borne in mind that until the Cardwell reforms of the 1870s, the standard way to acquire an army commission in cavalry and infantry regiments was to purchase it. Nevertheless, the purchase of commissions could only get an officer so far – no more senior than colonel – and so the United Service Club's emphasis on *senior* officers, with its fair share of admirals and generals, meant that a sizeable proportion of its members were appointed through merit rather than bribery. Accordingly, the United Service Club did not attempt to challenge the 'Establishment' nature of early Clubland; but it did try to redefine that 'Establishment'.

Creating a new middle-class club around the military caused some disquiet. There was a long-standing, centuries-old English ideology around maritime adventurism, which regarded land armies with deep suspicion, as tools of tyranny. This vestigial distaste for militarism was particularly strong so soon after the Napoleonic Wars, and the government feared a popular backlash against a military club. The prime minister, the 2nd Earl of Liverpool, wrote to the United Service Club's founders to notify them that he would refuse the use of any Crown land for the Club, and he cautioned against any royal patronage for such a venture. Liverpool warned that 'a general military club, with the commander-in-chief at the head of it, is a most ill-advised measure', and feared that 'it will inevitably create a prejudice against that branch of our military establishment'.[21]

Despite wider parliamentary opposition from the likes of the Radical William Huskisson and even the veteran Admiral the 1st Earl of Jervis, the United Service Club's founders pressed on, convened by newly ennobled General Lord Lynedoch. The Club's original Committee of thirty members contained seventeen generals, eleven colonels, one major and one representative of the East India Company.[22] As can be deduced from this, it was originally an army club only – a merging with the fledging Navy Club a year later would be the first major club merger.

In the wake of the United Service Club, other late Georgian middle-class clubs followed. These were aimed at specific groups in the professions, including the Athenaeum for artists, writers and scientists in 1824, and the Oriental Club founded the same year, for veterans of the East India Company, whose armies typically contained far more 'self-made men' and fortune seekers than the 'regular' British army. Newer clubs found that they were frequently treated with snobbish disdain by members of long-established clubs. The Duke of Wellington famously reflected when close to death that his two greatest life lessons had been, 'Never write a letter to your mistress, and never join the Carlton Club.'[23] This peculiar kind of Clubland snobbery, which continues to this day, is often punctuated by a race to find the earliest foundation date, even if some creativity is involved.

Clubs also played a different *kind* of role, in bridging social encounters. This grew more acute as they assumed more of a cross-class role. With the emergence of the middle classes, there grew an increasingly elaborate set of norms and expectations around only ever doing business with people to whom you had been formally introduced. To the landed aristocracy, this presented fewer barriers, because transactions were conducted between a small, familiar circle of interlocked (and indeed intermarried) families. To the emerging middle classes, it presented a major social barrier to trade.

This was where the different behaviours in a club were invaluable. It was entirely acceptable to do business with a complete stranger who was a member of the same club – the assumption was that even if you had not been formally introduced, a fellow member must at least be a friend of a friend, moving in the same circles. Clubs were, therefore, from a very early stage, invaluable in breaking down class barriers for commercial opportunities, and for networking outside one's existing social circle. For that very reason, there grew an increasingly insatiable appetite for club memberships among Britain's growing middle class, with all the promise they held for doors to personal and professional advancement. What better way to be in the same room as the great and the good while remaining behind closed doors and keeping the rest of the world at bay?

How people behaved behind those doors continued to be an issue. Entitlement in clubs continued as a marked phenomenon. Members were increasingly being told that their club should be treated as their home, and this began to have a number of implications. Why shouldn't they be able to keep drinking and gambling at all hours? Why shouldn't they be able to order a meal only a few minutes after the Coffee Room had shut? Why shouldn't they yell at and kick club servants? Why shouldn't they be in a state of near-permanent credit on their food and drink? Why shouldn't they cash a bad cheque? This mindset continues to this day and is particularly clear in the number of thefts which routinely happen in Clubland. Everyone purloins the crested notepaper – even the London townhouse of the stern, upright William Ewart Gladstone, which faced Pall Mall, was stuffed with stolen writing paper from the Carlton and United University Clubs.[24] But this approach moves to other areas, too. Anything with a club monogram is targeted – visitors want a souvenir, and members feel that their subscriptions have paid for it. And so an endless profusion of plates, teacups, towels and combs have all gone missing through the ages. Newspapers have been stolen from clubs for as long as clubs have been supplying them, even when rules say that they should never be removed. The cloakroom of most clubs is notoriously dangerous for hats, overcoats, umbrellas and other paraphernalia being purloined with alarming regularity.

At least the prevalence of theft has kept humourists in good spirit. P. G. Wodehouse, ever a popular chronicler of Clubland, had his hero Psmith stealing from his club's cloakroom for a noble cause — he donated another member's umbrella to an attractive woman he spotted outside in the rain, because the avowed socialist declares, 'Other people are content to talk about the Redistribution of Property. I go out and do it.'[25]

The nineteenth-century British economy was significantly decentralised, and this came to be true of clubs, too. In tandem with the Georgian growth of London Clubland, other cities saw historic clubs being established by a combination of local gentry and merchants, with a smattering of aristocratic patronage. This included prosperous slave-trading port cities, like Liverpool, whose Athenaeum club for the arts and sciences opened in 1797 (pre-dating the better-known London Athenaeum by twenty-seven years), and Bristol, whose Clifton Club in the city's leafiest suburb opened in 1818, with a number of slave-holders on the roll of founder members. From the outset, the Clifton Club had a heavy overlap with the Society of Merchant Venturers which had pioneered the British slave trade and remained at the forefront of lobbying for slave-trading interests. There were also clubs in old market towns like Chester, which saw its City Club founded in 1808. Across the Irish Sea, Dublin's Kildare Street Club was founded in 1782 and provided a home for the Anglo-Irish Ascendancy aristocracy, and kicked off a wave of Dublin clubs with a distinct culture of their own.

Nearby European allies involved in heavy maritime trade with these port city clubs also sprouted some of the earliest clubs in the anglosphere, including the Haagsche Club-Plaats Royal in The Hague from 1748, the Royal Bachelors' Club in Gothenburg in 1769 and the Koninklijke Groote Industrieele Club of Amsterdam from 1788, as well as the Factory House in Porto from 1790. Each had a strongly anglophone bent, and acted as a precursor to the 'new money' middle-class clubs of London.

Some of central Europe saw its own club culture start to flourish around this time, too. Geneva was a popular stopping-off point on the Grand Tour of English aristocrats, as was Lausanne across Lac Léman. Geneva saw its Cercle de la Terrasse established in 1754, and club-like literary circles would follow in the 1810s, most notably the Société de Lecture of Geneva in 1818, and the Cercle Littéraire of Lausanne in 1819. Elsewhere in the west of Switzerland, the Cercle de la Grande Société de Berne, and the Société du Jardin de Neuchâtel, had both launched in 1759. In Sicily, Palermo housed both the Circolo Unione di Palermo, founded in 1750, and the Circolo Bellini, which launched nineteen years later. Further north, the Kingdom of Lombardy–Venetia saw Milan's Società del Giardino launch in 1783.

Across the Atlantic, North American clubs of the type which had first influenced White's began to develop a shape of their own. The Schuylkill Fishing Company founded in 1732 in Andalusia, Pennsylvania, evolved into a distinctive and influential private members' club, now regarded as the second oldest of America's surviving clubs; while in 1769 the Old Colony Club was established in Plymouth, Massachusetts. Like North America's original South River Club, it was based in a modest, if historic, white-painted small wooden house. These eighteenth-century American clubs mirrored the 'aristocratic embrace' of the London clubs, albeit with their own

White Anglo-Saxon Protestant (WASP) notions of aristocracy on the north-eastern seaboard; each would be influential on the future shape of American clubs.

The result was that by the end of the eighteenth century, a distinctive club culture had begun to evolve, heavily influenced by London, but far from confined to it. A combination of elites built these early clubs, centred around immigrants and travellers, in cities highly connected by trade, and with considerable cultural capital. The 'aristocratic embrace' which gave these clubs an aura of exclusivity was conspicuous by the 1760s; but it would not last more than half a century before beginning to be significantly watered down. The nineteenth century would bring a peak of club influence and reach – but first they would undergo huge changes.

Chapter Three

Women, and the rivals to clubs

(1770–1865)

Women have long been left out of the story of Clubland. Most accounts focus on the *manliness* of clubs, and accept the assumption that women were at best an irrelevance in a world built for men, with the clubs providing a manly refuge from a gentleman's home life.[1] Even some of the pioneering accounts of women's clubs implicitly accept that women steered clear of clubs before the last half of the nineteenth century, that there had been something fundamentally masculine about the idea of socialising in this way which had put off women from even wanting to join.

The all-too-prevalent idea that Clubland was inherently a male bastion from the start is simply wrong. If we look at the supposed ancestor of the London club itself, White's, we have already found that on the death of its founder, Francisco Bianco, in 1711 the establishment was inherited by his wife, Elisabetta Bianco, who took over for the next eighteen years, running the club for as long as her husband had done. W. B. Boulton noted that 'Advertisements in the papers show that "Mrs White's Chocolate House, in St James's Street," was the place of distribution of tickets for all the fashionable amusements of the early years of the eighteenth century', putting Mrs Bianco at the centre of London's social scene.[2]

It was only after Elisabetta Bianco's death in 1729 that the clubs of London started to take shape into the organisations that are recognisable today. For all the protestations to the contrary, even early in their history women were far from disinterested in clubs.

Even if women were to be excluded from these very earliest clubs, then there were several attempts to mount stiff competition. These were mainly in two forms: salons, and early ladies' clubs.

Salons made the most of the 'separate sphere' ideas that held sway. If a woman's autonomy was to be confined to the home, then the salon was an attempt to turn this into an advantage. Women could still wield the power of exclusion from their homes, just as a man in his club could wield a blackball. A salon was often physically smaller than a club; and its whole social network was confined to the immediate personal social circle of the hostess and her immediate acquaintances.

Nevertheless, salons could operate on different scales. There were salons, and there were Salons. The really large-scale Salons were veritable institutions of their own. Instead of working out of pokey front drawing rooms, they occupied large halls that could entertain hundreds at a time for dances, in an era when the clubs were still occupying modest sitting rooms which only sat a dozen members per room. The Salons were showier and more prestigious than clubs. And they were entirely in the hands of Lady Patronesses.

There was a key difference between the Salons and the clubs – the Salons had no such thing as membership. Instead, regular visitors to a Salon had to negotiate each visit, buying tickets each time, as one might in a modern nightclub. The tickets were sought-after commodities, and this placed the Lady Patronesses in a uniquely powerful position in deciding who was allowed to participate in polite society. The Lady Patronesses were often 'spoken of as virtual despots' in their granting of tickets.[3] The same favouritism, bias and bigotry found in the blackballing of men's clubs was present in ticket selection for Salons – and the whole process was just as steeped in secrecy. Furthermore, for the unfortunate guest falling out of favour with a Lady Patroness, there was no formal committee structure to whom an appeal could be lodged. The informal nature of the Salon ticketing system made the Lady Patroness's discretion absolute.

The largest and the loudest of the Salons was Almack's Rooms, which opened for business in 1765 on the south side of King Street, running between St James's Street and St James's Square. Four adjacent houses were demolished, to be replaced by a grand set of reception rooms, focused around a ninety-foot-long hall. Almack's threw grand balls, and had abundant side rooms for eating, drinking, gambling and gossiping – in other words, all the activities of the nearby clubs, only in an environment where men and women could mingle freely. Although founded by William Almack as a business venture, Almack's Rooms was run day to day by six or seven Lady Patronesses. After Almack's death in 1781, control passed to his widow. By the 1790s, control had passed to the Willis family, and the Salon was renamed Willis's Rooms. At its height, Almack's or Willis's Rooms were noted for their snobbery. When the last of the Willis owners, James Willis, died in 1847, it was felt to be enough of a staple of London's clubbable life to be worth saving, and the premises opened under new management, lingering on until 1863.

While Almack's and Willis's were primarily social venues, the early Victorians insisted on mixing their business with a fair amount of pleasure, and even elaborate party rooms such as these could be pressed into practical use, as they were in 1859 – a meeting of Whig, Peelite and Radical politicians at Willis's on 6 June that year resulted in the formation of the Liberal Party which would dominate British politics for much of the next half-century.[4]

Yet it was the role of women in running the key Salons which ultimately made those venues so unpopular with men. So long as the Salons enjoyed a monopoly on fashionable London sociability, they pushed a small number of aristocratic women to the fore, as 'kingmakers' (or queenmakers) of polite society. Once the clubs started to provide a set of facilities which were serious rivals, then by the 1820s the day of the Salon was over. Club members could wander into comparable establishments simply by right of membership, without having to toady to the whims of a Lady Patroness each week for a fresh set of tickets.

Moreover, once the clubs started to explicitly 'pull up the drawbridge' against women visitors, their male members no longer needed to worry about Lady Patronesses at all. With the closure of Willis's Rooms in 1863, the Salons fell into abeyance, merging into less formal (and less prestigious) gatherings in private homes.

Men-only clubs can therefore be seen as a reaction to the women-controlled Salons; and the overlap was considerable, for, as we shall see, just as the last great Salons were winding down in the 1860s, so the first of the women's clubs opened for business. Women were never entirely excluded from the world of London clubs; but there was certainly an aggressive push by mid-nineteenth-century men to 'put them in their place', and to exclude them from the most prestigious clubs of London.

This proved to be quite a contrast to the early beginnings of clubs. Boodle's had been one of the earliest fully-formed, recognisable London clubs, convened by future prime minister the Earl of Shelburne in 1762, next door to the original Almack's premises, a tavern in Pall Mall, and benefited from service from their better-known neighbour. In its early years, it supported a separate but linked Ladies' Boodle's club, one of the earliest recognisable women's clubs.

Confusingly, London's early hospitality magnate William Almack operated *two* sets of premises around the corner from one another – Almack's, the original tavern on Pall Mall opened in 1759, before the better-known Almack's Assembly Rooms, detailed above. In addition to Almack's tavern serving both sexes, Horace Walpole noted that Boodle's next door to Almack's tavern intended to be 'a club of both sexes'.[5] It would do so through the establishment of a separate Ladies' Boodle's, known as the Female Coterie. Objecting to the largely masculine environment of a pub, by 1770 the Female Coterie was meeting in the backrooms of Almack's tavern. The Female Coterie were able 'to play cards, chat, or do whatever else they please'.[6]

An intriguing feature was that husbands automatically became members of the Female Coterie upon their wives joining. F. H. W. Sheppard noted another unusual feature: 'The most important rules were that all members were admitted by ballot and "the ladies shall ballot for men, and men for ladies"; thus "no lady can exclude a lady, or gentleman a gentleman".'[7] This distinctive approach to blackballing would not be replicated in future clubs, but it gave the Female Coterie its own unique culture.

The Female Coterie was small and overwhelmingly upper class, with 130 members in 1770, still very much part of the 'aristocratic phase' of Clubland, and the following year it took up more permanent premises in Arlington Street. It had all the trappings of a club, including the same balloting system with blackballs for electing and vetoing new members. Rumours abounded that the Duchess of Bedford had been blackballed – although her husband, the 4th Duke, subsequently joined.

Contemporary press coverage made much of the innovation, noting, 'those adventurous and spirited females, who seem resolved to break through the whalebone and buckram fences of modesty and decorum . . . A certain masculine air now distinguished the ladies [whom] . . . have arrogated the old Salic laws of libertinism, and openly set up a tavern in potent rivalry of Boodle's, Arthur's and Almack's.'[8]

The Female Coterie was to be a short-lived affair. It was wound down by 1777, for reasons that remain unclear. A heavily fashionable gathering in the early 1770s, it may simply have fallen out of favour within a few years. It also attracted, as Daniella Ben-Arie has noted, a heavy volume of negative publicity, which may have marred its image – although this was by no means unique, with many of the clubs of the day being lambasted for their hard drinking and profligate gambling.

Whatever the reason for its dissolution, the existence of the Female Coterie should not be minimised. From the very earliest days of London Clubland, there existed not only a major rival to the clubs in the form of women-run Salons, but also a blueprint for a mixed-sex club in the heart of St James's, long before most of today's clubs even existed. Women's participation in Clubland remained focused around the Salon for decades, but once these wound down, the experience of Ladies' Boodle's showed the potential for women's clubs.

There were also clear signs of a wider interest in women's clubs, from beyond the St James's district. A number of ladies' groups and societies *without* premises of their own convened in the late eighteenth century. T. H. S. Escott thought it significant that only one of these, the Ladies' Jockey Club for titled racing enthusiasts, was aristocratic in background. Of the rest:

> The Georgian ladies affecting what they called clubs, were certainly not in society. They belonged, in fact, to the lower and industrial portion of the middle class. Thus a Weavers' Wives Club met at a select pot-house in Spitalfields; there was a Milliners' Club not a stone's throw from the Royal Exchange,

a Mantua Makers' in St Martin's Lane, and innumerable others of the same kind elsewhere.[9]

Early women's societies modelled on clubs therefore foreshadowed the middle-class direction that men's clubs would take in the nineteenth century.

Furthermore, women were never kept out of the men's clubs entirely. Even men-only clubs had women admitted as part of their world: in 1802, Boodle's threw a vast ball for several hundred men and women under a large tent in Ranelagh pleasure gardens in Chelsea – 'separate spheres' had its limits.[10]

As the nineteenth century wore on, various men's clubs would introduce (and then repeal) bans on women visitors and women staff. This was not the case in the Georgian clubs, however. Although 'separate spheres' ideology meant that there were already considerable obstacles to women members and visitors 'upstairs', no such obstacles existed 'downstairs'. Female servants worked in clubs from their earliest days. The Travellers Club was established in 1819, and by 1826 it already had a female chef.[11] Yet the presence of mixed-sex staffing led to serious concerns about staff fraternisation from the outset. For instance, in 1836 there were complaints at the Travellers Club about women staff 'giggling and romping' in the Men Servants' room.[12]

Nor did the 'upstairs' rooms of Clubland escape women's interests. The French-Peruvian writer Flora Tristan visited several London clubs as part of her travelogues of London. In the course of four tours of the city between 1826 and 1839, she was convinced that a visit to Clubland would be insightful. She recruited the aid of a male friend (a time-honoured ploy for club-crashers to work in pairs, feigning being deep in conversation, so as to deter footmen from interrupting them), and she cross-dressed as a man. The ploy

61

seems to have been wholly successful – she recounts visiting clubs in Pall Mall, St James's and Carlton Terrace, and made no mention of ever being found out. At the very least, her descriptions tally with her having penetrated the Athenaeum, Carlton and Reform Clubs, on her 1835 and 1839 visits.

She was not impressed by what she saw. Tristan's descriptions of all-male clubs in the 1830s could be decidedly caustic, although that was in keeping with her sometimes snobbish remarks about London society in general. While she paid tribute to the clubs' architectural grandeur and luxurious range of facilities, she was less charitable about their members:

> What do those two or three hundred members of a club actually do all day? Are they looking to enlighten themselves, in good faith, on important social issues? Do they talk about business and politics? Literature, theatre and fine arts, perhaps?
>
> No. They go there to eat well, drink good wines, play and escape the boredom of the household; they come there looking for a shelter from the tribulations of the day, and not to indulge in fatigue sustained by discussion on any topic.
>
> Besides, to whom could they chat? They remain unknown to each other; the membership of a club does not entail the obligation to speak to one's associates, or even to greet them. And so everyone enters the lounges, a hat on his head, neither looking at, nor greeting, anyone. There is nothing more comical than seeing a hundred men gathered together in these large living rooms, as if they were furniture; one, sitting on an armchair, reads a new brochure; another writes on a table, next to an individual he has never spoken to; that one, sprawled across a sofa, sleeps; then there are those walking up and down; and not to disturb this sepulchral silence, there are some who speak low, as if they were in church.

'What fun can these men find, to be reunited in this way?', I thought when I saw them. All appeared to be very bored. Astonished by this singular mode of association, I at times imagined seeing a collection of automata. I asked the Englishman who accompanied me, why there wasn't more intercourse between the members of these societies.

'How would you', he replied to me, 'address a man whom you don't know; and about whom you don't know anything; so that you don't even know whether he is rich or poor, Tory, Whig or Radical, and risk hurting the opinions of which he is so proud, regardless of the consequences? Only the French could commit these kinds of impertinences!'

'Why', I replied, 'do you get people joining the Club when you do not know them?'

He replied, 'Because you need a certain number of contributing members to cover the Club's overheads, and we only need to know about the respectability of members, and that they were presented by two Club members and approved by the committee.'

This answer perfectly portrays the English mind; this company always offers its members, through its association, the scope to achieve a material advantage; do not ask your club to associate its thoughts, its feelings, its being moral; because it will not understand you. - This immobility of the soul, this social materialism, is something frightening.[13]

Tristan's testimony offers a unique insight from a consummate outsider – as a woman, a feminist, a socialist, a lesbian and a foreigner – yet tempered with a rare, candid 'ringside seat' on early Clubland.

Nor was Tristan an isolated example. There would be plenty of later cases of women cross-dressing to get into men-only clubs. Members of the Savage Club were suspicious about the appearance of one regular visitor in the early twentieth century who had attended a string of their weekly House Dinners. One member approached them, and declared, 'You must excuse me, but I don't like your "make up"', and tugged at the moustache, only for it to peel away. She sprang to her feet, grabbed her coat as she passed the exit, and bolted. Her host subsequently admitted that his wife had been a weekly guest for some time, and he protested that it did not breach the letter of the Savage Club's rules, for they only said that a guest must behave like a gentleman.[14]

The exclusion of women from London's early clubs mirrored the wider exclusivity which they cultivated in the Georgian period, as they were centred around formalising a set of luxury facilities, for a small group of well-connected men. Yet by the 1820s, clubs were to undergo a radical transformation, which would have far-reaching implications, including the admission of women.

The writer George Augustus Sala was an active clubman, who was a founding member of two Savage Clubs on opposite sides of the globe, one in London (1857), the other in Sydney (1885); clubs which were aimed at actors and writers who enjoyed combining formal dinners with donning blackface at club entertainments. He opined, 'I may say that it is a subject for sincere congratulation that there are no ladies' clubs. We have been threatened with them sometimes, but they have always been nipped in the bud.' Sala was writing in 1859, describing attitudes up until then. The following year, the first Victorian London club for women would open.[15]

Chapter Four

Reform or revolution?
(1820–1860)

The one thing that almost *everyone* knows about the Reform Club is that it was the starting point of its member Phileas Fogg's journey in *Around the World in 80 Days*.

Actually, there could scarcely have been a less representative member of the Reform Club than the literary Fogg. The loudly political Reform Club, founded in the aftermath of the 1832 Reform Act, still requires members to sign a declaration of their agreement with the principles of that Act. The Club was a hotch-potch of earnest Whig, Liberal, Radical and Reformer politicos from across Britain. Its members could not talk anything *but* politics.

Yet Fogg cuts a distinctly apolitical figure, and Jules Verne's explanation is decidedly unconvincing: 'The way in which he got admission to this exclusive club was simple enough. He was recommended by the Barings, with whom he had an open credit.'[1] This might have been a plausible enough explanation for many clubs, but not the Reform, with its growing waiting list and legions of avowedly political candidates queuing up to join, and pressing their case based on merit. It seems far more likely that Verne, who had never set foot in the Reform Club, simply chose the first name that he could find for a fashionable London club. This misleading image has been enduring, even though the clubs of London were about to go through a deeply political phase. Equally puzzling is how no one had any idea where Fogg's money came from; for the mid-nineteenth century was the era of the plutocrat, as the middle classes massively expanded – and clubs hugely reflected this, with members flaunting their wealth.

The arrival of professional middle-class clubs also brought a preponderance of nouveaux riches tastes.[2] These made themselves felt in fields from gastronomy to architecture. As clubhouses became more ostentatious, the members who frequented them around the clock began to expect ever more elaborate meals. As Roy Strong has noted, the nineteenth century saw a revolution in supply chains: 'New transport systems meant that diet ceased to be regionally based, and by 1900, thanks to the emergence of the processing industry, canning and refrigeration, food became international.'[3] This coincided with the Victorian craze for celebrity expatriate chefs who balanced a flair for novel recipes and publicity, including Louis Eustache Ude, *chef de cuisine* of Crockford's from 1827 to 1838, and his successor from 1838 to 1840, Charles Elmé Francatelli. Yet it was the celebrated Alexis Soyer at the Reform Club who would become the most famous Clubland chef.[4]

All three chefs were pioneers of popular cookbooks, with Soyer balancing out scholarly, historical tomes such as his updating of classical Greek and Roman recipes, with his affordable cookbook suggesting everyday recipes which could be made at home on a budget.[5]

Flora Tristan, as a visitor from France wandering the clubs of London incognito, observed the heavily continental flavour of the cuisine offered by clubs in the 1830s:

> Now we know that, for any Englishman, dinner is the big business, the purpose of existence. There is no club passably

well-established which does not have a French cook. The Head Chef (because the culinary artist keeps, on the other side of the Channel, his name grandiose) is the very soul of the establishment. In general, we dine very well in the clubs. In all, we eat French dishes, the Sauternes and Champagne are of first quality, and all at a very moderate price.[6]

At the Reform Club, Soyer personified the gregarious showmanship which came to be embraced by noted chefs. Everything about him was unconventional – his artisanal clothes offset by a velvet hat, even his business cards, which were octagonal rather than rectangular, were all intended to draw attention to the man. This was the antithesis of stuffy, invisible Georgian club servants in matching livery disappearing into the background – Soyer made his presence felt out in front as well as in the kitchen, seeing gastronomy as a theatrical experience, and delighting in ostentatiously carving roasts before guests, and flambéing pigeons before members. At the time of his appointment as Reform Club chef in 1838, Soyer was just twenty-eight (he would die relatively young, at the age of forty-eight); and he would be in post for twelve years, but the shadow he left was a long one – even today his name is mentioned in hushed tones, and one of this signature dishes, Lamb Cutlets Reform, made together from improvised odds and ends when he was dealing with a particularly fussy member late at night, is still served up in the Reform Club's Coffee Room.

After his stint at the Reform, Soyer would go on to be renowned as the creator of the 'magic stove', a versatile piece of equipment that would become a staple of the British army for nearly a century, permitting the cooking of hot meals in the field. First used in the Crimean War of the 1850s, Soyer's stove was still in use in the Second World War. It was this level of creativity that Soyer brought to the Reform Club's kitchen, comprehensively reimagining and redesigning a kitchen's layout to serve as both a laboratory and factory; a culinary counterpart to the Industrial Revolution which had overtaken Britain, all guided by meticulous research. The Reform Club moved to temporary quarters in 1838–41, at Gwydir House on Whitehall, while the present building was constructed. Soyer made the most of these cramped kitchen premises for the first three years, collaborating closely with architect Charles Barry on the main clubhouse, to produce a template for the nineteenth-century kitchen, which effectively worked as a factory production line for fine dining.

This reflected the other way in which nouveaux riches tastes made themselves most keenly felt, through Clubland architecture. The earliest clubhouses of St James's emulated the style of the aristocratic mansions which marked the district (now almost all vanished after the inter-war property boom made them more cost effective to demolish and sell off for the land).[7] Clubs such as Arthur's, Boodle's, Brooks's, Crockford's and White's were stately but modest buildings in the Palladian style, and in size they often resembled little more than voluminous townhouses. Generally, few rooms could comfortably seat more than thirty people – at Brooks's, the great Subscription Room on the first floor *might* hold up to a hundred people standing, provided they were of light build, packed in like sardines and held their tummies in.

Nouveaux riches tastes changed that. Club architecture became something of an 'arms race'. As with club rulebooks, the Union Club on New Square (now Trafalgar Square) was a trendsetter. Other clubs would emulate its large, airy rooms, and its principal floors all raised above street level, so that club members could peer down onto the world outside, while passers-by could not peer in. A relatively small circle of architects, mindful of the clubs' need for discretion, were to define what the 'typical' London club would look like.

A further opportunity was thrown open by the sale in 1826 of the Carlton House estate. Carlton House had been a sprawling mansion owned by George IV, used as his London base when he was Prince Regent. Once he became King in 1820, he chose to focus on redeveloping the old Buckingham House as Buckingham Palace, and took the opportunity to settle his spiralling personal debts by selling off Carlton House and its surrounding land.

Until this point, the clubs dotted along St James's Street had grown rather crowded into a small, overdeveloped space. Pall Mall, adjoining the bottom of St James's Street and stretching east into New Square, offered a chance to expand. The south side of Pall Mall, where Carlton House had stood, offered large, relatively inexpensive parcels of land for such a prime central location – and they went onto the market just as Clubland was taking off. It was an irresistible combination, with fashionable new clubs for middle-class professionals moving in, including the United Service Club and the Athenaeum.

Few buildings have been as influential on London club architecture as the Athenaeum, designed by Decimus Burton, a twenty-three-year-old prodigy when he was commissioned in 1824; although the commission may have also had something to do with his father, James Burton, being one of London's richest, most successful and well-connected builders.[8] It was James who seized the construction contract for the Club.

The Athenaeum was the first club to be built around a large, central atrium which the front entrance led into – a pattern which would be repeated by countless other clubs. This created easy flows walking in and out of the club, all revolving around the atrium. More importantly, it revolutionised how members would use their clubs. The atrium – typically covered by some skylight in most clubs – would become the heart of the club. No more hobbling around narrow, winding corridors past the front door, checking every individual room, one by one, to see who was dining, gambling or resting in each spot. Instead, lounging became the order of the day – one could lounge or loiter around the atrium, amiably keeping an eye on who went in or who came out. Guests could be greeted. Gossip could be picked up. Most helpfully of all, the temporary nature of being in the atrium meant that bores could be easily disposed of – one could potentially hang around in the lobby for hours on end; but at the first sign of an imposition, a bore could be fobbed off with a hurried excuse about needing to be in another room, and being on one's way. There was no commitment to endure company one did not enjoy. Club atriums gradually became the very hub of many a club for gossip, surpassing even the bar and the smoking room.

The Athenaeum building was also highly influential in several other ways. It was equipped with one of the largest and finest libraries in Clubland – it is still a marvel to stand amid its three storeys of book-covered walls.

Moreover, it presented a revolution in neoclassical design. Until this time, clubs had shown subtle influences of Classical architecture, but these were limited to the odd column here and there. There was no mistaking the Athenaeum for anything but a classically-themed club, from its gold statue of Athena over the front portico, to the scale reconstruction of the Parthenon Marbles frieze which ran along three of its outside walls. The Athenaeum building, with its strong influence of an ancient Greek temple, oozed that it was an establishment institution, representing *solidity* and permanence. It was a look which many subsequent London clubs were to emulate, including the Oxford and Cambridge Club,

Army and Navy Club, East India Club and (after a refit) the United Service Club. It transformed how clubs started to think about themselves. They were no longer small, fly-by-night gambling dens in cramped townhouses. They were substantive institutions which could not be ignored, and would not be moved. By the middle of the century, the whole of the south side of Pall Mall was a solid mass of palatial, newly built clubhouses. This, more than any site on earth, was Clubland.

By the end of the century, with Pall Mall space running out, much of the northern side of Piccadilly facing Green Park was dotted with an overflow of ever-larger London clubhouses, often stretching to four, five, or even six thousand members each. The clubs were increasingly *confident* – and their custom-built architecture was their way of declaring this to the outside world, building enigmatic citadels that filled outsiders with curiosity, in much the same way that heavily secretive Freemasons would build incredibly conspicuous halls in plain sight on main high streets.

One of the unsuccessful applicants to design the Athenaeum was the Prince Regent's favourite architect, the highly fashionable John Nash. Nash was, however, later commissioned to design the United Service Club building directly opposite, in 1826. Nash had been a mentor to the young Decimus Burton, and so after Nash's death it was Burton who extensively remodelled the exterior. Given the United Service Club's proximate mirroring position to Burton's Athenaeum across Waterloo Place, it was refaced as a consciously Roman-style building, both complementing and contrasting the Greek-style Athenaeum, but with shared materials and colour scheme. Taken together, they made a large, pleasing vista at the junction of Pall Mall and Waterloo Place, just behind the Duke of York Column which towered over them from 1832. Standing on that site today, peering down the still club-lined Pall Mall, marks the entry point to the very heart of Clubland. Burton also found himself called upon to redesign other clubs, most notably the two-storey Oriental Club in Hanover Square, to which he added one more storey.

Another of the influential architects of Clubland was Charles Barry, who designed two major London clubhouses, the Travellers and Reform Clubs. These are both in very different styles. The Travellers in the 1820s was really the last gasp of the 'English country house' style, with small but elegant asymmetrical rooms, compared to the increasingly grandiose European palaces which would surround it. It presents a 'missing link' between the small aristocratic clubs of the previous century, and the grander, bolder clubs which would follow.

So different is the Reform Club next door that it is difficult to believe it was the work of the same architect, barely more than a decade later. Yet Barry's Reform Club showed the shape of things to come. With an exterior strongly influenced by the Palazzo Farnese in Rome, as well as Barry's earlier buildings in the north of England, the interior comes as a shock, in assuming a completely different style from the exterior. It takes Burton's central atrium concept one step further, in a pillared symphony of marble, wood, tiling and glass. Surrounded by a first-floor saloon where members sip drinks while staring, panopticon-like, down into the central lobby below, the Club showed the possibilities ahead. While the building stands as a monument (or mausoleum, depending on one's view) to the Whigs and Reformers of the nineteenth century, lined in portraits of its founders, what it exudes above all else is *power*. Peter Marsh once said that the Club was 'a great stage in the theatre of politics', and that 'No one who enters the Reform Club can mistake it for a setting for democracy.'[9] It is little wonder that when Parliament came to be rebuilt after the great fire of 1834, the winner of the design competition was the Reform Club's Charles Barry.

Yet Barry, for all his influence, only ever designed two clubhouses. London's most prolific club architects in the Victorian era were probably the Smirke brothers, Robert and Sydney.

Sydney Smirke had originally made his name as a club architect designing the first United Service Club on Charles Street in 1819, now long since demolished. It was a stately building with neoclassical elements; but it was not long before the Club's eye was caught by one of the Carlton House plots of land, and they promptly commissioned John Nash to build something bigger and better, which was completed opposite the Athenaeum in 1830. The old, Smirke-designed building on Charles Street was instead bought up by the new Junior United Service Club.

Sir Robert Smirke, the older brother, was best known as the architect of the British Museum. In his Oxford and Cambridge Club building of 1835-8, he was clearly influenced by the Athenaeum's Grecian temple – though he couldn't help but garnish it with a few English touches, most notably in the terracotta panels of scenes from Classical antiquity at the front, which are incongruously joined by a Tudor scene.

Previously, Sir Robert Smirke had rather less successfully built one of the earlier little-loved clubhouses of the Carlton Club, for Britain's Conservatives, a clumsy building with Palladian touches. Accounts of this building were uniformly unflattering, pointing to poor lighting, and poor use of space with random, winding corridors that needed to be navigated to get from one room to another – a point reinforced by the building's surviving plans. As the Carlton Club was based across a narrow alleyway from its great rival, the Liberal Party's Reform Club, it had before it a very obvious model for a successor club, built in a quadrangle around an atrium, bigger and better in every way. The Carlton's members were so dissatisfied with their own clubhouse, they took the drastic step of demolishing it in 1854, and replacing it with a larger building (thanks to also demolishing some adjoining buildings and expanding onto them). Completed in 1856, this was entrusted to the younger brother, Sydney Smirke, and was in many ways a reflection of the Reform Club directly opposite, following a similar style and layout. Members were, however, treated to an even more souped-up central atrium, set around a series of staircases to give a sense of occasion. This sort of one-upmanship, and 'arms race' among rival clubs jockeying for ever more elaborate facilities, was to mark the nineteenth century, as clubhouses grew more ambitious. It was to prove extremely expensive, with crippling mortgages that were still being paid off well into the twentieth century.

Sydney Smirke also found his Conservative contacts were invaluable in securing the tender to design another major clubhouse, the Conservative Club of 1840, which was a breakaway from the Carlton, stemming from the latter club's growing waiting list, and catering mainly for those on the Conservative radical right, who had trouble getting into the Carlton. Sydney Smirke collaborated with George Basevi to come up with a highly eye-catching design – classical in its exterior, but with a gaudy, gold-leaf-covered Byzantine-influenced interior, and a large lobby looked down upon by a circular-banistered gallery above. This was a club for people who wanted to be noticed. Indeed, club members wanted their clubhouse's grandiosity to be acknowledged by outsiders, and this increasing architectural grandeur encouraged members to open up these clubhouses to outside guests.

The architectural 'arms race' among clubs foreshadowed an increasingly public role. Some clubs have always embraced discretion, bordering on secrecy – Boodle's still notes today, 'The club has never sought public attention.'[10] Yet the increasingly eye-catching architecture of nineteenth-century clubs was intended to draw attention.

The Athenaeum, for instance, is adorned with a frieze by John Henning Jr which was the first public exhibition of the Parthenon Marbles in any form in Britain, and being outdoors, was visible to all. While the Marbles had been acquired by the British Museum some years earlier, they remained hidden from public view in storage. Henning's frieze, adorning three sides of the Athenaeum building, represented an attempt to 'restore' the Marbles, complete with filled-in missing segments, in a copy approximately three-quarters scale.

As the nineteenth century wore on, even the most private of clubs began to assume a more public role. St James's Street and Pall Mall became regular routes for pageants and state marches such as funerals and jubilees. The profusion of grand clubhouses along Pall Mall made it a perfect vantage point for processions, such as the 1838 coronation of Queen Victoria. Instead of being routed directly along the main east–west thoroughfare of Piccadilly, they were diverted south down St James's Street, so that they could then run along the parallel east–west course of Pall Mall, passing the stately new clubhouses. Clubs accordingly began to erect temporary stands, and admission for men and women alike for these unique vantage points was 'the hottest ticket in town', particularly benefiting from the raised elevation of Clubland architecture. By the time of the Duke of Wellington's funeral in 1852, Pall Mall was accustomed to the routine, with temporary stands covered in black drapes of mourning,

The disadvantage of this public role was that it brought an increase in public scrutiny, from simple mockery to clubs becoming objects of protest. It was nothing new to satirise clubs: pioneering Georgian cartoonist James Gillray had lodged in the St James's Street rooms of his publisher and lover Hannah Humphrey, and whenever he needed divine inspiration he had but to look out of the window at the nearby clubs, frequently spoofing Boodle's next door, as well as

Brooks's and White's. Clubs as a target of protest became a growing phenomenon from the nineteenth century.

Public protests made the most of London's new open spaces. Trafalgar Square was completed in the 1840s, initially designed by club architect John Nash, and then redesigned by fellow club architect Charles Barry. Barry's design sought to minimise the space open to protestors so close to Parliament, by permeating the area with huge fountains, lest any crowds turn violent. With Pall Mall flowing into Trafalgar Square, the established route for protestors marching from Hyde Park made the march past the clubs of St James's a regular fixture, which it remains to this day. This led to predictable results, particularly when some clubs had strong political connections to the governing party of the day. In 1866, Lord Stanley recorded that a crowd of 10,000 pro-reform demonstrators shuffled down Pall Mall, and that 'They went off pretty quietly, groaning only at the Carlton.'[11] This was followed by a similar raucous protest past the Carlton in 1867.[12] So-called 'Black Monday' on 8 February 1886 saw riots breaking out across the West End of London, and they included a group of several thousand men peeling off from a protest of the Marxist Social Democratic Federation in Trafalgar Square, descending on Pall Mall and hurling stones at the windows of the Carlton Club.[13]

Anti-club demonstrations could turn even more violent. It was unlikely that a crowd would force its way into a clubhouse that was heavily guarded by club servants and had robust doors, with windows above ground level. Terrorism was another matter. Sneaky, isolated attacks on clubs sought to make the most of security vulnerabilities. One example was the terrorist bomb at the Junior Carlton Club on 30 May 1884. It was lobbed into an open window in the rear kitchen on St James's Square, which was located below ground level. The bombing was devastating, and it necessitated a full reconstruction of the building.

If anything, clubs as targets of terrorism grew worse after the nineteenth century. Well into the late twentieth century, terrorists would often target clubs due to their perceived (if not actual) power. The Irish Republican Army and its successors particularly saw clubs as valid targets. A bombing campaign in 1974 saw attacks between October and December on military-themed clubs including the Army and Navy Club, the Cavalry Club, the Naval and Military Club, and the Victory Services Club, as well as the National Liberal Club as a political club. The Naval and Military Club's long bar was devastated by a bomb thrown through the building's open front window. Remarkably, no one in the packed bar was killed; although, after a long, awkward pause and everyone being thrown off their feet by the blast, including the head barman Robbins, one member, Commander Vaughan Williams, broke the awkward silence: 'Another pink gin please, Robbins.'[14]

Mildly more baffling was the October 1974 bomb attack on Brooks's (by then avowedly apolitical), which injured three staff members. The only explanation anyone could come up with was that the home secretary, Roy Jenkins, was a member. The National Liberal Club was to suffer a second IRA bomb in 1992, although the shattered windows were all replaced the same day by the Club's efficient Secretary, Graham Snell. The most notorious terrorist attack on a club, however, remains the IRA's 25 June 1990 bombing of the Carlton Club, which wounded twenty people, and a Conservative peer, Lord Kaberry, died of his injuries nine months later.

Violence very much loomed in the background of the early nineteenth century, however. From the violent suppression in the Peterloo Massacre of 1819, to the mass demonstrations of the Birmingham Political Union in the 1830s, a series of large political protests sprang up around the issue of parliamentary representation (or lack of it).

These uprisings were long presented as examples of growing working-class involvement in politics, a backlash against the cosy power wielded in places like clubs. In recent years, historians have seen them more as battles among Britain's growing middle class. In particular, the Industrial Revolution had seen an explosion in the size of the middle class. The new members of this moneyed class wanted to find avenues for their new disposable income, and clubs were a perfect outlet for this, if only they weren't continually excluded from them. They also wanted to participate in politics – especially through gaining the franchise – and clubs were again to play a role in this. Recent estimates have shown that the 'Great Reform Act' of 1832 was not particularly 'Great'. It extended the vote from around 2 per cent of the population, to between 4 and 6 per cent of the population – scarcely a transformation. For decades more, voting remained an elite preoccupation, often closely tied to the kinds of people who belonged to clubs. The debates which persisted through much of the nineteenth century were *which* parts of the evolving middle classes were thought desirable and wise enough to be trusted with a vote. The vote was the ultimate middle-class status symbol. Club membership was not far off.

For the first three decades of the nineteenth century, there were demonstrations over Catholic Emancipation, and the vote itself, which risked seeing violence break out more widely – even if the crisis could sometimes veer into farce. Memorably, the Lord Chancellor Lord Brougham physically got down on his knees in the House of Lords in support of reform, telling his fellow peers, 'I implore you – yea, on my *bended knee* I supplicate you – reject not this bill!'[15] Unfortunately for Brougham, it was at that exact moment that his back seized up. The drama of the moment was considerably reduced as he had to ask his fellow peers to carry him away.

As the dust settled on the First Reform Act of 1832, clubs came to assume a central role. Part of this had little to do with reform, and everything to do with the Great Fire of 1834, which had burned down almost all of the old Houses of Parliament. There were no longer rooms in Westminster physically large enough to contain hundreds of MPs – other than in the clubs.

This was compounded by the changes to the House of Commons. Until 1832, political parties only existed in the very loosest sense – factions of half a dozen to a dozen aristocratic MPs, usually united by family (or family interest), who sat together. After 1832, with the Reform Act placing an emphasis on democratic mandates, it became important for parties to start winning votes of confidence in the House of Commons. That meant regularly putting together coalitions of two or three hundred MPs, all voting for the same cause on the same night.[16] Instead of clubs gathering a dozen MPs in a room, they needed to gather together three hundred in a room. In the 1830s and 1840s, with Parliament relegated to a building site and the existing Salons winding down, there were very few rooms in Central London big enough to accommodate this.

After 1832, there was a flurry of new political clubs. Defeat was often a great spur to reorganisation, and in 1832 the defeated Tories, flung out of power after decades, turned their electioneering office into the Carlton Club. Four years later, the Whigs and Reformers, who had already had their majority slashed in the 1835 general election, founded the Reform Club as a rival next door. Both clubs were meant to help regroup after defeats. Both clubs would be heavily politicised, and their proximity to power made them enormously prestigious – which only increased their appeal to those who were disinterested in politics, yet still keen to mix in the highest social circles. They were to prove popular templates for many of the clubs that followed.

The post-reform world these clubs appeared in was very new for all concerned. Almanacs started to appear. Originally, these almanacs were made necessary by the First Reform Act: MPs were no longer all aristocrats, inter-related and inter-marrying one another's families. As a new wave of middle-class MPs appeared, people started to ask 'Who is he?' To answer this need, *Dod's Parliamentary Companion* first appeared in 1833.[17] This was to be the first in a series of nineteenth-century almanacs such as *Vacher's*, and culminating in *Who's Who* from 1897. The section where entrants listed their memberships of 'Clubs' afforded some scope for showing off. In addition, some MPs, presumably feeling deeply inadequate at their own lack of social connections, tended to embellish and outright lie about which clubs they belonged to. The proportion was as high as one in ten MPs blatantly fibbing and claiming to belong to a certain club.[18] Then there were the MPs who, if not lying outright, then certainly embellished. In the 1830s, the newly elected Benjamin Disraeli told *Dod's* that his club memberships were 'Carlton, etc.'. In fact, having been blackballed by the Athenaeum, Grillions and Travellers Clubs, and expelled from the Westminster Reform Club for non-payment of his subscription, he only had one other club at the time, Crockford's, covered by the 'etc.'.[19] (By the twenty-first century, the reverse has happened – instead of MPs fabricating membership of prestigious clubs, many modern-day MPs play the prolier-than-thou card in public, but prefer to quietly omit any mention of the salubrious clubs to which they retire in the evenings.)

Yet the political clubs were far more than just a salon in which people could show off, close to the centres of power. They had aspirations to meddle in elections, and to control the destiny of the nation. My previous research into this has shown that their success at this was quite limited: they did indeed engage solicitors to act as election agents, in general elections and in by-elections up and down the country. The clubs' influence here was modest, though. The election interventions numbered in the dozens, not the hundreds; and they were mainly limited to the south-east of England. The sums they raised in each seat made up just a tiny proportion of the money spent on electioneering. For all the talk of 'club government', the actual 'golden showers of the Reform Club' and 'Carlton Club gold' were scarce.[20]

Where clubs did matter was in setting a framework for 'high politics', as Victorian Britain evolved. They provided inexpensive, respectable lodgings in town for MPs and those on political business. They provided offices, when the political parties had none. They were more than just rooms for MPs' meetings – they were an extension of the parliamentary estate, which remained a building site until the late 1860s, but was easily reached by hansom cab. They encouraged the discreet lobbying of politicians which has so long been a hallmark of the British political system.

For a few short years, in the 1820s and 1830s, the United Kingdom seemed to stand on the brink of revolution. By going for modest political reform, the threat of revolution retreated – for a while, at least. This gave way to a cosy, self-congratulatory orthodoxy. Where the English had once been branded a 'dangerous' people, 'mad, bad and dangerous to know',[21] this gave way to Victorian ideas of respectability, and the breezy confidence of club buildings, club rules and club mannerisms helped solidify that.

Richard Usborne echoed the belief that a club's 'hall porter was a reasonable picket against cads, creditors and hunch-backed foreigners'.[22] In reality, clubs had no shortage of cads and bounders; and politicians could be the most rum characters of all. Early Victorian MPs like Peter Borthwick fled their creditors through their clubs – the fact that they would not (yet) admit women, even as visitors, allowed him to evade several female creditors, including a

81

Mrs Lutton of Bath, and a Mrs Bates of Richmond. When the latter showed up at the Carlton Club in 1842 to demand the money due to her, Carlton members were far more upset at a woman getting as far as the main lobby than they were at one of their members being a fraudster who left a trail of unpaid bills. Instead, they passed a resolution, 'That the Porter have orders to prevent females waiting in the Clubhouse'.[23] Early clubs were full of wheeler-dealers 'on the make', like Peter Borthwick. But the gradual retreat into cosy bourgeois respectability would allow clubs to paper over the reality.

By the 1840s, clubs looked and felt different. They were grander, offering greater creature comforts to a wider audience of members increasingly drawn from the middle classes. Accessing these clubs, however, was increasingly dependent on ideas of respectability, and pursuing the right causes, which came to have a growing grip on nineteenth-century Britain. Club members were about to discover that the middle classes were not the only audiences for 'respectable' clubs.

Chapter Five

The rise and rise of the working men's clubs
(1858–1920)

The Reverend Henry Solly was a most unusual person. His original calling was as a Unitarian minister, but Solly found that the consuming passions of his life were ever less centred around religion. Instead, having been politicised by the Chartist movement as a young man, he grew increasingly consumed with Radical politics. In particular, he was fascinated by the idea of self-help as a way 'to improve the character and condition of the Working Classes in this country'.[1]

Unlike some of Karl Marx's disciples and collaborators such as Friedrich Engels, who had shown so much preoccupation about *The Condition of the English Working Class*, Solly chose a different outlet. He saw the potential to realise lasting social change through leisure. He was especially impressed with the organisational potential of the new clubs – and set out to imitate them. In the late 1850s, Solly's ministry in Lancaster put him in Britain's industrial heartland. He began speaking and writing around the idea of self-help, and clubs. By 1862, he was ready to launch the Working Men's Club and Institute Union.

What made Solly's approach so unusual was that it was the opposite to how the older clubs of London had evolved. They had grown organically. Their objects were extremely modest, self-indulgent even. By contrast, Solly was tremendously ambitious, with lofty goals of inspiring waves of self-improvement. He saw clubs as a vessel for social change. Crucially, he looked at how the elite society of London and the provinces coalesced around a handful of clubs, and he believed that more people could benefit from their fellowship.

Solly's working men's clubs were aimed at bringing a slice of Pall Mall into local communities. A working men's club would have far more modest facilities than the 'elite' clubs; but it would try to replicate all of their core functions. Members would be elected in the same way (unless blackballed); and within the Club, they would treat one another as equals. They would eat together, socialise together, and could attend talks together. The clubhouse would provide newspapers and games – at the very least billiards and card games.

For all the prosaic aims around self-improvement and fellowship, the working men's club had another major draw to working-class audiences: heat, light and warmth. At a time when homes were still heated – if they were heated at all – by coal and gas, the cost of energy was high. Poverty meant rationing heat in the winter months, or forsaking it entirely. Sharing rooms with others, from the pub to the club, meant a few hours of respite from a chilly home. While this could be true of the genteel poverty of many members of 'elite' clubs who were cash-poor, it was an existential question for many members of working men's clubs.

Clubs also offered other creature comforts. Just like the elite clubs, even the humblest clubs could offer sumptuous furnishings, and a pattern repeated over and over again was when members yearned for a level of luxury which their income could not sustain – a common factor in clubs promptly closing after only a short time. On the other hand, some clubs were so impecunious that they asked each new member to donate their own chair upon joining.

If the working men's clubs had radical origins, their delivery was distinctly conservative in its embrace of the 'Establishment'. David Doughan and Peter Gordon argue that 'Most of the clubs . . . were actually established by wealthy, and frequently titled, philanthropists courted by Solly; to take an extreme case, the Grosvenor Working Men's Club was started by the Duke of Westminster.'[2] Indeed, such was Solly's lobbying zeal to sign up 'respectable' aristocrats as patrons of the Working Men's Club and Institute Union, that it boasted as Vice-Presidents no fewer than four dukes, a marquess, nine earls and ten barons, not to mention twenty-three MPs to boost the Institute's 'Establishment' credentials.[3] John Taylor notes how 'Locally the same spirit of high patronage prevailed. Landowners and capitalists (sometimes in the person of their "ladies"), clergymen and philanthropists entered into the spirit of the exercise by setting up and running clubs in their own areas.'[4]

The Hall was the centrepiece of many such clubs. It could simply be a large room with barely more than some raised flats to serve in lieu of a stage, or it could have a professional theatrical stage set-up of its own. It allowed a wide variety of performances, not only the educational lectures, readings and concerts envisaged by Solly, but also more popular song-and-dance events; and blends of the educational and entertaining. John Taylor writes that in the Victorian and Edwardian eras:

> Dramatic performances featured prominently in the clubs' entertainment programmes: Shakespeare rubbed shoulders with Socialism, and melodramas and farces happily coexisted with brass bands and debates. It was an era during which the clubs flourished as the providers of a wide variety of dramatic presentations: 'there is hardly, however small, but boasts a stage and scenery, and a band of amateurs, giving periodical performances to their fellow members', wrote the Club *Journal* in 1888.[5]

Crucially, the emphasis was on making up numbers: as the name suggested, working men's clubs followed the patterns of 'elite' clubs and many public houses in only catering for men. However, the stage area was an exception to this, with women invited to performances all the same. This made the working men's club even more important as a community centre.

The very nature of a working men's club could be more community focused. Like the 'elite' clubs, the working men's clubs had the power to convene. Their very existence was important in providing a focal point for communities to gather together. In 1888, for instance, the Boro' of Hackney Club was by no means unusual in being able to accommodate 300 people in its Billiard Room, and 500 in its main Hall.[6]

The 'themed' elite clubs of Central London often brought together what we would now call 'imagined' or 'virtual' communities – people with shared interests and identifications who were geographically very spread out.[7] Working men's clubs could do this as well, particularly with the themed political clubs. Yet the typical emphasis of these clubs was on *physical* communities, bringing neighbours together in a shared space that they could literally call their own, without having to depend on the whims of a publican.

The absence of a pub landlord did not, however, mean that these clubs lacked patriarchs of their own. In reflecting the local communities, they often reflected their power structures, whether through 'labour aristocracy' of well-organised trade unionists, or a literal aristocracy, with the local aristocrats and squirearchy serving as patrons and subsidising such clubs.

Solly did not invent the working man's club. As we have seen, club-like organisations of a wide variety of descriptions and clienteles had recurred in many localities and countries, and these included working-class clubs long before Solly. Nonetheless, he was the first person to approach them systematically, with a manifesto. Moreover, Solly's ideas involved spreading the gospel of Clubland – and he had the zeal of a missionary – to new audiences.

Solly loomed large over the nascent movement, and the early working men's clubs were very much built in his image. He could be priggish and censorious, and so could the clubs he inspired. Nowhere was this truer than in his holier-than-thou attitude to alcohol. Solly was deeply concerned that the main alternative to the club for working-class socialising was the pub; and that if working men were to advance their interests, they needed to meet somewhere 'dry'. The working men's club was intended by Solly to be an alcohol-free haven. He was not alone in this desire: the very aristocratic patrons he courted (often themselves no strangers to a tipple) were convinced that the workers needed to lay off the booze, to increase productivity. As Doughan and Gordon note, 'It may come as a surprise to those who in the twentieth century have frequented working men's clubs that the Working Men's Club and Institute Union . . . was originally established in the mid-nineteenth century by well-to-do philanthropists to keep working men off the beer.'[8]

However, as these clubs grew, it became apparent that there was overwhelming demand for alcohol. An early stock-take by the Club and Institute Union in the late 1860s looked at why so many newly opened clubs closed after so short a time, and found that temperance restrictions were a key factor. Originally, the Union's shift in position was relatively minor – it argued that taken away from the evil influences of the local pub, members could responsibly drink alcohol in moderation, in the soothing confines of their club. Yet with the passage of time, the appeal of the working men's club became ever more focused around an inexpensive place to drink beer – somewhere that the community could use the bulk purchasing power of a club, to buy and sell alcohol at wholesale prices. The appeal to members was not that it was more virtuous than a pub, merely that it was cheaper. This was particularly true with the very modest subscriptions of such clubs, typically only a few shillings a year.

In many ways, this was a microcosm of what happened (and would happen) in the 'elite' clubs. New clubs would be set up in the late nineteenth century by high-minded, far-sighted founders, proclaiming lofty goals around nobles causes – the Arts Club for artists, the Eccentric Club for self-described eccentrics, and so forth. After a generation or so, the founders would often slip away or pass away, while the newer generations of members grew more interested in the comforts of nice furniture and cheap refreshment, the lofty goals being increasingly forgotten. And so it proved with working men's clubs, which had originally placed temperance at their core.

Most accounts of working men's clubs, written by socialist historians, tend to make the implicit assumption that Labour-affiliated clubs were the dominant force; and that as the interests of the Tories were so diverged from those of the working classes, that any Tory working men's clubs must be treated as freak aberrations. This was not the case until well into the twentieth century. For much of the nineteenth century, Conservative-affiliated working men's clubs were the most numerous of all the political clubs; followed by the Liberal ones. It was only with the emergence of a Labour Party as a major electoral force after the First World War that this changed.

In 1894, the Association of Conservative Clubs was formed, under the watchful eye of Aretas Akers-Douglas, the Tory Chief Whip. It sought to be an umbrella for Conservative-supporting working men's clubs up and down the country, with the tacit supervision of the Carlton Club.[9] As with so many political innovations in Clubland, it was borne out of electoral misfortune, and the need for a Tory Party then in opposition to reorganise and rebuild.

Intriguingly, the political clubs had a marked electoral impact, more so than the interventions of 'elite' clubs. When a constituency had political clubs of two or more major parties, there was no clear advantage in the political 'arms race'. Yet when a constituency only had *one* political club supporting one party, that party generally did better in elections. The working men's clubs could provide a real focus for political activity.[10]

It would also be wrong to imagine that working men's clubs were a happy, homogenous mass of working-class people all bound together in a common purpose. As with much of Clubland, they could be riven with rivalries, factions and personality clashes. The *Club and Institute Union Journal* observed in 1892:

> Numerous as clubs are in London, there are few where the clerk can be found . . . he scorns the idea of mixing with 'working men'. The clerk of 25s a week for monotonous work looks down on the plumber at £2 for 48 hours . . . There is a great gulf between them and they are often as wide apart as an aristocrat and a commoner.[11]

These inter-class rivalries pointed to a gap in the market. For while the working class and upper middle class were catered for, London's lower middle class often fell somewhere between these two groups; not enough social cachet to join an 'elite' club, but still too precious and status-conscious to join a truly 'inclusive' working men's club.

It was partly to meet this demand that the 'elite' clubs evolved. From the 1880s to the 1910s, Britain saw the launch of a new breed of more inclusive West End clubs. They had been a long time coming, with a sort of halfway house in the provincial political clubs. These existed in most of Britain's major cities, and the need to corral and mobilise political volunteers gave them an unusually wide social base, rather than just centring around the regional aristocracy. The template for these was set by the Manchester Reform Club established in 1867.[12] Other Liberal clubs followed, including the Liverpool Reform Club in 1879, and the Leeds Liberal Club in 1881. The Conservatives launched the Manchester Conservative Club in 1876, Edinburgh's Scottish Conservative Club in 1877, the Glasgow Conservative Club in 1880 and the Leeds and County Conservative Club in 1882.[13]

The ripples began to be felt in London, too. No longer were there clubs for five hundred or a thousand members. Instead, starting with the National Liberal Club in 1882 and the Conservatives' rival, the Constitutional Club in 1883, massive clubs started to be built for five or six thousand members at a time. Much of Pall Mall was full up by then – vast new sites were found, either facing the north side of Green Park, or else on the newly reclaimed artificial land that made up the Thames Embankment, which had been swampland just a generation earlier.

These large new clubs *felt* different. There was more emphasis on accommodation, often with over a hundred bedrooms at a time. The intended audience was not the middle-class London clubgoer, who had already joined one or more clubs, and did not need any more. It was the lower middle classes across the United Kingdom, offering the provincial, salaried worker a home from home when visiting London. As we shall see, they also embraced a much more cosmopolitan and international membership. It would be a stretch to say that they went in the direction of full-blown proletarianisation of Clubland; but one of the major effects of the working men's clubs was to transform how the major London clubs oriented themselves, especially the newest ones of the late Victorian age.

And there were attempts at daring 'hybrid' clubs between the old and the new. The New Reform Club was set up at 10 Adelphi

Terrace overlooking the Thames in 1899, for 'men and women of advanced liberal views'. Its address had impeccable provenance for its purposes, being the ground floor of the London townhouse of socialist playwright George Bernard Shaw, and many members 'worshipped at his shrine', and fawned over his occasional appearances in the shared hallway. However, Shaw was not always a sympathetic landlord, with tensions around the partitioning of the building by 'a little wicket gate on the staircase', and his being perturbed by the members' cigarette smoke rising up to his apartments. By 1912, the New Reform was just another failed London club.[14]

Even the more established clubs began to relax their restrictions. In 1893, the United Service Club began to admit junior officers for the first time, and one newly recruited army captain reported, 'the painted disapproval on the faces of the Club Staff when new members ventured to take the grand staircase at a run', and recalled an elderly Crimean War veteran marching in with whiskers and top hat, exclaiming, 'My God, what a nursery!', and storming out again.[15]

Over the years, this sense of a wider impact has faded. There has long been a narrative of decline for working men's clubs, with a sense that things were better for them yesterday, and that the glory years belonged to the Victorian age, with its sumptuous furnishings for even the more modest working men's club. The figures around working men's clubs tell a slightly different story. By 1868, the Working Men's Club and Institute Union numbered seventy-two clubs. By 1880, the figure had exploded to 520 working men's clubs. While the numbers fell back slightly in the 1880s, by 1905 it had hit 1,041, and by the outbreak of the First World War it had reached 1,613 working men's clubs. Unlike the 'elite' clubs of Central London, the working men's clubs did not go into terminal decline after the war; they flourished for over half a century more, and did not hit their peak until the 1970s, when they numbered over 4,000.[16]

The ultimate fate of the working men's clubs formed a sad coda to this. While their numbers continued to grow strongly through the first three-quarters of the twentieth century, they experienced the same fossilisation which we shall see took hold of the 'elite' clubs, undermined by an ageing membership.

By the post-war years, many were essentially part-time (or even full-time) bingo halls. By the 1980s, journalist Rupert Morris assembled a pen-sketch of how these clubs were starting to go to seed, noting of working-class Conservative clubs, 'Cheap beer and snooker tables are often their main attractions, and connoisseurs of such simple pleasures are only too willing to perjure themselves by pledging undying loyalty to the Tory party' to qualify for membership.[17] Like the Pall Mall clubs, many made ends meet by selling off or subletting parts of their building, exploiting their real estate to compensate for the fact that the basic club business model had ceased to work for them.

Subletting arrangements were frequently uneasy, and could spectacularly backfire. As a modern illustration, the Benton Conservative Club outside Newcastle, described by Morris in 1991, came full of creature comforts in its fine Georgian building, the ageing members dancing to wartime Glenn Miller recordings. It had a minor scandal in 2007 when they discovered the flat they sublet within the clubhouse was being marketed as a swingers' sex club, although the Club Secretary Paul McGivern noted, 'To be honest, it has been greeted with general hilarity among the club members.' The Club only found out about the creative use of their premises from a couple of would-be attendees asking for directions at the front door. Members promptly found a website advertising the premises, with reviews including, 'The place is a flat above a bingo hall and if you can hear the people below playing bingo God alone knows what they can hear from above', and 'Don't knock the pool table until you've tried it, or seen someone else try it.'[18] Few subletting arrangements end quite so amusingly, but they are rarely happy arrangements.

Yet the now-diminished world of working men's clubs is not the only legacy of the London clubs. Henry Solly's bold experiment may have been the most organised attempt to provide clubs for the masses, but it was far from unique.

Sports clubs have, somewhat improbably, been one of the great legacies of Clubland. As with some of the eighteenth-century clubs, these had decidedly aristocratic beginnings, with 'gentlemen's sports' such as sailing through the Royal Thames Yacht Club from 1775, cricket from the Marylebone Cricket Club after 1787, and racing, whose enthusiasts gathered at the Turf Club from 1790. Nor were these confined to London – the very earliest exports of empire included early Indian clubs such as the Calcutta Cricket and Football Club in 1792, and Calcutta Racquet Club the following year.

In each case, the London club provided a template for a rule-book, and a system of election. It was no coincidence that with the evolution of county cricket from the eighteenth century, cricket clubs became more club-like. Association football, likewise, mush-roomed in popularity in the nineteenth century, with many clubs initially having a rulebook based on the London clubs. Again, this was exported to colonies, as organisations like the Hong Kong Football Club of 1886 offered a halfway house between the luxuries of a premier clubhouse, and professional association football.

One of the most far-reaching modern legacies of this club business model has been the modern gymnasium. Gym membership is closely built around the idea of club membership, making the facilities available in exchange for a subscription fee, and building a community around that. The biggest practical difference is the emphasis of gym membership on monthly rather than yearly payment, as found in traditional clubs. Yearly payment creates a greater sense of belonging and permanence, as members pay their annual dues (if they don't have to resign on financial grounds). Monthly payment creates a far more transient membership – if they are not actively using the gym that month, they can always resign and return later. That sort of 'come and go' attitude to membership is rarely found in the 'elite' clubs and the working men's clubs – but the root of the behaviour patterns is in how they popularised club membership.

Other groups looked to clubs for inspiration, too. A number of early clubs like the Athenaeums of Liverpool and Manchester had long operated successful lending libraries. In 1841, the London Library was spun off from the library of the Travellers Club, run as a private members' club, but offering a template for the lending libraries open to the public which would sweep the nation in the second half of the century.

Clubs, therefore, had a wide footprint. They were not simply about a few dozen aristocrats sipping port in a small West End room. They were emulated, popularised and modified. They inspired much popular British culture that followed, especially in how people socialised together.

Chapter Six

Clubonomics

(1860–1900)

Clubonomics is the economics of clubs.[1] It is often stark, raving mad. Clubs behaved in a unique way, compared to nearly any other business. They could be highly lucrative in the short term – and an almost sure-fire way to lose a fortune in the long run. Yet the high demand for clubs led to hundreds of speculative ventures in 'failed' clubs, from the 1860s to the 1900s. Despite the many setbacks of club bankruptcies, and some high-profile cases of former members being sued for liability, the public appetite for creating new clubs seemed insatiable. Club waiting lists were often full, a new stream of clubs kept opening to meet fresh demand, while major provincial clubs sprouted up in every major British city. Furthermore, a range of leisure organisations began to copy the club business model, from subscription libraries like the London Library, to cricket clubs up and down the country.

Here we consider the economics of clubs – including supply and demand for places, the mysteries and intricacies of 'blackballing' which could befall a candidate (but which was actually a staggeringly rare occurrence), the professionalisation of clubs with the development of a whole range of club servants, and the business cycles of clubs which went from 'boom' to 'bust'. By the second half of the nineteenth century, the club 'system' was in full swing, and it is worth also looking at the lives of 'outsiders' caught up in all this – servants and candidates. If that sounds overly dry, then the tales involved show that it was anything but.

The purest expression of supply and demand was found in something that could involve no money changing hands: 'blackballing', and the whole secretive world of being elected to a club in the first place. In some ways, no price could be put on this, for it was the most valuable commodity any kind of club has to offer: the acceptance and approval of its existing membership. The supply and demand of places for membership was a valuable commodity in its own right.

Club members have long built up a mystique around 'blackballing', with its process of anonymous voting for new members, using white balls for 'Yes' and back balls for 'No'. Or, as one popular if apocryphal story had it, club members were sent a ballot paper with three options for electing new members: 'Yes', 'No' and 'Good God, No'.[2] By the nineteenth century, the popular press was filled with stories of so-called 'blackballing scandals', with members retaliating against other members who had blackballed their friends, by ensuring the friends of the blackballers were also blocked from joining.

The reality was rather more mundane. The long-standing popular image has it that one solitary blackball, issued in wrath by one permanently recalcitrant member, could be enough to veto any applicant and paralyse a club, with no new members joining for years. As we have seen, by the nineteenth century it was almost unheard of for one blackball to be enough – it was usually a *proportion* of all votes cast. The more elitist institutions opted for just one in ten balls being enough to veto a candidate. These clubs did indeed see 'blackballing scandals', yet the end result was to make 'blackballing' even harder as clubs responded by raising the bar to one in three members being needed to put in a blackball.

The other major shift of the nineteenth century was that clubs stopped letting all of their members ballot new applicants. Instead, the power was delegated from the whole membership, to a committee of no more than ten members. These were often the same committee members preoccupied with balancing the books, which made retaliatory blackballing much rarer. They preferred to take the money and run. They also tended to have a firmer idea of what was involved in the balloting process, although that was not always the case. One persistent blackballer in an Edinburgh club had managed to veto all new applicants for two years, until he realised he had misunderstood the process – in casting his ballot for 'No', he believed it meant 'No objection'.[3]

Interestingly, blackballing set a major historical precedent, in providing for anonymous voting. Until 1872, British and Irish elections to public office were still conducted in public – a voter had to go to the local polling station, to publicly declare their vote for a candidate, before witnesses. At the end of the election, lists of how every voter had cast their vote could be published and circulated. This made elections a haven for bribery, since a corrupt politician could agree only to hand over bribes to voters *after* they had cast their votes 'the right way'.[4] By contrast, club members were using secret ballots over a century before the rest of British voters.

This irony was not lost on club members. The double standard arguing for public votes in public elections, and secret votes in private clubs, was often pointed out. The Whig politician Sidney Herbert offered a robust – if strained – defence against a charge of hypocrisy. Opposed to granting the secret ballot to voters in public elections, he told his fellow MPs in 1853:

I hold there is no analogy between the two. One is political, the other social. The object of the ballot in clubs is to enable you to act upon predilections and aversions which you cannot perhaps justify, and dare not care to avow, and it rests upon the ground that everybody has a right to choose with whom he will associate. Beyond that there is no principle involved. It is the right you claim of selecting your associates and friends without giving any public reason, or without being able to give any reason or justification of the aversions and prejudices which you may entertain. That is exactly why the ballot is useful in clubs, and why you should prevent its use in the exercise of public functions. You want every man to feel the weight of responsibility which falls upon the exercise of public functions. It is absurd to imagine that there is no responsibility in giving a vote for a Member of Parliament.[5]

In other words, the defence for secret voting in clubs rested around its frivolity, and its positively inviting an irrational prejudice, which could not easily be defended in public.

In many ways, this epitomised the Whig mindset, which was a Clubland holdover from the 'aristocratic phase'. Whiggery was hard to define at the best of times, for it transcended issues, and was often as centred around birthright and aristocratic tradition – albeit a tradition of dissent. Yet, by the 1850s, Whiggery was dying. Within twenty years, the position came to be reversed on secret ballots: public elections began to use the ballot in 1872, while clubs began to delegate the whole area of blackballing away from the entire membership, towards a committee. This remains the normal position today.

Blackballing was exported to clubs worldwide, both across British colonies, and to the clubs of America, Portugal and Spain which all looked to the British clubs for cultural influence. When the handsome but wooden Hollywood star Victor Mature tried to join the Los Angeles Country Club in the 1940s, he had his application blackballed on the grounds that the elite club did not admit actors at the time. He protested, 'I'm no actor! And I've twenty-two screen credits to prove it.' They were not amused.

Blackballing has tended to be analysed by historians as a symbol of the British class system – and snobbery and prejudice undoubtedly played a major role.[6] Yet it was just as much a product of clubs being businesses, buying and selling their most valuable commodity, in membership.

Members' attitudes to blackballing could vary considerably. Some clubs took fairly inclusive attitudes – more so than society at large – in welcoming a varied membership; this was particularly true of clubs with strong international links. By contrast, other clubs measured their exclusivity, and so their sense of worth, by how frequently applicants were blocked. An extreme example of this attitude was an anonymous letter writer in 1888 who howled in protest at his club having admitted someone he had never met before, suggesting that if he had not missed the ballot, he would have blackballed them there and then. He believed the committee had a duty to 'keep every other man in London outside the Club walls'.[7]

This exaggerated attitude rarely held sway over clubs. Indeed, the opposite was often true: it was far safer to apply to a club as a complete unknown, than with any kind of a track record, which was bound to have proved divisive or controversial. One Edwardian account noted, 'No one who has lived into middle age is sure of election at any club. The unknown neophyte will be much more certain to win admission by his negative qualifications.'[8]

In reality, blackballs remained rare. Where they were wielded was in a handful of 'blackballing scandals', which were typically over political decisions, not reflections on individual candidates, nor financial decisions. Indeed, every club needed a healthy supply of new members, so frequently deploying a blackball made little financial sense, and was akin to a club shooting itself in the foot. Where blackballing scandals happened, waves of retaliatory blackballing and counter-blackballing followed, so that it soon became very difficult to elect anyone, as rival factions of the Club craved revenge. After Gladstone's first Home Rule Bill of 1886 sought to introduce self-government for Ireland, the resulting deep political polarisation affected a range of clubs, including Brooks's, which experienced one of the largest blackballing scandals in history. Unionists and Home Rulers alike blackballed one another's candidates, so that by 1887 the Club's Chairman had to appeal to members to bury their differences if the Club was to continue at all.[9]

These instances were rare, though. My own previous analysis of Club balloting books shows a remarkably consistent pattern across clubs. When a club was newly established, sooner or later it let most applicants in. At the Reform Club, the acceptance rate was as high as 98 per cent in its first few years.[10]

This had its own logic: bluntly put, new clubs were desperate for members, and needed the cash. Whether paying extortionate rents to a temporary landlord, or commissioning architects and builders for a palatial new clubhouse at astronomical costs (or both), new clubs incurred vast expenses; not to mention the tasks of furnishing a clubhouse and filling it with artworks. Newly established clubs tended not to be that picky, which was one of the reasons why they were so appealing to applicants who had been blackballed from 'older', more established clubs.

New clubs were also highly speculative ventures, and a number went bankrupt very early on: the Westminster Reform Club, for instance, only existed from 1834 to 1836, and it never recruited more than 105 members. Yet its members rented prestigious rooms off Parliament Square, and they spared no expense on increasingly elaborate furnishings, even as the monthly trade figures showed losses increasing. Its closure, before it was even two years old, was a fate shared by many other ill-fated clubs.[11]

However, if clubs *did* survive, they became pickier. My previous analysis of club blackballing shows that typically, in the twenty to thirty years after a club's foundation, the acceptance rate would drop from over 90 to around 70 per cent.[12]

Restricting the use of the blackball from the whole membership became a strict necessity. As Sidney Herbert suggested, it could be deployed irrationally, to settle old scores. Blackballing made a particularly potent mix with Clubland's own brand of snobbery. Once a new member had got in, especially at one of the more aristocratic Georgian clubs, they could be keen to pull up the drawbridge behind them, and to ensure that others from their own social background would not follow. Stripping the entire membership of the blackball, and delegating it to a sub-committee, had the effect of professionalising the whole process. The whole matter of scrutinising candidates would at least involve some active deliberation and discussion, instead of a knee-jerk response.

Where the eager young club applicant had difficulty in joining, it was rarely caused by the blackball. Instead, there were two other sources of frustration.

Firstly, even if blackballs were rare, the *fear* of a blackball was common. Although it was not always true that a member proposing a blackballed candidate was expected to resign in disgrace, it certainly reflected badly on the sponsoring member. Accordingly, club ballot books show that a far more common reason for a candidate failing to get elected was the withdrawal of the application, whether by the candidate, or by their proposers. If it looked likely that the candidate might be blackballed, they faced considerable pressure from their proposers to avoid a decisive defeat. They might then be free to apply again another time (or they might not).

Secondly, there was the dreaded waiting list. No club has ever explicitly set out in writing that it would set up a waiting list. Instead, a waiting list is the inevitable symptom of a separate cause: a cap on the number of members. Most London clubs have had a cap on numbers, on the grounds that club facilities should not become overstretched.

Caps on the number of club members were never terribly well-thought out. Most clubs have abandoned them in the centuries since. As clubs found to their cost, the problem with a cap was that it only afforded two ways of joining an existing club: waiting for an existing member to resign (typically through failure to pay their subscriptions on time), or else waiting several decades for the existing members to die of old age. A close study of candidate balloting books bears this out: Victorian applicants really did have a thirty-year wait for major clubs such as the Athenaeum or the Carlton.[13]

Nor did the cap on members necessarily have any bearing on the usage of a club by its members, which could vary hugely by season (or even time of day), which made a mockery of the idea of a club being 'full'. Where clubs have in the past drawn a line in the sand, suggesting that they could not possibly contemplate any more than a certain number of members, today they easily accommodate three or four times that number.

For this reason, clubs regularly found themselves patching on an extra hundred or so members to their absolute limit, only to find that this barely dented the growing queue of applicants.

Faced with spiralling numbers on the waiting lists, with some clubs having thousands of outstanding applicants by the 1880s and

1890s, it is little surprise that members sought out the alternative: founding their own new club. While financially riskier, it at least meant that they would not have a thirty-year wait to make use of some club facilities. Accordingly, the 1890s and 1900s saw the largest boom in construction of 'new' clubs across Central London.

The result was that, over time, it became quite normal to belong to multiple clubs, with all the applications that had been notched up over the years. Some resulted in swift election, others in years of waiting. In the 1850s, MPs had an average of two and a half clubs. By the late nineteenth century, it was not unusual to belong to five or six clubs. This had advantages of its own. Stephen Potter's delightfully catty 1950s study of *One-Upmanship* argued that 'it is essential to belong to two clubs if you belong to one club. It doesn't matter if your second club is a 5/– a year sub. affair in Greek Street [located in bohemian Soho]; the double membership enables you, when at your main or proper club, to speak often in terms of regretful discrimination about the advantages of your Other One.'[14]

Clubs could have a very different 'feel' from one another (and still do). It used to be said that there were two types of club: those where you went to meet people, and those where you went to avoid meeting people.[15] In reality, the latter was just the former type of club which had grown stale. Most clubs would experience peaks and troughs, and a sudden influx of new members – or a marked lack of new blood for decades – could seal a club's fate.

Successful clubs were marked by a degree of informality, which made members feel at home. This particularly extended to dress, for dress codes wouldn't be imported to London clubs until the second half of the twentieth century, as a symptom of decline. In successful clubs, casual dress ruled the roost. At the Arundel Club, a literary club off the Strand, Francis Burnand remembered the Club's early days in the 1860s, when 'shirt sleeves were *de rigueur*, in very hot weather, as the costume suitable for the billiard room adopted by all, whether they were players or not'.[16]

Indeed, until the 1940s the move in London clubs was towards further relaxation of dress. The Edwardian Clubland historian Arthur Griffiths observed in 1907, 'There is a freedom and independence nowadays in the matter of costume, which would have ineffably shocked the beaux and dandies of the past', contrasting the relaxed casualwear of clubs with Beau Brummel's legendary fastidiousness. Griffiths elaborated, 'Through the day men wear very much what they please, tweeds, dittoes, soft hats and straws', and that the sole smartening up of dress, around formalwear for dinner, was an 'unwritten law' rather than a cast-iron rule, occasionally shunned 'for recognised reasons, such as the hurried meal snatched on the eve of a journey, or the dinner swallowed immediately, with the knowledge that it may be interrupted at any moment by the division bell'.[17]

The most impressively capable Club Secretary of my acquaintance observed that successful clubs have three components: their members, their staff and their building.[18] We have already seen the mad scramble through the nineteenth century for fashionable and extravagant architects to make a statement in club buildings, and to imbue even the newest clubs with a feeling of permanence. Yet there is a tendency for books on clubs to overly focus on the members.

It is worth, then, looking at the oft-neglected world of club staff. Like the ephemeral Jeeves, the most successful club staff are often imagined to be those who flit in and out invisibly; and so histories of clubs routinely overlook staff – some do not mention them at all.

'Club servants are the making or breaking of any club,' insisted Ian Fleming.[19] Yet clubs require far more than *servants*, they need *staff*. Far from merely doing the bidding of their sometimes irrational members squabbling on committees, club staff must proactively take initiatives when reconciling the often-irreconcilable whims of different members. Some of the most successful club staff have been tyrants – only with elegance, wit, charm and flair.

How each club has dealt with the twin pressures of professionalism (by the staff) and democratic accountability (by the members) has often said much about the culture of that club. Of course, not all staff are professional, and not all members are democratic. Indeed, in looking at the professionalisation of clubs over the last two centuries, one of the most noticeable things is how so many clubs had (and have) distinctly unprofessional set-ups. One Club Secretary once confided to me that the job revolved around 'knowing how to treat gentlemen when they don't behave like gentlemen'. There is a degree of affectation in this, particularly as most members did not come from particularly landed or aristocratic backgrounds. Nevertheless, it speaks volumes of the double standard as to how members expect to be treated – as distinguished gentlemen when it suits them, but not when it involves inconvenience. Indeed, it remains true that the members who are the loudest in their pedantic upholding of obscure club rules are usually the first to flout them.

As Clubland flourished, so the profusion of jobs grew ever more specialised, each focused around members' varied interests. Club jobs started focusing on the gastronomic side, with cooks and waiters. The very first surviving London club rules, from White's in 1736, justified the subscription on the grounds of paying 'towards a good cook'.[20] As the clubs' catering operations grew more complex, so did the ranks of waiters, stretching up to the exalted heights of Steward and Head Steward, for the British have always loved to replicate the class system in every bureaucracy they create. As clubs began to vie for gastronomic innovation and excellence, so clubs started to recruit celebrity chefs. A far cry from the 'school dinners stodge' image of declining clubs of the twentieth century, when clubs were on the up in the nineteenth century they were identified with catering creativity. It was into this scene that the likes of Alexis Soyer made their mark on Clubland.

Not all clubs could afford to hire celebrity chefs. Indeed, to hire chefs at all was an inherently risky venture, prone to temperamental unpredictability. From the very earliest days, a number of clubs have discreetly outsourced their cooking to more dependable caterers. This practice started in the very first clubs, with Almack's club on Pall Mall ordering in meals from Almack's tavern next door. It continued through the nineteenth century – the epitome of aristocratic gambling clubs of the 1830s, Crockford's on St James's Street, ordered in food from James Ellis, the same 'refreshment contractor' who prepared meals for theatres such as Her Majesty's and for the Lyceum, concert venues like the Prince's Concert Rooms, as well as Salons such as the Hanover Square Rooms.[21] They were differently packaged, but they were identical meals. The practice discreetly continues in some London clubs to this day, and at least one outsources its kitchen to a global catering giant, often with members none the wiser. Yet the supposed reliability of outside caterers could not always be taken for granted: the University Club for Ladies off Grosvenor Square depended on the Grosvenor Restaurant for all of its catering in the late 1880s. When the restaurant refused to continue with the contract in 1890, the Club found that no other caterers were near enough to serve hot meals, and it had to resort to salads and cold sandwiches.[22]

A club's chef was invariably a matter for frenzied discussion among members and guests alike. One Edwardian account observed: 'His quality, whether inferior, doubtful, or first-class, is a subject for perpetual, and not seldom heated, debate.'[23] Sometimes, tensions arose between the chefs who cooked the food, and the member-facing staff who would wait on tables in the Dining Room. In extreme cases, all-out war broke out between the two. One Dining Room Manager in a leading London club had not spoken to the Head Chef in twenty years, each holding the other in mutual contempt. The Dining Room Manager had even developed a code with his favourite members: 'Chef's not in today', he would grin, meaning the food was quite good when cooked by young apprentice chefs. Alternatively, 'Chef's in today', he would scowl, meaning that everything on the menu was suspect, and to try something like the oysters was to place your life in mortal peril.

A successful club chef was not only gastronomically inventive, but a great economist as well. A huge amount of recycling prevails in any club. The day often starts after last orders have been taken at dinnertime the night before, when the Head Chef takes stock of which leftovers can be recycled the next day, and which fresh supplies will be needed. Those in turn dictate the affordable 'menu of the day' so beloved of regular members, as well as the free meals doled out to club servants.

With clubs becoming sought-after destinations, the need for security increased, and the doorman gradually evolved into that Clubland institution, the Porter. A club's night Porter once gave a description of his job, namely that there was considerable worry among members that two particularly elderly habitués of the Club would die in their sleep as they snoozed overnight in armchairs; and it was his job to turn them over every hour or so, to check they were still alive. He bemoaned that if he *did* turn them over, they verbally abused him for waking them, and if he *didn't* turn them over, they complained afterwards that he might as well have left them for dead.[24]

This gentle self-mockery aside, the Porter's job was an essential one – he set the tone for the whole club. He was the first point of contact of members and visitors setting foot in the premises.

Typically recruited from a military background, and with the manners (or lack thereof) to boot, the prompt, peremptory Porter did much to promote the image of a club as being unattainable and detached. Nevertheless, expectations of porters were high. A club's claim to 'exclusivity' often lay on the Porter doing a thorough job in filtering out members of the public. The very best at their craft were expected to know every club member by sight – potentially several thousand individuals – and to keep abreast of deaths, resignations and members owing money.

The Porter was also one of the most important figures in a club for another reason: they presided over the mail. It was the Porter who received the daily torrent of letters, parcels and circulars, sifting through them to decide which to forward and which to dispose of. They could also be known to read members' mail, too, making them an excellent source of society gossip, ever popular with prying journalists.

As the activities within clubs flourished, so the range of specialised staff promulgated. At the top of the tree were the Club Secretary and House Manager, who would typically be on hefty, upper-middle-class salaries, but clubs also had a profusion of other wages to pay. A club's kitchen operation could be prodigious. As well as the Head Chef, there would typically be a secondary chef handling soups and sauces, and often a third chef to provide cover. The lion's share of the remaining work was often done by an army of specialist kitchen maids: a fish maid, roasting maid, broiling maid, vegetable maid, and a variety of scullery maids and odd maids, to do odd jobs. Then there was the army of specialist member-facing staff. These included the house steward, porters, barber, librarian, bathman, barmen, dining room manager, dining room waiters, smoking room waiters, wine butler, billiard markers, card room attendants, housekeeper, housemaids, cleaners, pageboys and shoe-shine boys. Like a larger version of a country house, a club's full staff could stretch to over a hundred.[25]

A cornerstone of this profusion of jobs was the principle of cheap labour. The country house which proved so fashionable in the nineteenth century was something the clubs attempted to echo through the provision of luxurious amenities with as much individuality and personality as a private home. It did, after all, strike at the roots of clubs, as communal versions of the aristocratic mansions of St James's. To this day, the Victorian tradition continues of refusing to tip club servants, on the grounds that a club is an extension of the member's home, and one would never tip a servant in one's home. In theory (if not in practice), it has long been considered a sacking offence for a club servant to accept a gratuity. This is a custom devised by members, for the convenience of their fellow members, and one suspects that few club servants have ever enjoyed what might be called consultation on the matter. Certainly, the notion of rank-and-file staff involvement in the governance of a club was unheard of. This was the flipside of member-owned clubs – staff welfare always came secondary to members' convenience. In practice, the 'no tipping rule' has long kept miserly wages even lower. By the 1970s, one Club Secretary rued how it 'should have been deleted from rulebooks thirty years ago'.[26]

Of course, the *theoretical* position was quite different. Arthur Griffiths set out in 1907 how clubs could be benevolent, stable, long-term employers:

> To be attached to a high-class club is, for the domestic servant, practically a provision for life. There is something patriarchal in the system; places often descend from father to son. The child enters at a tender age, like an apprentice; he passes on and upward, till in time he occupies an excellent position and is

honoured and respected by his employers. The club servant has, as a rule, a very snug billet; his wages are probably a fraction above the market price, the work, save at special seasons, is not unduly severe, pensions are granted in the end when health and strength break down, while there are clubs in which subscriptions *ad hoc*, or some well-managed benevolent institution, afford a present help in time of trouble and domestic distress. No club servant cares to forgo the manifest advantages of club service, and they act in the manner of a premium upon good behaviour. There are never many changes in the staff, and those who join come to stay. The members, indeed, do not like to see new faces about them, and look upon their people as personal retainers. The servants in return render old-fashioned fealty to their masters and take a deep interest in all that concerns them, a pride in their success, and a cordial sympathy in their sorrows and affliction.[27]

Yet this presented a somewhat idealised fantasia. Even in the nineteenth century, it is doubtful that this happy picture held true. A 'core' of long-term servants remained in the more senior roles, but turnover could be high in menial jobs, and court records attest to no shortage of petty (and not-so-petty) larceny by club servants, who helped themselves to everything from cash in the till, to laundered tablecloths sold on the black market, complete with incriminating club monograms. Nor should staff tactfulness towards members necessarily be mistaken for actually caring about the day-to-day lives of the procession of bores, tyrants and lunatics who could walk through a club's doors and make their lives miserable.

The precarious position of club staff is something all too easily overlooked. In even the wealthiest clubs, the servants have often been on what can at best be described as 'poverty wages'. The long-standing rationale for such low wages was that clubs provided accommodation (even if only rudimentary dormitories) for staff; although as pressure for space increased, staff accommodation was often the first thing that club committees sacrificed, usually to make way for members' bedrooms. Besides which, Victorian Britain was marked by a lack of secure employment – there was a large pool of casual labour available to do a job if the existing servant was not able to do so. It remained not uncommon for club servants who spent their days waiting on aristocrats to insist on promptly finishing work around 5 p.m. This was in order to secure either a bed at the nearest homeless shelter, or, at the very least, a suitable park bench.[28]

The loneliest staff job of all lay at the top of the tree: the Club Secretary. Effectively the chief executive of a club, these professionals emerged from the Stewards of eighteenth-century clubs, yet the role evolved into something much greater. Their responsibilities included organisation of the full range of members' services, from catering to building maintenance. They dealt with the endless building needs of a club, from construction to paying off extortionate mortgages on elaborate premises. They also managed the day-to-day financial affairs of the Club. Given the historical vulnerability to fraud, large and small, across the whole club sector, Club Secretaries broadly fell into three categories: those fighting a constant war against junior employees defrauding the Club; those too lazy or ineffectual to prevent other staff defrauding the Club; and those actively engaged in defrauding the Club themselves. And as the name 'Secretary' implied, they also provided secretarial support, not only to a club's governing Committee, but to a baffling array of Sub-committees on every topic under the sun. It was (and remains) an almost impossible job to do well.

What made the Club Secretary's role so lonely was that neither members nor staff saw the Secretary as 'one of us'.

To the members, the genial, welcoming Club Secretary might occasionally meet them for a drink in the bar; but strictly in a subordinate capacity, in much the same way as a Master of Foxhounds might meet in the pub with a stable lad ahead of a hunt, never on terms of equality. Furthermore, the Club Secretary's role in providing administrative support for committees made them favourite scapegoats for members.

To the staff, the Club Secretary remained an aloof figure. It was largely unheard of, until well into the late twentieth century, for the Club Secretary to be recruited from the ranks of servants – the highest the staff might aspire to reach in promotion was the middling rank of Steward. The prevailing attitude was that servants were not really cut out for a higher calling, and the standing advice was, 'You might get [to be Club Secretary] eventually, but never in the Club you worked in as a "servant." It would be antisocial and you would never have the respect of other servants.'[29] Instead, an 'officers and men' military attitude prevailed, and Club Secretaries were overwhelmingly plucked from the services, typically retired majors, colonels and commanders. (Anything more senior than that, and a Club Secretary's post might seem like a climb-down in social status.) Few had experience of what we might now term 'hospitality', which explains much about how clubs came to develop such a reputation for poor service in the ensuing decades. Occasionally, clubs recruited someone from the professions, such as a solicitor or a journalist, but this was itself somewhat unusual.

There was money to pay for this ever-growing battalion of club staff, because the demand for clubs remained high throughout the nineteenth century – and kept growing exponentially until the First World War. Even though the Union Club model was the popular template in the Victorian era, with a premium on member-owned clubs, this did not deter the considerable scope for entrepreneurship in the area of clubs.

Especially popular was the hotel-owned club. This typically involved several 'clubrooms' within a hotel. It lacked any of the social prestige of the long-established clubs, but it had advantages of its own. Just as the club members of Almack's club in the eighteenth century were able to benefit from the staff and facilities of Almack's tavern next door, so the Victorian hotel-club member could enjoy the very latest in luxurious facilities. For the hotel proprietor, it was a licence to print money: the overheads were already paid for in the hotel; and for the cost of freeing up a few rooms as a lounge area, a lucrative stream of membership subscriptions rolled in. This was revenue which a hotel would not normally be able to enjoy.

These proprietary clubs *did* recruit people with a hospitality background – the late nineteenth century saw the development of the grand Central London hotel, which also contained some 'club' rooms within – and it was normal for the hotel manager to double as Club Secretary. However, as we shall see, this type of club was among the shortest-lived and least enduring, and so the overlap between Club Secretaries and hoteliers remained limited.

Yet the model has proved remarkably resilient; indeed, it has had something of a resurgence in recent decades, both in London and globally.

However, the hotel-club is also an excellent example of another major facet of clubonomics: identity. When looking at the patchy survival rate of clubs, a club's identity frequently trumps its financial health. Over the years, plenty of clubs with healthy assets and much going for them have gone to the wall; while clubs with decidedly ropey finances and a strong identity have often survived, in spite of all common sense. The reasons are worth setting out.

From a purely financial point of view, membership of a club makes no sense at all. The member pays for facilities which are often offered elsewhere, either more cheaply, or even for free. Furthermore, while a club's offer to its members remains fairly static, a member's needs change over the course of their life. A young man-about-town who finds his club a convenient watering hole on his way home from the office when he is in his twenties may later find his tastes changing. He starts a family, moves out to the country and spends less time in London. Instead of dropping in for a drink three times a week, he is barely in his club once or twice a year. By this stage, the hefty financial outlay of the subscription is hard to justify. Sooner or later, any member who looks at the situation rationally will tender his resignation, and save the money squandered on a subscription.

This phenomenon goes some way to explaining why most clubs are failed businesses. London has had at least 400 major historic West End clubs over the years. Only some forty of these historic clubs have survived. That is a failure rate of 90 per cent for London's clubs. A look at other club-rich cities around the world also suggests a similar 90 per cent failure rate. The club business model – particularly the more commercially-oriented variants like the hotel-club – have proved an excellent way of making hefty short-term profits; but an almost sure-fire way of losing money in the long term. If simply run as businesses, they are not sustainable.

Which London clubs have survived, then? Which make up the resilient 10 per cent? The answer has little to do with economics. It lies in *culture* and *theme*.

As recognised above, a member retaining their club membership for any length of time is behaving irrationally. Yet humans are irrational beings. It is no coincidence that those clubs which have survived have tended to have a strong *theme*, or, at the very least, a strong *culture*: the Carlton Club for Conservatives, the Travellers

Club for diplomats, the Oxford and Cambridge Club for Oxbridge graduates, and so forth. Each of these presents their members with a unique, cohesive culture and identity. Ongoing membership may well present woeful value for money, in some cases – no matter. If it is the passport to a member's social life and circle; if they feel they need to keep this culture alive, even through subsidy, then they will readily retain their membership. It is the *long-term* members of clubs who provide them with a firm financial base, as well as institutional memory and culture, and it is the *culture* which helps them to survive.

By contrast, the more purely 'social' clubs have tended to be the most vulnerable. In the short term, these clubs often draw the most lucrative receipts, in the bar and dining room. Yet they are also shorter-lived. Their offer is a more transactional one, based on giving members value for money. While this may be enormously appealing for a while, it is almost impossible for any social organisation to consistently offer value for money year in, year out, for centuries. As clubs have waxed and waned, the successful ones have been able to fall back on a sense of identity and attachment among their members. Clubs without a strong identity have simply gone to the wall, once faced with difficult times.

Many of these issues were fleshed out – in a different context – by Robert D. Putnam. In his landmark book *Bowling Alone*, Putnam looked at the idea of social capital, mainly through the phenomenon of suburban bowling clubs in America. Putnam argued that there were two types of social capital: *bridging capital* (bowling clubs socialising with friends from the world outside) and *bonding capital* (a bowling team socialising with their teammates). A team which has no bonding capital lacks cohesion; whereas a team which lacks bridging capital is little more than a sect. A team needs both bridging and bonding capital.[30] Obviously, each of these propositions applies equally to clubs.

Little of this was apparent during the Victorian era, when clubs were at their height. True, there was already a high turnover of newer clubs, run as speculative ventures and often only in business for two or three years before bankruptcy ensued. Yet the exponentially increasing demand for clubs helped mask this – if one club went bust, two or three more were set up in its place. It was only during the long, slow, painful decline of clubs after the First World War that it became clear how much that decline owed to the peculiar clubonomics which took root in Victorian Britain.

Of course, clubs of all shapes and sizes still did their best to have a strong, superficial offer for members, particularly where creature comforts were concerned. As noted, clubs hired the most fashionable architects of the day, in an early 'arms race' to create 'temples of luxury and ease'.[31] As the century progressed, emphasis moved on to comfortable interior furnishings. This included luxurious furniture, from 'love seats' in the lobby to semi-recumbent divans in the lounging areas. It encompassed a range of dining facilities, including different rooms for eating different courses.

It also positively embraced technology in the pursuit of pleasure. Pall Mall had been served by the very first use of gas lights in London in 1809, and clubs like the Carlton, Reform and United Service made heavy use of this from the 1830s. Brooks's installed a telegraph wire in the 1850s. By the 1880s, the National Liberal Club was London's first building to use electrical light throughout (as well as the first building outside the United States to use a steel frame), and had the first passenger lift in London.[32] The Travellers Club fitted a telephone in 1896, and a passenger lift in 1905.[33] The National Liberal also made heavy use of tiling to maximise the amount of wipe-clean surfaces, so as to be suitable for the fashionable activity of smoking – where other clubs had ageing velvet furniture and thick wallpaper that was all drenched in tobacco fumes, the newer clubs sought to use technology to accommodate smoking. Indeed, at the Athenaeum, an entire attic storey extension had been colonised for the use of smokers by the turn of the twentieth century.[34]

(At the other end of the spectrum, clubs could often be reluctant to upgrade once-pioneering technology, so that by the 1970s the National Liberal Club's lift had become something of a death trap.[35] Anyone who used the Reform Club's minuscule lift in the 2010s will have sympathised.)

The maintenance of these elaborate clubhouses created a culture of its own. The annual cleaning of a clubhouse in the summer – typically around August – meant temporary closure, which offered a welcome opportunity to explore other clubs. An elaborate network was set up by the mid-nineteenth century of scores of London clubs offering temporary hospitality to one another's members during overlapping summer closures. The idea of reciprocity was born, within London at least. As we shall see, over time, this would be extended internationally.

Where clubs attempted to offer 'value for money', it was often in the provision of 'intangible' benefits around business opportunities and networking. There is a view, commonly promoted by clubs in decline in the twentieth century, that one should always 'keep business out of the club'. Victorian club members would not have recognised this at all. Clubs traded heavily on the way their prestigious reputations allowed members to make new professional contacts, and this was a major superficial appeal for club recruitment (if not retention). Even when there were rules preventing anything so gauche as talking business, Marrisa Joseph recognises how there was a widespread understanding that clubs would 'promote male personal and professional relationships, as it was a space where men could promote their ambitions'.[36]

Meanwhile, clubs across London adopted a collective identity, viewing different clubs as equals, superiors or inferiors. By 1865, this sense of cross-club identity was enough to see the launch of the *Pall Mall Gazette*, produced by club members, for an audience of club members. Its publication history, until 1923, almost perfectly spans the peak years of London clubs.

Pressure for space was high. The first wave of clubs of the eighteenth century had focused around St James's Street for social reasons, as the hub of the fashionable aristocracy. Later waves of clubs included those from the 1820s to 1840s along the south side of Pall Mall around the ruins of Carlton House, and those from the 1880s along Piccadilly, because it accommodated large buildings facing Green Park. Already by the 1840s, 'Clubland' was a recognisable geographical area, entering the *Oxford English Dictionary* in 1885. Such was the cachet of the area, that although new clubs could crop up in any locality, those that were hungry for prestige sought out anywhere – anywhere at all – which was in 'the right area'. In 1877, even the Kennel Club, for lady dog-lovers, squeezed into an improbable extension at 29A Pall Mall, just so they could claim the social standing of a Pall Mall address.

Some buildings played host to multiple clubs. A palatial abode which stood at 66–68 Pall Mall, for example, sandwiched between the Guards Club and St James's Palace, successively played host to the Junior Naval and Military Club (1875–9), the Beaconsfield Club (1880–87), the Unionist Club (1888–92), the New Oxford and Cambridge Club (1894–1920) and the Old Colony Club (1920–30). Given how many of these clubs were ill-fated, the premises were thought to be cursed.

As fashionable new buildings were created, newer clubs took to them. In the 1880s, the ten-storey, marble-pillared Whitehall Court was an early precursor of countless later blocks of mansion flats.

With its commanding views of the Thames, it hosted a baffling array of later Victorian clubs. The Royal Automobile Club started in its apartments in 1897, before decamping to its own premises in 1913. Other clubs in the flats included the Authors, the Auxiliary Forces, the Chemical, the Flyfishers, the Northern Counties, the United Sports, the Westminster and both the Golfers (for male golfers) and the Lady Golfers' next door (which later merged into the Golfers Club).

The building itself had a colourful history. Whitehall Court was constructed by the Liberal MP Jabez Balfour, who enjoyed considerable success as a builder. He was also a fraudster, operating a massive pyramid scheme as he raided the savings of his investors. The prestigious Whitehall Court development was the icing on the cake of his property empire, in which he shuffled money between companies with such zeal that few could keep track of where all the money belonged. Balfour was exposed in a major scandal in 1892, and, while he fled to a life of 'sultanic luxury' in Salta, Argentina, he was eventually brought back to England to stand trial. His defence – 'Judge me not by my morals, judge me by the quality of my buildings' – remains one of the more innovative defences for fraud. He served eleven years in jail.[37]

As clubs declined in the twentieth century, it became more common for them to amalgamate. This typically involved the grander clubhouses absorbing small, defunct clubs, which would maintain a presence of their own with an independent clubroom within the larger clubhouse. Some clubs proceeded like vampires, feasting off the corpses of bankrupt clubs, for a fresh influx of members – even then, it was no guarantee of success. The United Service Club would absorb a wide range of smaller clubs, including the Constitutional, Union and Royal Aero Clubs, but none of this was enough to save them from eventual bankruptcy in 1977.

Many of the prevailing patterns of doing business worked well enough when clubs were doing well. They would also be the undoing of clubs once they became trapped in a cycle of decline a century later.

The very idea of the member-owned club is a prime example. Compared to the proprietary club, it is immeasurably more appealing. Joining a member-owned club carries with it the feeling of importance and participation, in helping to sway the destiny of an institution. Yet it also carries with it both responsibility and liability. It involves turning up to meetings and reading paperwork, assuming the Club even confides in its members. When clubs fall on hard times, members begin nervously looking over their shoulders at who would be left to foot the bill in any bankruptcy proceedings.

Owning a share of your own club, however small, is a tempting prospect. Clubs moved to this form of mutualisation throughout the nineteenth century: even the existing, proprietary clubs of the eighteenth century staged 'management buy-outs' from the members, so that they became member-owned clubs. But this could be a dangerous set-up for clubs once they were in decline.

The biggest threat was demutualisation. When membership numbers dwindled, each member's share was increased. The temptation was to sell off one's club and pocket the proceeds. Given the years of assets built up, including valuable artworks and expensive land, it is easy to see how this temptation increased with the passing years, particularly once Mayfair's land values skyrocketed through the twentieth century. This was further exacerbated by members holding multiple memberships: if they belonged to three or four clubs, would it really matter if one of them was sold off? By the post-war years, once-fashionable clubs like the Marlborough did precisely this, selling its site and sharing the proceeds among its members just prior to dissolution. From the 1930s to the 1970s, this became a torrent, accounting for dozens of London clubs.

White's club, relocated down St James's Street after a fire in 1733. These sorts of scenes, with debtors arrested by bailiffs, were not uncommon in 18th-century St James's, when there was plenty of pressure to spend beyond one's means. William Hogarth, *The Rake's Progress IV: The Arrest* (1734) *(© Sir John Soane's Museum, London)*

The fashionable gambling 'hell' of White's club is shown vividly in all its sordid glory. Hogarth, *The Rake's Progress VI: The Gaming House* (1734).
(© Sir John Soane's Museum, London)

The Union Club had pretensions to being a parliament of clubs, mirroring the union of Great Br[i]
and Ireland. James Gillray took a rather more cynical view in his *The Union Club* (1801), showing
leading politicians of the day running riot. *(Peter Jackson Collection/Bridgeman Images)*

Clubland always retained an air of chaos. George Cruikshank's *Exterior of Fishmongers Hall, a Reg[ular]*
break down (1824) shows members peering out of Crockford's club. William Crockford had beer
a fishmonger before he branched out into lucrative club management, so his club was known as
'fishmonger's hall'. *(Album/Alamy Stock Photo)*

n when clubs went through their 'aristocratic phase' as men-only institutions, big showcase
ts still revolved around women's participation: Thomas Rowlandson's *Fete at Boodle's Club, in
or of George III* (1802) shows a grand ball in a marquee erected at Ranelagh Gardens.
President and Fellows of Harvard College/Bridgeman Images)

A PEEP AT THE GAS LIGHTS IN PALL-MALL.

bs tried to stand out by offering the latest technology available. In Thomas Rowlandson's
ep at the Gas Lights in Pall Mall (1809), passers-by flock to see Britain's first public gas
*etlights. Clubs on the street would soon scramble to tap into this.
don Metropolitan Archives/Bridgeman Images)

French-Peruvian travel writer Flor
Tristan gave a unique insight into
Clubland in the 1830s, when she
successfully gatecrashed several m
clubs in drag, and published her
acerbic impressions. *(API/Getty Imag*

THE FEMALE COTERIE.

Well, this is certainly one of the most usefull institutions!

The first women's club was 'The Female Coterie', otherwise known as Ladies' Boodle's, in the 177
Women would elect men, and men would elect women, while spouses would become associate
members. Thomas Bonner, *The Female Coterie* (1770).
(Reproduced by kind permission of the British Library/Bridgeman Images)

es Barry's Travellers Club library, designed and built in 1828–32, influenced the shape of clubs to

(Reproduced by kind permission of the Travellers Club)

The largest library in Clubland today remains that of the Athenaeum. Members donate books they have written. Michael Faraday died in the wheelchair in 1867, which is still kept as a curio.
(Reproduced by kind permission of the Athenaeum)

s Reform Club coffee room – the name for a dining room in the earlier clubs, when coffee was luxury item. *(Reproduced by kind permission of the Reform Club)*

nd women touring the newly opened clubhouse in William Radclyffe (after G. B. Moore), *The Club: The Corridors of the Saloon* (1841). *(Eraza Collection/Alamy Stock Photo)*

Pall Mall, capital of Clubland, was the place to be seen – and the south side was lined in clubs. Fr
left to right: the United Service Club, Athenaeum, Travellers Club, Reform Club and Carlton Clu
Anonymous artist, after Thomas Shotter Boys, *The Clubhouses of Pall Mall* (1840s).
(Reproduced by kind permission of the Carlton Club)

A family occasion: W. E. Gladstone and Catherine Gladstone celebrate their 50th wedding anniv
at the National Liberal Club in 1889. *(Reproduced by kind permission of the National Liberal Club)*

None of this was apparent in the Victorian era. As far as the clubs were concerned, they were building steady institutions, with the members in control of their destinies. It was only decades later that it became apparent just how great the temptation was to 'take the money and run'.

Clubs have a unique culture of their own, particularly if they are successful and long-lived. This has tended to be treated in isolation, like some mysterious phenomenon. In reality, much of the culture was the product of economic decisions taken very early on, and the unique, idiosyncratic and sometimes just plain bonkers model of clubonomics.

Chapter Seven

Clubs and empires
(1827–1913)

Anthony Sampson wrote, 'The Empire was built round clubs.'[1] He was not exaggerating. The earliest Georgian clubs had been a colonial import to London, from the north-eastern seaboard of America, influenced by the prototype clubs of Maryland and Pennsylvania. American independence after 1776 signalled the death of the First British Empire. As the Second British Empire took shape throughout the nineteenth century, clubs came to be centres of power for Britain's expanding colonies. The British model of club came to be one of the nation's most enduring cultural exports.

'Wherever three Englishmen are gathered together, two of them will form a club, for the purpose of keeping the third one out', ran an old joke. Yet the clubs of the British Empire assumed a far more central role in the identity and the discreet administration of British colonies. While the British Empire would grow to span the globe, the physical British presence in these colonies was invariably small, often limited to a tiny 'British quarter' of cities like Madras, India, and Colombo, Ceylon. The clubs which sprouted up as British exports from the 1820s onwards loomed large in how the British in their empire worked and played.

The very first British colonial clubs were in India, beginning with the Bengal Club, founded in 1827. British India occupied a huge area, including modern-day Pakistan and Bangladesh. As Pavan Malhotra has argued,[2] the spread of clubs across India followed the spread of the British presence in India. The first clubs were in the original British capital of Calcutta, in the east; then in the vital trading post of Madras in the south, as well as the cool hills across the south where the British avoided the summer heat; then in the west around Bombay as the port grew in size and significance. The north of India saw clubs as a relatively late arrival – the capital only moved to Lutyens' Delhi in 1911, which is why the oldest clubs in the city only arrived thereafter – the Imperial Delhi Gymkhana Club in 1913, the Chelmsford Club in 1917 and the Roshanara Club in 1922.

The earliest Indian club founders and members were dominated by the East India Company and its interests. Early accounts of the East India Company reflected the Victorians' 'strong sense of embarrassment about the shady, brutal and mercantile way the British had founded the Raj', William Dalrymple reminds us.[3] Britain had not colonised India as a state; instead, a rapacious British corporation, protected by a large private army, maintained and expanded its interests, ruthlessly bartering deals, extracting resources and quelling opposition where necessary. So lucrative was the East India Company that the merchant alliance first forged in the 1590s evolved into the largest company in history, controlling nearly half the world's trade. For the British state, it was considered too big to fail.

Thus the Bengal Club was formed from a meeting of the EIC-dominated merchants, at Calcutta's Town Hall in 1827. Disease and mortality were high for the Europeans who worked along the lucrative trade routes. All the greater was the demand for creature comforts. The Bengal Club made its home in the heart of the administrative enclave of the British capital, surrounded by military and government buildings. Even amid the humidity and storms of Bengal, to which the British were unaccustomed, life was luxurious for those living in this enclave, underscored by sprawling grounds, and slavery which provided domestic servants. The white European founders of the Bengal Club were no strangers to associational culture either – they clung to organisations and trappings which might remind them of home, from Freemasonry to sports clubs; before the Bengal Club, Calcutta already had clubs for racket, cricket and football founded in the 1790s. Again, they were for white Europeans only. The strong streak of overt racial discrimination which marked these clubs made them far more exclusive than their London counterparts.

With military forces – particularly the East India Company's private army – being so central to British rule through much of India, it was unsurprising that Calcutta soon added in 1829 the United Services Club. Over the next few decades, clubs proliferated in Calcutta, many of which survive today – indeed, modern-day Kolkata remains the global city with the third largest number of clubs, after London and New York. It is closely followed by Mumbai. The British-dominated clubs of Calcutta set a template for many of the clubs that were to follow throughout India, and indeed the British Empire. There were those such as the Bengal Club which were purely social, although a reactionary outlook somewhat invariably went with it. Then there was the profusion of clubs around the various sports: the Royal Calcutta Golf Club of 1829, the first of its kind outside the British Isles; the Royal Calcutta Turf Club of 1847, whose grandstand views on the one day of the month they operate still offer the best views of the racecourse, and arguably the city; and those catering for aquatic sports such as the Calcutta Rowing Club of 1858 and the Calcutta Swimming Club of 1887. Collectively, they represented a particular view of how the British abroad could eat, live, socialise, exercise and remain cool.[4]

Women had a similar position in imperial clubs as in British clubs: most of the Indian clubs reflected a nostalgic recollection of the England left behind, and so they tended to reflect the clubs of yesterday, even by nineteenth-century standards. Most had avowedly men-only memberships well into the twentieth century, although a number of women-only clubs were set up as well. However, with the British community closely bound together in India, most men's clubs had far greater integration of women. In London, men's clubs often had only one room in which women visitors could be received at certain times of day. Across India, it was far more common for clubs to have only one room that was men-only. This only reinforced the idea of a safe enclave – so long as you were British.

There were some exceptions, however. The position of women could depend on the innate conservatism or liberalism found across different provinces. In Karachi, the city's premier Sind Club notoriously had a sign reading 'NO WOMEN OR DOGS ALLOWED', which hung until the independence of Pakistan in 1947.[5]

What differentiated the Indian clubs and the colonial clubs that were to follow was their scale. Unlike the Georgian and Victorian London clubs, they were not hemmed in by a city already built around them. Land was easily available to the British – by coin or by seizure – and it became the norm to occupy vast, palatial grounds, which could accommodate a vast array of sporting facilities. The Tollygunge Club of Calcutta, for instance, took over a 1780s-built merchant's house when it was founded as a club in 1895, in a leafy southern suburb of the city. Surrounded by over 100 acres, it still commands a wide range of facilities, including a golf course, stables, a nineteenth-century outdoor swimming pool and an indoor swimming pool added in the 1930s, as well as its own one-time racetrack, though the land for the latter was subsequently seized for the city. So large are the Tollygunge Club's grounds that it has its own ecosystem – various flora and fauna that were bred from European species and local Indian species, including a unique type of jackal that still stalks its grounds.[6]

Indian clubs also provided accommodation, but of a very different type from the London clubs. Heat and humidity meant that many clubs often avoided being high-rise (or if they were, took particular effort with fan coverage, first manually operated by servants, and then operated electronically). Instead of shunting their overnight guests into bedrooms upstairs where heat gathered, it became normal through the nineteenth century to build cottages dotted around the grounds. This made the most of what Indian clubs had in abundance – land. Allocated their own cottage, usually with servants stationed twenty-four hours a day outside to see to their every need, British club members were able to live in grand style. Little wonder, then, that as well as the usual transient guests flowing through any city, Indian clubs began to attract their own measure of 'permanent residents', like a modern-day bed and breakfast, only rather grander.

Given such scale and sumptuous facilities, it is easy to see how colonial expatriates could shelter behind such walls, and live comfortable existences which were detached from the grinding poverty just outside – in some cases, literally on the doorstep, as Indians starved by the front gates. These clubs were an integral part of British rule. They allowed small social networks to thrive, centred on a few dining rooms and bars; and they enabled the British to retreat into their own private world. Psychologically as well as organisationally, they were key in encouraging an outlook that all was well in India, even at times of famine. The rebellion of 1857 came as a considerable shock to this cosy British mindset – and if anything, the incentive was even greater to retreat ever more into the clubs, building cosier and more elaborate realities behind their massive walls.

British merchant vessels returning home from Calcutta frequently stopped off at Madras, a trading port even older than the capital. It was unsurprising that Madras followed with clubs of its own, beginning with the Madras Club founded in 1832, occupying a succession of three stately clubhouses. Like Calcutta, Madras would expand to have clubs themed around sports: the Madras Race Club in 1837, the Madras Cricket Club in 1846, the Madras Boat Club in 1867 and the Madras Gymkhana in 1885. Each would be centred around one of two sites: Fort St George, the traditional British compound dating to the seventeenth century, and the River Adyar some six miles south, whose still waters were perfect for rowing.[7]

Deep inland, the garrison cantonment of Bangalore came to provide an administrative centre for the British across southern India, and its military presence ensured a similar concentration of clubs by the late nineteenth century, including the Bangalore United Services Club founded in 1863 (now simply the Bangalore Club), and the Bangalore Golf Club in 1876, both heavily catering to off-duty army officers. To this day, the Bangalore Club still displays a ledger showing an unpaid thirteen-rupee debt incurred as a bar tab by one of its members in 1899, Lieutenant Winston Churchill, whose first club it was. The Bowring Institute established in 1868 also provided its own distinctive halfway house between a club and a literary institute, fuelled by Victorian notions of self-improvement, and founded with the patronage of Mysore and Coorg commissioner L. C. Bowring.[8]

The clubs of Bombay could scarcely have looked more different from Bangalore. They cropped up not from off-duty army officers, but from catering to the city's wealthy merchant elites. Like much of Bombay, they were unusually tall for India – land prices were at a premium in this port city built on solid rock, and buildings rose high. Further to the north of the city are some 'typical' cottage-strewn Indian clubs occupying vast grounds, though these tend to be much later establishments, like the prestigious Willingdon Sports Club, not founded until 1917.[9]

Sitting by the dock of Bombay were found far larger, more palatial seafront buildings like the Royal Bombay Yacht Club, established in 1846. The Club's original riverside clubhouse was demolished by the post-independence municipal authorities in 1947 – the lease renewal coincidentally came up in the year of Indian independence, and in a show of defiance this building which came to epitomise so much of British rule was razed to the ground by the new authorities. Since then, the Club has retreated to what was originally built as its chambers – apartments for members – and, if anything, this tall, gothic edifice only further emphasises how distinctly the clubs of Bombay stood out.[10]

Delhi was quite a late addition to India's Clubland. The British moved their capital there as late as 1911, in response to growing political discontent in Calcutta. An attempt to resolve dissent through the partition of Bengal in 1905 only aggravated matters and provoked increasingly militant anti-British demonstrations, so that within six years the partition was undone and the capital moved far away. Within two years, the Delhi Gymkhana was founded, at the heart of Lutyens' Delhi, following the by now well-established Indian sports club model. In 1917, it was joined by the Chelmsford Club, which still stands close to the Central Vista constructed by Lutyens and Baker from 1921 to 1927. Delhi's clubs were thus part of the grand design of the development of an imperial capital. Demand for European clubs soon spread to Old Delhi, too, partly met by the building of the Roshanara Club in 1922.[11] These Delhi clubs synthesised all that had come before them in the clubs of India. They included informal as well as formal spaces, which would be invaluable: in 1931, Mohandas Gandhi and the British viceroy, Lord Irwin, were keen to meet, but neither could agree on a suitable venue. In the end, the Nawab of Bhopal broke the impasse – as a member of the Delhi Gymkhana Club, he was able to host them in some discreet alcoves off the central ballroom, with curved walls that meant they could not be seen or overheard.[12]

Although Calcutta remained the titular capital for the rest of the nineteenth century, British toleration of the hot, humid climate did not improve. For decades, British traders had already retreated to cooler hill stations for long holidays in the summer months. (Popular hill stations included 'Ooty' in the Nilgiri Hills of the south, where British expatriates in the Ootacamund Club famously invented snooker in the 1880s.) By 1864, the entire administration recognised this practice, and Shimla in northern India became the summer capital of India for over six months of the year, from April to October. It, too, acquired its own clubs, despite steep and challenging topography. The Amateur Dramatics Club was formed in 1868, staging frolicsome, lightweight plays that featured the likes of Rudyard Kipling. When the Gaiety Theatre complex was built over The Ridge at the heart of the city, in the style of a Scottish baronial hall, it embedded a wing for the Club, which remains to this day.[13] Out of town, colonial administrators could unwind at the nearby Naldehra Golf Club.

Working as a member of staff in these clubs was not a salubrious prospect. As well as the instability of employment and threat of instant dismissal which came with working in any Victorian-era club, there was the additional burden of endemic racism, and the day-to-day abuse which was heaped on through that. Hours were long and wages were paltry.

A question worth answering is whether slavery formed part of these colonial clubs. This is difficult to prove, because the surviving archives are often slim to non-existent, and staffing matters are some of the least documented items on record. Nonetheless, it would have been exceptionally unusual if the earlier Indian clubs had *not* used slaves. Although Britain formally abolished slavery in 1807, and the slave trade from 1833, slavery continued in many parts of the empire. By the 1830s, over a million slaves were recorded in India. It was not until changes to the Indian Penal Code in the 1860s that slavery in India was formally abolished. Even then, the relationships between masters and servants did not progress much further than slavery. This could be clearly seen in the tea plantations of India – and their many accompanying tea planters' clubs – where the workers had a bare subsistence level of existence. Just as the luxurious buildings of London clubs were often founded on cheap labour, so the splendid facilities of the Indian clubs were often built through mass exploitation.

Amid all this, the nineteenth century saw the emergence of a small Indian middle class, who appropriated European manners and fashions, training for and performing professional roles in the ever-growing British bureaucracy. They could be found working both in the Princely States, and in the British-controlled provinces. Their relationships with the British were complex – they could be everything from nationalist in outlook, to staunchly pro-British. But they were long excluded from clubs which were for Europeans only.

The response to this was the founding of a series of Cosmopolitan Clubs – clubs which looked and felt just like the British clubs, and indeed tried to outdo them for architectural grandeur, but which admitted Indians on an equal basis. The first of these was the Cosmopolitan Club in Madras, set up in 1873. Today, it remains an imposing building, every bit as grand as the British-founded clubs of Chennai, the only noticeable superficial difference being that the oil paintings are mainly of Indian subjects, rather than the moustachioed European administrators whose pictures usually line Indian clubs. This was followed by other Cosmopolitan Clubs across the autonomous Princely States of southern India, in Coimbatore in 1891, Mysore in 1895 and Calicut in 1898. In the north, a similar establishment arrived in the capital with the Calcutta Club of 1907.[14]

These cosmopolitan clubs were only ever a minority pursuit. They did not admit vast numbers of Indians to club membership, just the small number who worked in legal, clerical and professional roles. They did have an impact on the admissions policies of the European clubs, but this, too, was limited. By the early twentieth century, many of these older clubs began to elect their 'first Indian member', though invariably it was a local maharajah, diwan (prime minister), or similarly exalted celebrity. For even the majority of the Indian elite, the European clubs remained out of reach until after Indian independence in 1947, save as a servant.

An alternative approach to cosmopolitanism in Indian clubs was sectarianism. This was most clearly seen in Bombay. The city's grand Bombay Gymkhana opened in 1875, with unrivalled sporting facilities at the time. Yet membership remained strictly open to the white British only. As Bombay underwent further expansion in the 1890s and 1900s, a flurry of further sporting clubs opened, each founded on a sectarian basis, often built side by side along a narrow coastal strip further north-west, and so within decades, the Bombay Gymkhana had as rivals the Parmananddas Jivandas Hindu Gymkhana of 1878, the Parsi Gymkhana of 1888, the Muslim Gymkhana of 1890 and the Catholic Gymkhana of 1912.[15]

To describe the clubs of the major Indian cities might give the impression that they were urban phenomena, and indeed many of the largest and best-known clubs of India were (and are) found in these cities. Yet their spread across British India was phenomenal, and they were to be found in almost every city, large or small, as well as many which existed as stand-alone settlements, far from any city – this was particularly true of hilltop clubs built at high altitudes. Today, the 300 surviving colonial-era clubs of India stand testament to their popularity as a way for the British to unwind at the height of empire – not so much behind closed doors as behind sealed walls.

India's clubs grew exponentially, yet the country was far from unique among British colonies. Others saw the exporting of clubs as a central part of British imperial rule. In particular, key strategic naval ports saw clubs crop up early on in the Victorian British Empire.

Hong Kong island initially became a British colony in the early 1840s, after the First Opium War. By 1846, the Hong Kong Club was established, emulating the first wave of the Pall Mall clubs of London. This was followed by a series of club-like sporting institutions over the following decades, mirroring the Indian pattern, including Hong Kong's Cricket Club in 1851, Football Club in 1886, and both the Golf Club and the Jockey Club in 1889. As British rule on the neighbouring Kowloon Peninsula deepened, this, too, sprouted a range of clubs by the early twentieth century.[16]

Singapore had been colonised even earlier, from 1819, but it was the slow dismemberment of the East India Company in the 1850s and 1860s which saw control transferred to the British state, with large-scale urbanisation underway. Singapore began with a Turf Club in 1842 and a Cricket Club in 1852, followed by the more socially-oriented Tanglin Club in 1865, and a brace of further sporting clubs in the 1880s, the Recreation Club and the Polo Club, providing just about every outdoor sport imaginable.

Alongside this, Singapore's status as a key trading post made it a melting pot for an increasing range of expatriate groups. Excluded from the socially conservative British clubs, they each began to set up their own rival English-style clubs. This began as early as 1856, with the creation of a German Association, and in the following decades they were joined by the Swiss Club in 1871, the Hollandse Club in 1908 and the Japanese Association in 1915.

On the other side of the globe from London, two colonies embraced clubs as pillars of British rule: Australia and New Zealand. Both had their indigenous populations largely disregarded by the British, and so were viewed as blank slates to be moulded into a model society – where clubs would have a central role. The same reforming voices in the British Parliament who urged the First Reform Act of 1832 were also keen to impose a new social and political order in Australia, through legislation like the South Australia Act 1836.[17]

The first club on the Australian mainland was Sydney's appropriately named Australian Club, founded in 1838, which survives to this day, often making headlines because of its continued refusal to admit women. With the expansion of Melbourne and Sydney as major cities, both grew a range of downtown clubhouses, as did other growing nineteenth-century Australian settlements like Brisbane and Perth.

Closely following the Australian Club, only a few months later in 1838, was the Melbourne Club. While Melbourne's bay had been inhabited by Aboriginal Australians for 40,000 years, the city of Melbourne was only founded three years before the creation of the Melbourne Club; thus colonial-era Australia came to be bound up with these clubs, and those which followed. Melbourne added an Athenaeum Club in 1868, and its own Australian Club in 1878, while a Melbourne Savage Club, based on its London counterpart, started in 1894. With women excluded from these clubs, they eventually set up their own Lyceum Club in 1913, affiliated to the sister club in London of that name.[18]

This was paralleled by the growth of Sydney. Already its Royal Exchange of 1851 was offering club-like facilities, followed by a Union Club in 1857 modelled on the London club of that name; and in 1858 a Tattersall's Club sprouted up in the centre, prompting a further City Tattersall's Club in 1895. As with Melbourne, these male-only clubs prompted the creation of a rival Women's Club in 1901, followed by the ladies-only Queen's Club in 1912.

Yet it was the island of Tasmania, one of the most anglophile corners of Australia, which actually saw the country's first British-style club: the Union Club of Hobart, which began in 1834. While this is now defunct, Tasmania still has surviving clubs, including the Launceston Club from 1882, and the Athenaeum Club of Hobart dating to 1889.

Across the Tasman Sea, in New Zealand the Wellington Club was established in the capital in 1841, barely two years after Europeans first settled the area. As with Australia and India, clubs sprouted up across the rest of the country in roughly the order of European expansion, including the Christchurch Club of 1856, the Dunedin Club in 1858, the Hawke's Bay Club of Napier in 1863 and the Northern Club of Auckland in 1869.

The earliest British clubs across Africa were along coastal South Africa, reflecting the strategic importance of the Cape of Good Hope. Before the Suez Canal was built, all British shipping routes to India passed the Cape. Among the small white British population of the colonies, the new clubs played a major role in regulating social and professional life, and soon spread inland from the ports. As the British Empire massively expanded in the 1880s–90s 'scramble for Africa', so did the popularity of clubs across Africa. British clubs across Africa tended to be even more overtly tied to the country's colonial mission. In India, the dual structure of Princely States as well as British-administered regions forced at least some measure of cultural synthesis, even if the British clubs were regarded as sanctuaries from that. Across much of Africa, British engagement with local tribal identity was minimal, and this was reflected in the clubs. Major African clubs such as the Salisbury Club of 1893 and the Muthaiga Country Club of 1913 in the capitals of Rhodesia and Kenya respectively were overtly founded to support the colonial elite and maintain them in lifestyles that emulated the luxuries of Britain.[19]

In line with the nature of British rule in these countries, these African clubs carried a particular propensity for enforcing racial segregation – to a degree not seen in many of the London clubs they were trying to emulate. They sought to build a fantasy world of what the colonists imagined London clubs to look like – and that meant ensuring that the only black faces in sight were among the servants.

As was often the case with racial barriers, these were rarely overt. Instead, they were couched in encouraging cultural norms, customs, dress and, of course, that favourite code word, 'standards'. It was the British colonial clubs across Africa and India in the 1890s which introduced the very first club dress codes, for the express purpose of keeping out non-white members and guests. London clubs remained distinctly more casual – and cosmopolitan – and would not adopt dress codes until the mid-twentieth century.

The *post*-colonial legacy of these British colonial clubs was almost as important as their imperial role. They moved in a number of directions. Many clubs in Africa often served as a whites-only enclave, decades after decolonisation happened; where an ageing, dwindling membership of once-powerful farmers would convene in the ever-shabbier ruins of formerly grand buildings, nostalgically looking back on the days of white minority rule. In the case of Ian Smith's rogue state of Rhodesia in the 1960s and 1970s, this often meant club government, by the membership of the whites-only

Salisbury Club, a couple of doors across Cecil Square from the Rhodesian Parliament. By contrast, the experience on the Indian subcontinent was very different. British clubs continued to be seen as socially prestigious in post-independence Bangladesh, India and Pakistan. They were rapidly appropriated by the emerging new middle classes after independence. A typical pattern was for an Indian club to have refused to admit non-Europeans until 1947, for it to have elected its first Indian General Committee members by the 1950s, and its first Indian Chairman by the late 1960s or early 1970s.

There could be unexpected developments in post-colonial clubs. Early optimism that Indian clubs would reach a new era of inclusivity was to be dashed. However vast their facilities, they were only ever built to accommodate a small minority of the vast populations of Indian cities, and by the 1980s it was common to find these clubs 'full', just like nineteenth-century London clubs with long waiting lists. Part of the added complication was that immediately after independence, many of these clubs had also become family clubs. While this had some advantages in opening up the clubs to women and younger members, it also had unforeseen effects on numbers. In practice, if you were related to an existing member, you could jump to the front of the waiting list. This means that Indian clubs today often have memberships that serve as a who's who of the children and grandchildren of the Indian middle class of 1947. Far from providing greater social mobility, it has ended up fossilising the Club's composition around the families of yesterday's elites.

An unexpected lifeline came to the aid of the Indian colonial clubs in recent years. Each faced huge financial pressures, and concentrating on a small number of middle-class Indian families was not necessarily a recipe for financial prosperity. In recent years, many of these clubs have cashed in on their prestige, through

'Corporate Membership' – companies can pay the equivalent of millions of pounds to elect a handful of senior executives to a club, for as long as they remain in post, when they would normally have languished on the waiting lists for decades. This secret has filled the coffers of several major Indian clubs, as well as letting some 'old' money give way to 'new' money – although it does create two classes of club members.

The British were far from being the only colonial exporters of clubs. Through the mid-nineteenth century, both Spain and Portugal adopted British-style clubs in their major cities, and went on to export them to their former colonies across Central America and South America.

The clubs of Spain merit a book of their own, spreading through the country at least as comprehensively as they did through Britain. Spain's oldest club remains the Casino Antiguo at Castellón de la Plana in Valencia, founded between the last of the Napoleonic Wars in 1814. This was one of a number of cultural casinos, which were to form the basis of Spanish clubs. These were not gambling casinos – in fact, gambling remained forbidden on the premises of most – but social organisations. This earliest casino was something of an outlier, with only a couple more clubs following in the next quarter-century, the Casino de Madrid in 1836 and the Sociedad Bilbaina of Bilbao in 1839. However, the 1840s and 1850s would see an explosion in the number of major clubs and cultural casinos across Spain, including in each major city.

By this time, Spain had already begun shedding its empire, with the wave of independence movements of former Spanish colonies from the 1810s onwards. Unlike the British, Spanish clubs were never exported as pillars of empire. However, Spain's commercial and cultural links with Latin America remained strong, and it is no coincidence that from the 1850s onwards, former Spanish colonies began opening clubs of their own, heavily influenced by Spanish architecture, and often larger and more impressive than their Spanish and British counterparts.

In Portugal, the two biggest cities of Lisbon and Porto saw a crop of clubs, primarily founded by the cities' British expatriates. Porto, with its major supply role for transatlantic shipping, and its major port wine industry dominated by a number of British (often Scottish) families, opened its first club in 1790, well before most London clubs. Factory House – named after the archaic term 'Factor', for one engaged in trade – was (and is) only open to British owners of port houses. Its membership is tiny, but its weekly Wednesday lunch has long been the means by which business has been transacted in the port wine trade. The nineteenth century saw a flurry of further clubs for the city's expat populations engaged in commerce, including the Oporto Lawn Tennis Club in 1855, the Clube Portuense in 1857, the Ateneu Comercial do Porto in 1869 and the Clube Fenianos Portuenses of 1904 – the latter nicknamed the 'Fenian Club', not on account of any sympathy for Irish nationalism, but after its founders sent a delegation from Porto to a Brazilian carnival in 1903, all draped in green cloaks, only to be told that they 'looked like a bunch of Fenians'. Lisbon saw its first club in 1846, the Grémio Literário, and a succession of naval-themed clubs sprouted up in the ensuing decades.

Like Spain, Portugal had already begun shedding its colonies long before clubs caught on at home, most notably with Brazilian independence in 1822. Indeed, clubs would not catch on in Brazil for some time, with Rio de Janeiro not seeing its first clubs, themed around sports, until the 1920s and 1930s. São Paulo was an earlier adopter of clubs, in the late 1880s, tying in with the expansion of the city. Nonetheless, compared with much of Spanish-speaking South America, Portuguese-speaking Brazil was a late adopter of clubs. Across Latin America, these represented a clear influence of European culture – but without the colonial administration overtones of British imperial clubs.

In Portugal's remaining colonies, there were some overtly military clubs set up, like the Club Militar de Macau in 1870, which followed the British model. In Goa, Portuguese army officers built a rather more modest beach shack in the capital of Panaji in 1926, which was the Clube Gaspar Dias, open to men and women. Eight years later, an American magnate, Josephine Hogaz, introduced and sponsored tennis courts, and it gradually evolved into the Clube Tennis de Gaspar Dias, with an increasing sports and social emphasis, moving away from the Club's colonial roots.[20]

Interestingly, despite France having had the second-largest empire of the nineteenth century, the French did not appreciably follow the British–Spanish–Portuguese model of exporting clubs to their colonies. France was a relatively 'late adopter' of clubs. France's two oldest clubs, the paradoxically named Nouveau Cercle de l'Union ('*New* Union Circle') of 1828 and Jockey Club of 1834, were aristocratic haunts that predated the vast majority of London clubs. Yet these elite institutions can be considered outliers, and for all their social prestige they were not looked upon as examples to be emulated. Opera-lovers have long reviled the Jockey Club's boorish behaviour at the 1851 première of Wagner's *Tannhäuser*, arriving late, heckling the opera throughout with boos and rattles, and even invading the stage midway through the performance.[21]

While a smattering of other clubs followed, like the Cercle Anglais ('English Club') for English expatriates in Pau in southern France from 1859, most of Paris's major clubs did not originate until much later – the Cercle Suédois of 1891, the Automobile Club de France of 1895, the Travellers Club of 1903 (closely modelled on the ethos of its nineteenth-century London namesake, and housed within a hotel on the Champs-Élysées), and Paris's largest club, the Cercle de l'Union Interalliée, was not founded until 1917, as a wartime club for American, British and French officers on furlough in Paris.[22] Perhaps due to this relatively late development of francophone clubland, clubs were never exported to the French colonies in quite the same way.

Germany had few clubs of its own. A Museum Society formed in Bremen in 1783 gradually evolved into a club-like institution by the early twentieth century, and a smattering of English-style sports clubs cropped up in the late nineteenth century. The few recognisable social clubs on the English model were not to survive into the second half of the twentieth century. The Münchener Herrenclub (literally 'Munich Men's Club') formed in 1851 was representative of their fates, as it was shut by the Nazis in 1934. The Nazis deeply distrusted German clubs, for they saw within their memberships two groups they held in particular contempt: Freemasons and Jews.

Not all clubs proliferating around the globe were the product of empires. Clubs had started in North America, so it made sense that they would proliferate in the United States of America after independence. The clubs that followed acquired their own very distinctive flavour. Far more than the London clubs, they came to be synonymous with elites, and exclusion. As more cities were developed, further west, so clubs arose in each of them. They usually mirrored the local sources of economic power – hence the Fifth Avenue clubs of nineteenth-century New York, and the proliferation of at least one major club in every city of the United States by the early twentieth century. By the mid-twentieth century, petroleum clubs were one of the most common form of American clubs, closely tracking the source of wealth of key oil-producing towns.

The big American development was the Country Club, far closer to an Indian club in its scale and scope, occupying vast grounds that almost housed towns of their own, with a variety of restaurants and bars and even multiple clubhouses between all the sporting fields. American Country Clubs also acquired something of the reclusiveness of the Victorian clubs of India, heavily guarded behind high walls.

This exclusivity made them ideal for being 'restricted', which usually translated as 'No blacks and no Jews.' Other religious and ethnic minorities such as Catholics and Hispanics were slow to be admitted to American Country Clubs, too, reflecting the white Anglo-Saxon Protestant outlook of much of the 'new' money (which rapidly restyled itself as 'old' money) on the north-eastern seaboard. Few of these clubs were so gauche as to place obvious barriers, like defining their members' ethnicity in their rules. Instead, it so happened that over and over again, across thousands of members elected in each of several hundred clubs, no black or Jewish member had ever been elected. There were usually subtler ways of restricting admission – such as charging one-off entry fees fifty or even a hundred times higher than that of London clubs, so that the only people who could afford to join were overwhelmingly more likely to be white. By the First World War, the level of discrimination was becoming so obvious that rival clubs were being set up – like the Hillcrest Country Club in Los Angeles, set up in 1920 for Jewish members of the Hollywood film industry, who had been excluded from the Los Angeles Country Club which had been operating since 1897. Clashes over ongoing racial exclusion around some US country clubs continue to this day.

The Country Club had a significant impact on the flavour of American clubs in the cities, as well. Geographically, they were worlds apart – the urban clubs downtown in a city's central business district offered luncheon facilities for businessmen, whereas the Country Club could be deeply ensconced in rural areas, or else became a staple of the far-flung upper-middle-class suburbs. Yet the services they were both expected to offer converged. Downtown urban clubs, even of a social type, were expected to have vast gymnasiums and athletics facilities. From the 1880s onwards, many came to occupy their own skyscraper or warehouse-sized clubhouse. These urban clubs were not looking to the pokey townhouses of Georgian London for their model, but to the need to outshine sprawling country clubs closer to home.

North of the border, the clubs of Canada offered a sort of halfway house between the clubs of Britain and the United States. Club-like organisations such as the Toronto Cricket, Skating and Curling Club of 1827 and the Toronto Hunt of 1843 had cropped up, but it was in the 1860s that the first recognisably English-style clubs of Canada began to appear along the coast in Halifax, with the Rideau Club following in the capital of Ottawa in 1865. Over the next quarter-century, Anglo-American-style clubs would be founded in every major Canadian town and city. Nor were they limited to English-speaking Canada, either. The Club Saint-James of Montréal founded in 1857 was one of the earliest francophone clubs in the world, pre-dating most of the clubs of Paris, and most of the anglophone clubs of Canada.

Where this all came full circle was reciprocation.

From the 1870s onwards, clubs around the world began to reciprocate. The principle was simple but effective: clubs in different countries could form a reciprocal agreement, so that members of one club could use the other club, for a limited number of days a year, while staying abroad. This global network of clubs initially built up very slowly. It tended to focus around similarly themed clubs (such as yacht clubs); and even then, it would not really reach its full scale until after the Second World War.

Nonetheless, the existence of reciprocation made clubs see themselves differently. For one thing, it helped to raise professional standards.

Until the 1860s, the clubs of London were still quite parochial in outlook: if thought was ever given to 'raising their game', it only meant in comparison to nearby rivals a few streets away, or even a few doors away. Suddenly, with members returning to London from postings in far-off colonies or business trips to the United States, they came back with tales of how facilities measured up compared to their own London club. And they began to copy one another. Menus further diversified, as did mealtimes. Sports facilities – unthinkable at the start of the century – began to be introduced. Even certain items of furniture started to become staples of clubs, with increasingly low-slung chairs for lounging. To this day, almost any British imperial club which was in business in the nineteenth century still has one particular item: a weighing chair. Members used it to weigh themselves before and after a heavy meal.

London clubs were always international in their origins and their running. By the last third of the nineteenth century, they had become embedded in a global web of clubs, across the British Empire and beyond, influencing and being influenced.

Chapter Eight

Clubs and race

(1850–1914)

The clubs of London had their own distinctive racial identities. Picture a stereotypical London club, and a cluster of white men invariably comes to mind. This was an entirely accurate picture of London clubs by the middle of the nineteenth century. Yet over the next few decades, clubs would accommodate an immeasurably more nuanced and complex series of religious, racial and ethnic identities, reflecting London as a city of many cultures.

As we have seen, the earliest clubs of the eighteenth century had gender-neutral rulebooks, and much of the template of the nineteenth century clubs came from the Union Club, the first member-owned club, whose rulebook was copied by newly established clubs, especially after an 1821 reconstitution specified that its members would be men.[1] But club rulebooks from this point on also began to specify that members would be British nationals.

This nationality requirement had previously been superfluous, because the nature of clubs was that they were limited to small, intimate, local circles, and would grow organically. The expansion of clubs meant redefining who could – and could not – belong. For the first time, Clubland 'outsiders' overlapped explicitly with nationality; and while there was not an overt racial barrier in most clubs, the nationality requirement provided a tacit barrier. Yet ideas around this would evolve in the coming decades.

For one thing, there was the notion of 'invisible minorities'. Up until then, areas of religious difference within clubs had largely been confined to Christianity; Catholic versus Protestant members, nonconformist versus established church. The precarious status of Jews in British public life was a more dramatic example. The passage of the Jewish Relief Act 1858, allowing Jews to take seats in Parliament without fear of prosecution, signalled something of a softening of attitudes (and indeed allowed the swearing in of the first Jewish MP, Lionel Nathan de Rothschild, who had been elected in 1847, but was unable to take his seat for eleven years).

Up until this point, Clubland, as with so much of London society, had not been particularly receptive to Jews, or even those with Jewish ancestry. True, the young Benjamin Disraeli had been able to secure election to the Carlton in 1836; but he was the Anglican-baptised son of a convert from Judaism, Isaac D'Israeli, who had anglicised his surname. He was also something of an outlier. It was to be another twenty years before anyone else of Jewish descent applied to the Carlton – Sir Massey Lopes in 1857 – although the 1860s then saw five more Jewish-descended members elected, Henry Drummond Wolff, James Disraeli, Albert Grant, Edmund Francis Lopes and Sir Charles Lopes. It was not until 1873 that the Carlton elected its first Jewish member, the banker and philanthropist Henri Louis Bischoffsheim. Nevertheless, the Club was something of a trailblazer in this respect. Indeed, Bischoffsheim's seven-year wait in the candidates' book, from 1866 to 1873, was actually relatively quick, compared to the average thirty-year waiting list the Club operated at the time. Bischoffsheim was a Dutch immigrant who moved to Britain in 1849, naturalised in 1854 and married an Englishwoman two years later. He eagerly endeavoured 'to maintain the position and perform the duties of an English gentleman'. Later in the 1870s, the Carlton's rule allowing Members of Parliament to vault over the waiting list allowed the first two practising Jewish Conservative MPs to join, Saul Isaac in 1874 and Baron Henry de Worms in 1878. Jews continued to be treated as 'The Other' well beyond the nineteenth century; but increasing sections of Clubland – in London, at least – began to accommodate Jews as members.[2]

Other examples of 'invisible minorities' were the considerable number of mixed-race Britons, including those who could be found in the military service clubs. Clubs with strong overseas service connections, most obviously the Oriental Club and East India Club, each had their own share of mixed-race members, often the descendants of male East India Company members who had lived and worked for years in India and married while serving there; this topic was still considered something of a taboo at the time, tacitly understood but seldom mentioned in polite society. Indeed, such was the social stigma around mixed-race ancestry in nineteenth-century Britain that not only were such things often left unsaid, but in some cases members had been left unaware by their own parents of 'the family secret' of a non-white ancestor two generations or more earlier.

Service clubs like the East India would also elect the first explicitly non-white members of London clubs, who were able to satisfy the nationality requirements. Even though the early nineteenth century saw a temporary blocking of club membership to non-British nationals, this never entirely equated to a strict racial bar. Moreover, there was never a racial bar on club visitors. Thus, even at the height of the 'aristocratic embrace' of London clubs in 1789, we find a black French composer and fencer of African descent, Joseph Bologne, le Chevalier de Saint-Georges, visited White's. Having taken London society by storm over a two-year visit with his proficiency with swordsmanship, le Chevalier de Saint-Georges visited the Club, 'to give his very hearty t[h]anks, to all the noble Lords, Dukes, Earls, Barons, Knights and Gentlemen, for being so good as to receive him in so illustrious [a] Club and so good company'.[3]

Probably the first 'visible minority' member of London's Clubland was not necessarily a paragon of progressive values: the fabulously wealthy opium trader Sir Jamsetjee Jejeebhoy, who grew rich in partnership with the East India Company, and profited particularly from Britain's Opium Wars, aggressively opening up opium markets in China. Jejeebhoy had a curiously paradoxical approach to suffering – he could not abide it in any form in animals, yet showed few qualms about the human misery caused by the opium trade. Knighted by Queen Victoria in 1842, and then elevated to a baronetcy in 1857, he rose from humble beginnings to become a pillar of Victorian respectability. With his East India Company links, he joined the Oriental Club. A year after his death in 1859, his son Sir Cursetjee Jamsetjee Jejeebhoy joined the East India United Services Club.

Such admissions to non-white members were still rare, though. At the East India Club, the younger Jejeebhoy's membership was an honorary rather than paid one; and indeed he would have been barred from 'regular' membership, which as late as 1879 still welcomed only '*European* members of the Uncovenanted Services'.[4]

By the 1880s, however, rulebooks began to change. Newer clubs in particular, catering to larger mass memberships, preferred to adopt the phrasing of members being British subjects, rather than British nationals. At a stroke, this allowed hundreds of millions of subjects of the British Empire to become *potentially* eligible for London club membership – even if the actual number of applicants remained quite small. Nonetheless, the effect on the culture and diversity within London clubs soon became apparent.

One of the more obvious examples was at the National Liberal Club. With a membership already inclined towards radicalism, its first Club Secretary was William Digby, former editor of the *Madras Times* and an outspoken critic of British imperial policy in India. Under Digby's direction, the Club founded in 1882 set about recruiting Indian Britons, one of whom was Dadabhai Naoroji.[5]

Naoroji was a successful Bombay-born Parsi merchant and former professor of mathematics, who would come to be known as 'the Father of India'. As an economist, Naoroji was most closely associated with the 'drain theory' he advanced around British imperial rule, arguing that, for all its associated benefits, British rule in India had placed a great drain upon the natural resources of the subcontinent. Consequently, he was one of the nineteenth century's most prominent – and articulate – advocates of Indian self-governance, and a co-founder of the Indian National Congress, advocating moderation. Although he had worked in Britain intermittently since the 1850s, it was in the 1880s that his political activity accelerated, through Britain's Liberal Party. At the hastily convened 1886 general election, Naoroji secured the nomination for the recently created seat of Holborn in north London, only to lose the election by a two-to-one margin against the national backdrop of a Conservative landslide.

And that should have been that. While Naoroji was not the first non-white British general election candidate, he was certainly a pioneer when this was still extraordinarily rare, and his failed candidacy seemed to be proof for all who sought it that white British voters would never elect someone with darker skin than their own.

Only this was exactly what the Conservative prime minister, Lord Salisbury, openly said in Edinburgh in November 1888. To approving laughter, and cries of 'hear, hear!', Salisbury told his audience:

> I doubt if we have yet to go to that point of view where a British
> constituency would elect a black man. I am speaking roughly,
> and using language in its colloquial sense, because I imagine
> the colour is not exactly black, but, at all events, [Naoroji] was
> a man of another race.[6]

The prime minister's comments prompted a series of national debates in the press. The first of these were a number of rather esoteric and insensitive discussions as to whether Naoroji actually was 'black'. This, in turn, gave way to a series of debates as to what, if anything, this should signify in a post-slavery world. Salisbury's remarks, apparently intended as an audience amusement, had the unexpected effect of prompting a backlash, catapulting to national celebrity someone who had hitherto been a relatively obscure figure outside Indian economics and Liberal politics. The debates were not straightforward ones along racism versus anti-racism; nonetheless, they allowed for a far-reaching examination into questions of race in Victorian Britain.

Since 1885, Naoroji had been a member of the National Liberal Club, which already had a growing membership drawn from London's large Indian diaspora. Far from shrinking away from the controversy, the Club positively embraced it, holding a banquet in solidarity with Naoroji. Much of the Westminster press pack was invited, and encouraged to convey details like the menu intended to taunt Lord Salisbury, with its 'Purée Indienne', followed by 'Consommee a la Black Man', and 'Curry a la Salisbury', washed down with 'Café Noir'. The banquet had an unusually broad composition, including former Viceroy of India the 1st Marquess of Ripon presiding, giving it impeccably 'Establishment' credentials; yet its 230 diners included radical MPs such as Charles Bradlaugh, and one press account noted the sizeable contingent drawn from

London's expatriate Indian community 'clothed in flowing robes of green and gold, and red and silver, with splendid turbans'. Naoroji's thanksgiving speech to the dinner said that 'It marked an epoch in Indian history.'[7]

The National Liberal Club's banquet for Naoroji was not an empty gesture. Firstly, because of the lengths taken to promote the occasion with articles, poems, cartoons and published speech transcripts, the dinner made the news in its own right, for this kind of multi-racial dining at the heart of the British Establishment was still highly unusual in 1889. Secondly, these accounts in turn prompted further controversy, including a denunciation of the banquet in *The Times*, which only further fuelled debate. And thirdly, it consolidated Naoroji's eminence in the Club, which became a fertile support base for his political career. Fundraising through the Club and tapping its political network, he was selected for the north London seat of Finsbury at the next election, and elected to Parliament in 1892, becoming one of Britain's first non-white MPs. Digby at the National Liberal Club acted as his agent and chief fundraiser. Naoroji followed his political career in Britain with a further political career in India.

As a figurehead for the British Indian community, Naoroji built up a substantial personal following, and made his own club his Westminster base; it was more welcoming than the aloof atmosphere of Parliament, and while his tenure as an MP was relatively brief at just three years, the National Liberal Club continued to welcome him long after he lost his parliamentary seat. He served on its General Committee for twenty years. Around him, he built up a close cadre of followers. Some, like Muhammad Ali Jinnah (later founder of modern-day Pakistan), became NLC members themselves; others like the young Mohandas Gandhi were content to remain visitors.

Yet racial discrimination in clubs did not follow a simple trajectory towards greater enlightenment and the breaking down of barriers. There were examples of a range of attitudes to race across Clubland, which suggested that bigotry was alive and well in some corners. The origins of the name of the Savage Club, founded in 1857, are somewhat obscure – the original account by Andrew Halliday of the Club's founders' choice of name leaves it ambiguous as to members' reasoning. On the one hand, Halliday records the anecdote of countless writers and poets from Johnson to Shakespeare being rejected as far too pompous to be the namesake of the new club, until 'The Savage' was suggested: 'If we accept Richard Savage as our godfather, it shows that there is no pride about us.' On the other hand, the Savage Club went on to embrace the iconography, with its founders also averring in that same opening meeting that 'the Wigwam [should be] a *lucus a non lucendo*'.[8] The Savage Club certainly took this iconography to heart. Countless menus of the ensuing decades depicted instances of blackface, redface, and members dining in white tie and tails revelling in the placement of any number of ceremonial spears, drums and other 'Savage' imagery. The Club even sent a delegation to the Royal Albert Hall in native American headdresses. For every example of racial integration and dialogue in London Clubland, the crude racial pantomimes of the Savage Club remain a powerful counter-argument.

Additional racial barriers were incurred in clubs, as can be seen in the role of the National Sporting Club in lobbying for a 'colour bar' in boxing from 1911.

The National Sporting Club had been formed in 1891 at 43 King Street, overlooking Covent Garden's main piazza, to bring together sports lovers. Like several sporting clubs, it played a key regulatory role in several sports, including boxing. The Club attempted to rehabilitate boxing from its unruly reputation, holding matches on gentlemanly terms after dinner, with strict rules in place.

Throughout the nineteenth century, there had been a number of black boxers fighting in Britain, including former slaves Bill Richmond and Tom Molineux. A young Winston Churchill bunked off from Harrow in 1892 to watch the black Australian boxer Peter Jackson fight at the Club in 1892. However, the Club's founding President, the 5th Earl of Lonsdale, was a long-term opponent of inter-racial boxing. By the Edwardian period, a widespread frenzy of scientific racism reached fever pitch amid concerns for the fitness of the white British race, and its separation from other races. This culminated in 1911 in a proposed fight in Earl's Court between white British boxer Billy Wells and the black American heavyweight champion Jack Johnson. Lonsdale and the National Sporting Club led a wave of demands for separation of the races in fights, and this triggered an intervention from Winston Churchill – by then the home secretary – cancelling the fight. A 'colour bar' in British boxing then persisted until 1948, with black boxers denied the chance to compete in the top tier.[9]

Other clubs could provide sporting opportunities for members from different racial backgrounds. When the National Liberal Club opened its new clubhouse in 1887, a feature was the suite of billiard rooms under the terrace, enabling practice. One member who honed his skills was the Anglo-Indian member Mohamed Abdool 'Arthur' Vahid, born in Agra.[10] He went on to win the Billiard Association Championship of Great Britain, hosted at the National Sporting Club between 15 January and 2 February 1893. His reign was brief, however, as he took up a position as a billiard marker in March and duly resigned the title, because his new occupation made him a professional rather than an amateur.[11]

Meanwhile, complicating the patchwork of different cultural and racial traditions across Clubland, London's multiplicity of expatriate groups saw several set up their own clubs. Many of these were linked to Britain by reason of trade. In 1910, an Argentine Club launched just off Hyde Park Corner, for expatriates of what was at the time one of the wealthiest nations on earth. (In 1948, realising that London's dwindling contingent of Argentinian immigrants was not necessarily enough to sustain a club, it was broadened to embrace those with a connection to South America as a whole, and rebranded the Canning Club, in honour of George Canning's various treaties deepening British ties across Latin America.)

Scandinavian clubs were particularly popular. The first was the Danish Club founded in 1863, with clubrooms in Soho's Morland Hotel. This was followed in the 1870s by a Scandinavian Club at 80–81 Strand, with a large Swedish membership. Den Norske Klub was convened for Norwegian expatriates in 1887, on Norway's national day, 17 May, initially as an informal association meeting in a succession of pubs and taverns for its first few decades, before its financial situation stabilised after the First World War, and in 1924 it settled on a clubhouse in Cockspur Street, just off the junction of Pall Mall and Trafalgar Square, for the next seven decades.

Other national groups also acquired clubs of their own. A French Club cropped up on Adelphi Terrace in 1883, a West Indian Club was formed on Norfolk Street in 1898 and the Nederlandsche Vereeniging (Dutch Club) on Sackville Street launched by the end of the century; the latter two would continue until the 1970s. German expatriates could join the German Athenaeum Club on Mortimer Terrace founded in 1868, although it predictably vanished overnight on the outbreak of the First World War. Thus, even in the heart of London, Clubland was not exclusively British, or even English, given the Caledonian Club and several successive Irish Clubs.

London's Clubland was not a bastion of racial harmony; but neither was it the reactionary racist stereotype often presented. It was large enough to encompass a wide variety of different clubs and attitudes; and even if it was overwhelmingly 'Establishment', it occupied a broad enough notion of *what* Establishments those might be, to accommodate a growing number of racial and cultural traditions in the late nineteenth century. It could not help but reflect at least some of the sheer diversity of London as a city.

Chapter Nine

Women in clubs
(1840–1920)

The earliest clubs of Georgian London had strictly men-only memberships. But over the nineteenth century, women were able to increasingly access these clubs, first as staff, then as guests, and then as members. Much of the mystique of 'men-only' Clubland had already been shattered by the enterprising journalist Flora Tristan in the 1840s, who successfully gatecrashed several clubs in drag, writing about her experiences. In the ensuing decades, Erika Rappaport notes, 'For over half a century, roughly between the 1860s and the 1930s, thousands of women founded and joined clubs to satisfy their physical, economic, social and political desires.'[1]

There is still a widespread belief that men's clubs were the only type of club in Victorian London. 'Until relatively recently, almost all the doors of Clubland were closed to the fairer sex', insists one of the most recent histories of Clubland.[2] This was not how the late Victorians would have seen things. Edwardian-era club historian Arthur Griffiths noted, '"My club" is a phrase as often heard on charming feminine lips as on those of the most determined club *habitué*.'[3] In reality, the first recognisable private members' club for women, the Ladies' Institute, opened its doors in 1860.[4] The facilities they offered were considerable, and as Doughan and Gordon have argued, they 'provided a haven for middle-class women from the demands of family, children, servants and tradesmen'.[5] All the advantages of men's clubs were just as manifest in women's clubs, including the very 'flight from domesticity' which is usually given as a reason for the appeal of men's clubs. In particular, the provision of inexpensive, safe and reputable accommodation in Central London was invaluable.

By 1874, London also had its first mixed-sex club, Mayfair's fashionable Albemarle Club and by 1884 the Alexandra Club kicked off a wave of further women-only clubs over the next thirty years. Some 50 out of 400 Victorian-era clubs were mixed-sex or women only, carving out a distinctive 'U'-shaped niche north of Piccadilly, close to Regent Street so as to cater for women in town on shopping trips – one of the few times Victorian women could enjoy agency and financial independence. They included grand buildings like the Empress Club on Dover Street, and the Green Park Club on Grafton Street, which was founded to encourage 'lady cyclists' to enjoy this sport in the nearby park, offering comfortable club hospitality before and after excursions. These clubs marketed themselves on their ability to offer afternoon tea facilities around shopping trips; but from the very beginning they were deeply rooted in feminist thought, and aspired to be more than a mere social venue. Furthermore, their geographical concentration just north of Piccadilly made 'Ladies' Clubland' a recognisable entity.

The opening of the Ladies' Institute at 14a Prince's Street in 1860 was a turning point. Like many of the clubs that would follow, it was optimally located for shopping, on a narrow street between the department stores of Regent Street and the respectability of Grosvenor Square, parallel to Oxford Street. After a few months, they moved to 19 Langham Place, opposite the site where one of London's grandest hotels, the Langham, was still being built. Yet the Ladies' Institute aspired to be more than just another set of leisure facilities. Its founders included pioneering feminist writers such as Barbara Bodichon, Bessie Rayner Parkes, Jessie Boucherett and Emily Faithful. Since 1858, Bodichon had been co-editor and majority shareholder in the *English Woman's Journal,* and this new club was intended to provide a home for its ideals, arguing for women's rights in the workplace.

This dual purpose as a publisher and a club gave the Ladies' Institute an important role. Yet it was not easy to run both a successful magazine and a successful club, and the financial pressures of each began to affect the other. By the middle of the decade, drastic action was needed. In the event, faced with spiralling debts, the *English Woman's Journal* closed down in 1866, to be replaced by *The Englishwoman's Review* (which would be longer-lived, persevering until 1910), while the Ladies' Institute closed its doors in 1867.

The Ladies' Institute did not go unnoticed, however. Many men felt threatened by it, casting aspersions on the type of 'unfeminine' women who would join such a club, while many women broadly welcomed its existence. Within a year of its closure, a new Working Women's Club took its place; renamed a couple of years later the Berners Club as it moved from Newman Street to Berners Street – both were just off London's main shopping thoroughfare of Oxford Street.

From the 1870s, dozens of other women's clubs were to sprout up, first within easy walking distance of Oxford Street and Regent Street, and then across London. 'From small beginnings, they [women's clubs] have grown into prominence, many owning fine establishments, supported by large constituencies and commanding substantial revenues', commented one Edwardian observer.[6]

Education was a strong driver of women's clubs. The cause of women's education found a particularly fruitful outlet in the establishment of two women's colleges in Cambridge, Girton in 1869 and Newnham in 1871. The leading women's education reformers, including Barbara Bodichon and Emily Davies, were also concerned as to what would happen to women students *after* they graduated – there was little point in women passing through the previously all-male bastion of Cambridge University, only to find themselves ostracised from London society on graduation, still excluded from Clubland. Thus the Somerville Club founded in 1878 noted that many of the key exponents of women's education were behind this ladies' club on Berners Street, and the University Club for Ladies was founded out of the same ideals. Initially, the University Club started as a series of discussions in 1883 among alumni of Girton College, Cambridge, hosted by Gertrude Jackson, who had graduated three years earlier, at her house in Portman Square. Over the next few years, she found a growing community of women graduates wanting a club of their own, which embraced women who had graduated from all the universities, not just Cambridge, as well as professional women practising medicine.[7] By 1886, Jackson had reached a critical mass of 200 members, with the Club opening on premises at 31 Bond Street, again conveniently located for shopping. It proved to be the most resilient of the Victorian women's clubs, and is the only one to still exist today, as the University Women's Club on Audley Square.[8]

Other professional groups followed. The exclusion of women from the Authors' Club founded early in 1891 led to the establishment of the Writers' Club as an all-women breakaway that same year, soon to be augmented by the Women Journalists' Club in 1894.[9]

Two of the most luxurious and celebrated of the women's clubs were the Pioneer Club off the Strand, and the Empress Club on Dover Street. Each was a fairly 'late' club of the 1890s, offering the most sumptuous accommodation. They combined elaborate tearooms adorned with large, prestigious artworks, with capacious lecture rooms used for evening meetings around fostering self-improvement. As with the working men's clubs, the combination of the social and the educational made it possible to spend much of one's life in the club, developing a particular school of outlook.

Women's clubs contained many luxuries within, but an additional incentive to spend time there was that they were often besieged from outside. There was a lasting, and influential, line of argument that women were unclubbable, and clubs were unfeminine. Certainly in a 1943 history of Clubland, Bernard Darwin asserted, 'women are not, or perhaps it is merely that they have not yet had time to become, quite as clubbable as clubmen. It may merely be that they are less fond of good things to eat and drink, and less given to sitting on their shoulder blades in deep armchairs.'[10] This is, of course, nonsense. Feminine Clubland had no shortage of demand, and no shortage of deep leather armchairs; although it was true that the furniture design has been less given to resting horizontally. Indeed, well into the modern age, in mixed-sex clubs it is usually women members who have asked for fewer items of furniture that necessitate resting in an almost indecently horizontal position. In Victorian men's clubs, such louche divans were all the rage.

From their earliest days, women's clubs often placed an inordinate emphasis on 'respectability', including ensuring a supervision of members and guests throughout their visits, and anyone who had unsuccessfully tried to join was banned from even visiting the Club. This had been necessary to overcome the jibes often hurled at them, that they were unfeminine, or a pale imitation of male clubs. Doughan and Gordon write:

> Women's clubs have above all been an attempt to claim social and physical space for women especially in city centres. In

the case of the wealthier clubs, this was mainly just claiming equality with their menfolk, but they nevertheless made it possible for less well-off middle-class and professional women on their own in major urban centres to have the sort of social base for activities that could have otherwise exposed them to risk. They helped considerably to establish women's right to be in the city.[11]

This simple right to exist on equal terms should not be underestimated – and in itself would prompt further backlash.

The natural response of women's clubs was only to stress further their reputable credentials. This in itself did not necessarily help, as it only made them more vulnerable to a charge of priggishness. It may also not have been true. Women's clubs do not appear to have been any more or less reputable, or indeed 'naughty', than men's clubs. Clubs have always been a place of assignation, heterosexual or homosexual, as long as they have contained people. For instance, in 1882 the Committee at Brooks's found out that a member had been receiving a lady in the lower dressing room outside of the hours when ladies were permitted into the Club and had been entertaining her, ostensibly for refreshment, and that the practice had been going on over a period of several years.[12] In another case, one Victorian man tried to call upon a woman of his acquaintance, looking for her at her club. The Porter confessed that he had no idea whether she was in or not, but invited the man in, to look around the Club's public rooms. While he found no sign of her, another woman fixed him with a meaningfully suggestive gaze: 'You want Mrs So-and-So do you? She is not here, I know. Won't I do as well?'[13] History does not record what followed.

Women's clubs also existed as a microcosm of the ways in which clubs could help any marginalised group which set up their own club.

For instance, they 'helped with networking: like-minded women [who] have been able to communicate in a way that men have always taken for granted'.[14] This holds true of other marginalised clubs, too, for example for expatriate groups in London that allowed 'outsiders' to become 'insiders', even when they were not members.

At the more ambitious end of the women's club movement was the Lyceum Club, founded on Piccadilly in 1904 by the artist and playwright Constance Smedley, in a building which lives on today as the RAF Club's capacious clubhouse. London's Lyceum Club was a grand affair, though like many Edwardian women's clubs its tenure was limited, and it closed down within Smedley's lifetime, in 1933. What made it far more enduring was her plan for it to lay at the centre of an international sisterhood of women's clubs, encouraging women the world over to visit each other's club, seeing this as 'the future' of clubs. Smedley also launched the International Association of Lyceum Clubs, and it continues to this day, with women's Lyceum clubs worldwide, containing large concentrations in Australia, Finland, France, Germany and Switzerland.[15]

Women's clubs did not exist in isolation. Just as men-only clubs catered to what may now be recognised as 'the pink pound', with serious money to be made in catering for unattached men, so the women-only clubs were part of a wider explosion in for-profit businesses catered to women, single or attached, including teahouses, shops and restaurants. Such was the mix of feminist thought and blatant consumerism found in women's clubs that Rappaport has called them 'the most fully documented and longest lasting aspect of what might be termed feminist commercial culture'.[16]

The shopping dimension was central to the distinctiveness of ladies' clubs. These establishments were not only influenced *by* shopping; they also began to influence shopping. Major department stores such as Harrods opened their Ladies' Club room in 1905, comfortably furnished in an ostentatiously feminine style that was rare even in ladies' clubs, with facilities aimed at rivalling much of the experience of ladies enjoying afternoon tea at their clubs. Just as hotels had done with the hospitality revolution of the Savoy and the Ritz, so the great department stores were able to wade in and set up clubs.

When the rival department store Selfridge's opened its flagship Oxford Street shop in March 1909, it made a point of embedding separate men's and women's clubrooms within the shop. Selfridge's did not merely see Clubland as a franchising opportunity, but as a rival business. The new store's advertisements urged women to 'give up' their clubs 'in favour of Selfridges . . . since Selfridges gives you everything the Club does with lots of things it does not begin to do'.[17] That keen chronicler of Clubland the *Pall Mall Gazette* saw this phenomenon happening across London. In May 1909, it observed 'the whole of London's shopping centres, from Knightsbridge to Tottenham-court Road, has of late been transformed into a vast feminine club, run on a gigantic scale, that caters for a universal and unlimited membership'.[18] Indeed, the whole club business model eased the wheels of the department store. With regular shoppers being members of the in-shop club (and vice versa), it was far easier for shoppers to charge items to their account – and for the shops to know where their debtors were.

The shop-run clubs had one major advantage as a rival to the traditional clubs. Even though they started out with gender-segregated clubrooms, they rapidly allowed more mixed-sex dining through the Edwardian era.[19] By the First World War, it had become immeasurably easier to dine with a spouse, parent, child, friend or lover in a shop or a restaurant than in a men's club – unless that guest happened to be of the same sex. For heterosexual club members, the club was immeasurably less flexible for entertaining, unless one waited for the designated time of week or year when members of the opposite sex could be corralled through the back entrance to dine, usually attracting considerable comment from fellow members. This only reaffirmed men's Clubland as a haunt of 'confirmed bachelors'.

Despite these genteel surroundings, the women's clubs found themselves under attack in the press from the outset. Their very existence seemed a threat to the idea of Clubland as a man's retreat from home, and so they were portrayed as a bastion of every trope imaginable: 'new women and shrieking sisters, the newest and the loudest; man-hating, but mannish in their dress; and women's-righters, without a single right notion in their heads'.[20] In reality, the primary appeal was exactly the same as in men's Clubland: a discreet, personal space to meet friends over a cup of tea or a meal, and enjoy the occasional stimulation of newspapers and talks.

For all the strides the women's clubs made for women's equality – or at least parity – they were noticeably restrictive in the women for whom they catered. With their emphasis on creature comforts and education, they remained a middle-class preserve, much more so than the men's clubs. There was no great wave of working *women's* clubs, to mirror the growth of working men's clubs. However, these clubs did a considerable amount to advance middle-class women. Much mid-nineteenth-century political activity had been restricted to the aristocracy. Just as men's clubs expanded in the Victorian era, to cover first upper-middle-class and then lower-middle-class men, so the same was true of the women's clubs by the early twentieth century.

Not all women's clubs celebrated independence. Some identified their female members by a husband's interests – and so membership identity was effectively acquired through marriage. Most conspicuous were the women's Service clubs, for the wives of army and navy officers. Examples included the Union Jack Club founded in 1907 by nurse Ethel McCaul, as a club for both enlisted soldiers (rather than just officers), as well as their spouses. Sometimes, admission to such clubs could involve tenuous connections – one woman applied on the basis that she had once been engaged to a militia officer, before she had called off their impending wedding.[21]

In time, a further logical evolution grew, in the form of women's Service clubs for women who actively served themselves, rather than seeing themselves as the chattel of a male officer. Nursing corps for women were founded as early as 1884 for the navy, and 1902 for the army, while the cumulative effect of the Boer War and the First World War meant that by 1920 there were already tens of thousands of women who had served in the auxiliary forces. The creation of the Voluntary Aid Detachment for nurses in 1909, and its leading role in the First World War, led to the creation in 1920 of the VAD Ladies' Club on Cavendish Square (later the New Cavendish Club). The creation of further auxiliary and territorial units in the late 1930s saw over half a million women serve by the end of the Second World War – more than enough to sustain several women's service clubs.

Not all the women's clubs were conspicuous bastions of progressivism. Some advocates of women's rights could still be distinctly reactionary in other areas, and Rappaport notes that 'especially after the turn of the century, women's clubs were no longer necessarily liberal, feminist or progressive'. The Ladies' Army and Navy Club was one of the more successful clubs, signing up 3,500 members within a year of opening in 1908. Yet by the 1930s it was advertising that it was open to 'Ladies of English race only'.[22] There was certainly a parallel with the way that men's clubs of all kinds would be set up for a specific object; but within a decade or so, creature comforts increasingly became the priority, and the founding ideals were gradually abandoned, and even overshadowed by blimpishness.

Despite the dozens of women's clubs in London, mainly focused around the West End, they had a much lower survival rate than their all-male counterparts. Men's clubs took their names from their business structure – they quite literally involved members 'clubbing together', to share the risks and costs of a highly speculative enterprise. There were far fewer financially independent women, so women's clubs came to depend on a small number of wealthy women patrons. Their fate is represented by that of the prestigious Ladies' Athenaeum on Dover Street. It heavily depended on the formidable Lady Randolph Churchill — and so when she died in 1923, the club promptly went under. From the 1920s, as a generation of wealthy patronesses died out, female Clubland had been reduced to a rump.

The reputation of Ladies' Clubland was dealt a further blow by the Oscar Wilde scandal of 1895, which was prompted by an incident at the mixed-sex Albemarle Club. As we shall see, it came to play a big role in how homosexuality and bisexuality were tolerated in clubs; but it was cited for years to come as a scandal that denigrated women in clubs, too. Mixed-sex clubs did not cease entirely, not least as some new ones still opened, such as the Sesame Club on nearby Dover Street later that year. Nevertheless, they struggled to reacquire the trendy 'buzz' of the late 1880s and early 1890s, and were increasingly seen as something of a social pariah. The assumption started to be that the kind of man who joins a club alongside women members was either exceptionally effeminate, or else had something to hide through over-compensation.

Furthermore, members of men-only clubs who advocated women's advancement began to be regarded with suspicion. This tapped into a wider controversy around the suffrage movement, and this mistrust was exacerbated by women chaining themselves to the railings of politically prominent clubs like the Carlton and the National Liberal in the early 1910s. Meanwhile, at the Reform Club, when a member, Frederick Pethick-Lawrence (editor of *Votes for Women*), was imprisoned for conspiracy to incite damage to property by the Women's Social and Political Union, he was promptly expelled.

Women's clubs were seriously overlooked for a long time. Many of the histories of Clubland have been written by men with little apparent interest in or even awareness of Ladies Clubland, and coverage of women's clubs has been superficial at best, and often outright dismissive. Anthony Lejeune, doyen of 1970s Clubland, opined that ladies were not really clubbable, attributing this to his belief that 'women grudge spending money on food and drink for themselves',[23] while as recently as 2019, Stephen Hoare argued that men-only clubs were 'a personal choice' which was 'an important link to the past and an emblematic statement', while having surprisingly little to say on women's clubs.[24] Hoare instead insisted that an 1863 visit to the Travellers Club was 'the first recorded example of clubs admitting women as guests', overlooking the decades of previous visits by women before 1863; and he added 'Membership for women would have to wait until the last half of the twentieth century', while women's clubs only appeared 'by the 1920s', apparently unaware that London's first women's club had already opened in 1860, and that dozens more would follow over the next forty years.[25] Hoare is by no means alone in believing this to have been the case.

In recent decades, however, the full scope and significance of London's women's clubs has drawn renewed attention. This has been left to Clubland 'outsiders' rather than 'insiders'. It has been academics, mounting studies of neglected facets of Clubland, who have been at the forefront of this rediscovered tradition. A key turning point was historian Erika Rappaport's 2000 study of women's shopping habits in Victorian and Edwardian London.[26] Rappaport threw welcome light on the shopping roots of early women's clubs that lived side by side in the same ecosystem as London's main department stores. Subsequently, major work was done by David Doughan and Peter Gordon in mapping out women's clubs across Britain, and Barbara Black has highlighted them.[27] To this day, women's clubs tend to be treated as 'outliers' or exceptions, rather than as the substantial part of Victorian Clubland which they formed.

Chapter Ten

Clubs, bisexuality and homosexuality
(1830–1935)

The secretive nature of clubs has lent them to be the centre of every conspiracy theory imaginable – Freemasons, spy rings, powerful cabals in business and politics, and even Methodists. Yet one of the most enduring is the real or imagined frisson of gay sex in an all-male (or sometimes all-female), or indeed mixed-sex, environment. This is nothing new.

It is also ironic, as clubs can convey a deeply asexual image; there is nothing terribly sexy about a group of obese old duffers asthmatically wheezing for the port to be passed around. Yet club members are no more or less prone to displaying the full spectrum of human sexual behaviour than anyone else. And alternative, non-conformist approaches to sex and sexuality have long been part of Clubland's identity.

In the 1830s, the French-Peruvian socialist and lesbian writer Flora Tristan discussed the domestic upset that clubs could cause in heterosexual families, blaming how:

> clubs cause a lot of disorder in the households; husbands, abandoning the house, leave the poor woman at home alone to dine on a piece of beef that has to last all week, while these gentlemen

go to their clubs to have sumptuous dinners, to drink luxury wines, and to lose their money gambling.[1]

Yet, in contrast, Tristan spied an opportunity for homosexual members, concluding her musings on clubs, 'When I left, we talked about establishing clubs for *singles*, where subscribers could go to bed with other singles ...'. Tristan's comments came in an era when clubs were still single-sex.

Many club members were (and are) gay, lesbian or bisexual. Long before the 'pink pound' was identified as a phenomenon in the twentieth century, homosexuality played a central role in clubonomics, and in clubs doing a roaring trade catering to gay and lesbian members. Bachelors and spinsters were spared the cost of child-rearing and building up family homes, and so were free to wield a disproportionately large spending power. Single-sex clubs were the perfect homosocial, as well as homosexual, environment in which to unwind. This was particularly true as queer men and women were driven further underground by the increasing criminalisation (and prosecution) of homosexuality. Indeed, gay subcultures were major drivers of the push to keep clubs as men-only spaces, to maximise the scope for discretion in maintaining clubs as a popular meeting spots.

As we have seen, the Industrial Revolution had a transformative effect on clubs, particularly through the creation of a growing middle class, who wanted to share in creature comforts. It also transformed society in a number of ways. Growing urbanisation meant anonymity, and this anonymity had a number of implications. Law-breaking spiralled, for no longer were most crimes confined and resolved within a local parish, where the miscreant was usually already personally known to everyone. Sexual habits also changed with this new-found anonymity, and were no longer confined to isolated rural communities. A modern, industrial metropolis meant that anonymous sex thrived in all its forms, free from the judgements of a small community.

While clubs would come to be seen as elderly and infirm, and to promote a chaste image, the reality was that they were just as embedded a part of this social milieu as the rest of London. Indeed, they came to play a key social role in introducing gay men to one another, even if they took their liaisons off-premises – it was not unusual for contemporary police reports around homosexual prosecutions to note that a group of gay men, 'were introduced by M. at our club'.[2]

Much of this remained a taboo within Clubland circles, until the 1895 trials of Oscar Wilde thrust many of these issues prominently into public view.

On 18 February 1895, the 9th Marquess of Queensberry paid a visit to the Albemarle Club, appropriately located on Albemarle Street. This was a singular institution, at the intersection between traditional men's Clubland, and the nearby ladies' Clubland on the parallel fairways of Dover Street and Grafton Street. As London's first mixed-sex club, the Albemarle then enjoyed something of a 'family' reputation, where different generations of the same clan could be safely and reputably entertained.

Yet Queensberry's purpose in visiting was not a social call. He was already an aggressive, unbalanced figure, with a fascination for physical violence – he lent his name to the Queensberry Rules for boxing, practised through the International Sports Club, which he had founded. He was particularly aggrieved at the semi-public affair that one of his sons, Lord Alfred Douglas, was conducting with Oscar Wilde. Having tried in vain to confront Wilde at the theatre, he headed to the one location he thought he could guarantee to find the author: his club.

In the event, Queensberry was disappointed to find that Wilde was out. Wilde's latest play, *The Importance of Being Earnest*, had premiered only four nights earlier, and was playing to an acclaimed run, with the playwright being the toast of the town. Queensberry accordingly left a calling card bearing a hastily scrawled message with the Club's Porter, Sidney Wright. There is some dispute as to what that card said. It now appears to have said 'To Oscar Wilde posing Somdomite', for Queensberry had famously misspelled 'Sodomite'. When Wilde first received it, he read the last part as 'ponce and Somdomite' At the subsequent libel trial, Queensberry claimed it said 'posing as a Sodomite', a far easier charge to defend against a libel action.

There was an interval of ten days before Wilde showed up at the Club and collected the card. He had made a habit of lodging in hotels in the vicinity, ostensibly to assist with the solitude he required when writing, although they also afforded more opportunities for meeting with male prostitutes nearby. Having earlier exhausted the hospitality of the Albemarle Hotel over his antics with assorted male visitors, by early 1895 Wilde was staying at the Avondale Hotel on Piccadilly, a short walk from the Albemarle Club. Whatever Queensberry's note said, its tone was unmistakable – even the Porter, who had not been able to decipher its precise meaning, could tell it was intended as an insult of sorts.[3] Amy Milne-Smith argues that in Queensberry taking his insult to Wilde's club in such provocative terms, 'With a single word, a minor club scandal became a major topic of conversation and a historical legacy.'[4]

Wilde felt the airing of the 'Somdomite' label in his club changed everything; that it made the allegation public within his social circle. He believed he had little choice but to sue Queensberry for criminal libel. It was to prove a catastrophic miscalculation. The case collapsed after Queensberry's legal team unearthed extensive evidence of Wilde's

CLUBS, BISEXUALITY AND HOMOSEXUALITY

relations with male prostitutes, and Queensberry was acquitted. Wilde was bankrupted by his defeat, yet he declined to leave the country, even though some six hundred other Englishmen reportedly left for France in a panicked hurry that night.[5] Instead, the Crown made out a prosecution of its own, and Wilde was arrested for 'gross indecency' only three days after his original libel trial had opened on 3 April 1895. This trial ended on a hung jury; but Wilde then received a *second* prosecution from the Crown and was duly jailed on 25 May 1895. It was the first time the 1885 legislation criminalising male homosexuality had been used, having lain dormant on the statute book for a decade, and from then on its use became known as the 'blackmailer's charter' – although male and female homosexuality had already long been pilloried for centuries, and subject to a range of creative prosecutions. Wilde also felt he had little choice but to 'resign from his clubs before an inevitable expulsion'.[6]

The effect on the Albemarle Club was considerable. Overnight it became a synonym for vice and impropriety, where it had before enjoyed an unimpeachable family image. Furthermore, mixed-sex clubs as a whole started to have aspersions cast upon them. People began to ask why a man would shun a traditional men's club in favour of a mixed-sex club, and speculated that he might have something to hide, for why else would he be over-compensating in surrounding himself with women in his own club? Mixed-sex clubs went from being some of London's most fashionable spots, to increasingly being regarded with suspicion.

The downfall of Oscar Wilde was important, because it thrust into public view a discussion of how a gay man who made little effort to hide his proclivities had been embraced at the heart of London society; Clubland, no less. The reality was that a wide range of sexualities and sexual behaviours had long thrived in clubs, just as they had across British society.

The Wilde scandal loomed large in how clubs reacted. Most men-only clubs felt a new-found urge to assert the manliness of their members, something reflected in contemporary coverage in Clubland's in-house paper, the *Pall Mall Gazette*. Mixed-sex and women-only clubs felt a new-found urge to express greater separation of the sexes, to dissociate themselves from the effeminate men. Meanwhile, in a small number of cases, some of the more discreet underground clubs thrived by letting it be known that they were gay-friendly – effectively, the 'singles bars' of their day, with the added discretion of being private members' establishments. Just as the legal status of a club had proved useful a century earlier to opt out from the gambling laws, so it could be in Victorian London, to signal a separate realm, outside laws and conventions on sexuality.

Gay subculture in particular was well established in Victorian London, with its own argot, and accompanying series of nods, winks and signs for mutual identification. Gay men considered themselves to have 'the freedom of the West End', from seven o'clock in the evening.[7] 'Is he musical?' remained the preferred widespread euphemism for a man enquiring if another was gay.[8] Further light on this is shed by an 1895 privately published dictionary of Polari, the distinctive slang used among gay men; it noted a particularly esoteric line of enquiry was to ask, 'Are you inordinately fond of Wagner?' Asking for a cigarette light remained a popular opening line for a pick-up, for heterosexual and homosexual encounters alike.

Clubland overlapped with the fringes of this hidden world – for instance, in the mid-twentieth century the Labour MP Tom Driberg noted that he was able to repair from his club in Covent Garden, the Garrick, to a public lavatory on the narrow lane just opposite the Club's front door, which was a favourite spot for the practice of 'cottaging'; and then returning for dinner at the Club afterwards.[9]

Pubs, cafés, music halls, theatres, parks and public lavatories were the most common places for encounters, used for both cruising and for anonymous sex. Clubs existed side by side with this world, and indeed were part of it as well – club lavatories could themselves be a hotbed of 'cottaging'. Another option was the Turkish bath, although it was relatively rare for London clubs to have their own in-house Turkish bath, as was the case with the Royal Automobile Club on Pall Mall after 1913.

One favourite gay haunt in the heart of Clubland was the London Hammam which opened in 1862 at 76 Jermyn Street, one of the pioneers of the Turkish bath craze of Victorian Britain.[10] However, there is contradictory evidence as to whether (and if so, how typically) sexual activity took place here in the Victorian era. There are occasional references in surviving paperwork which may or may not be taken as euphemisms, around 'falling standards' and 'evil' found among the regular bathers. There were certainly cases of bathers being banned over misbehaviour, but these appear to have been relatively rare. In particular, unlike other Turkish baths with curtained cubicles offering privacy, the Jermyn Street hammam had open cubicles. Victorian Turkish bath historian Malcolm Shifrin believes that, at least initially, gay cruising in Clubland's favoured bathhouse was simply limited to the eyeing up of bodies while arranging to meet elsewhere.[11] Whether using the baths for sexual encounters or not, it was noted before 1900 that they were already seen as a magnet for queer bathers, with visiting American tourist Edward Stevenson remarking that they had gained a reputation for 'a small group well-recognised as homosexual rendezvous'.[12]

However, by the 1910s, this had changed; the baths were joined by a new Savoy Turkish Baths further up the road at 92 Jermyn Street, which had fitted curtains to encourage privacy; and soliciting for sex in the baths became far more open. By the 1930s, these baths, 'had acquired an almost exclusively queer clientele'.[13] (They later featured in a minor scandal when the Hollywood actor Rock Hudson was 'thrown out for importuning in 1952'.)[14]

In 1931, a Mr Otter-Barry was unable to book an overnight room in his nearby club, so he decided to spend the night in the Savoy Turkish Baths on Jermyn Street. On his way to the cubicle, he noticed a man who stared intently at him; but Otter-Barry tried to ignore him, drawing the curtains. After a few minutes, the man half opened the curtains and peered in. Otter-Barry did not respond, but the man paced up and down outside for fifteen minutes, peering in three times. He was awoken twice more in the night: once by another man who was also peering in, and then to find a further man who was straddling him, 'attempting to force his penis . . . into . . . [his] hand'. As Otter-Barry pushed the man off and demanded he leave, he was wistfully asked, 'Are you quite sure there is nothing you want to do?'[15]

As with the Garrick's nearby public lavatory, the Jermyn Street baths allowed clubs to outsource such amorous liaisons, so they were conducted off-premises. The Northumberland Avenue Turkish baths immortalised in *Sherlock Holmes*, next door to the Constitutional Club and around the corner from the National Liberal Club, performed a similar function for the clubs of Whitehall.

Even the most august and historic of clubs could serve as cruising spots, particularly the steps leading up to them, in much the same way as those steps were popular with gossip columnists – they were outside the jurisdiction of the Club and its rules, but carried the immediacy and confidence of that world. In 1906, twenty-year-old Albert Smith was imprisoned for twelve months and given thirty lashes for 'loitering outside White's Club in Piccadilly and trying to engage men in conversation'.[16] And, of course, the clubs themselves could actively be a popular spot for gay and bisexual men searching for partners: the diaries of George Ives record his liaisons with a string of gay men around the clubs of St James's, including fellow Clubmen Oscar Browning, Edward Carpenter, Robert Ross and Oscar Wilde, among others.[17]

The British class system loomed large over this subculture. The emphasis was often on certain stereotypes who were thought more amenable to sexual acts – and they were therefore more likely to be propositioned. Among the aristocracy, Guardsmen were often thought to harbour latent gay proclivities, as products of boys-only public schools where pederasty could be the only form of sexual contact they had ever known. It became something of a popular cliché to find Guardsmen cited as being found in compromising positions in the bushes with other men in St James's Park, a stone's throw from Clubland and nearby barracks.

Even more common – in every sense of the word – was the notion of 'rough trade'; that young, working-class men would be willing to perform sexual acts with their social superiors in exchange for some financial compensation. Indeed, it was Wilde's proclivity for 'rough trade' that first set tongues wagging as to why a noted society wit should so often be seen in the company of strapping young working-class lads with little evident education.

Much of 'rough trade' was predicated on carrying out homosexual acts while denying that you were yourself homosexual, and indeed a great many men in and out of Clubland combined this into a sort of double life, with a happy, married life running side by side. The fact that they had a club allowed them to compartmentalise their lives even more easily, and gave their homosexual experiences a dissociative touch.

Trade could simply mean a temporary exchange of sexual partners for one encounter, or it could quite literally involve bartering sex for money. Gifford Skinner recalled such encounters in the early twentieth century: 'The rough people were quite conscious of the fact that *they* weren't gay, and that they were only doing it for the two bob.'[18]

Indeed, a later landmark study found that a significant number of married men engaging in homosexual affairs still identified as heterosexual.[19] This was significant, because Victorian attitudes to homosexuality had relatively little focus on the idea that homosexuality or bisexuality was a sexual preference or identity; although there was a tendency in sensational literature to treat anything other than heterosexuality as a disease. Victorian thinking separated out 'inverts' (cases of congenital homosexuality, who were thought to make up a small minority of cases) from 'perverts' (those thought to have been corrupted). Instead, the focus was on homosexual *behaviour*, and homosexual *acts*. This informed much of the thinking behind legislation and behavioural norms, with the prevailing idea that if *acts* of gay sex were clamped down upon, then the phenomenon could be stamped out entirely. This found expression in club rules, which emphasised *behaviour*, while turning a blind eye to inclinations.

Yet clubs could be particularly well suited to catering to members' inclinations, and to not asking too many questions. In 1868 the Prince of Wales, the future King Edward VII, was supposedly so incensed by the refusal of White's to move with the times and permit him to smoke that he set up his own club that would permit the fashionable pastime, the Marlborough Club.[20] This story was widely told yet was almost certainly a complete fabrication. Prince Edward had his pick of the London clubs, including a great many which positively encouraged smoking. He did not go to the lengths of setting up an entire club on Pall Mall, with himself as sole proprietor wielding a veto over applicants, just to be able to smoke in peace. His wider problem was that as a man of louche temperament with a taste for slow card games and fast women, Clubland was filled with gossips, whose discretion could not be assured. He therefore set up his own 'club with more liberal ideas', containing only the most discreet members, to ensure that he could spend time in a club without unfavourable publicity emerging.[21]

Other clubs were favoured by gay men, such as the well-named Bachelors' Club on Piccadilly, which gained a reputation for being frequented by confirmed bachelors during its relatively short existence.

Club members could also be supportive in a manner that was rare in the outside world, as there was less need to justify themselves in public. This allowed heterosexual members to rally around their homosexual peers. When Robert Ross was embroiled in a libel action with Lord Alfred Douglas over his own homosexuality, he found that despite calls for him to resign his Reform Club membership, most of the members were privately very supportive. Nor was he alone, with Lord Somerset having similar experiences in the highly aristocratic Turf and Somerset Clubs.[22]

The single-sex atmosphere of clubs – otherwise known as homosociability – made them perfect venues for the discerning (or not-so-discerning) homosexual in search of company, whether social or sexual. More broadly, there was a curious double standard around single-sex company. Larger hotels continued to insist that no unaccompanied ladies should dine there, while men continued to be able to dine alone, or in any company that they chose. Erika Rappaport notes, 'Once prostitutes plied their trade less openly, the catering industry constructed their own version of history, which asserted that the large, modern restaurant and hotel had emancipated women and introduced a new moral tone into public life.'[23] In reality, the late-nineteenth-century popularisation of the hotel, on an industrial scale, made the social habits of Clubland more widespread. Furthermore, given the complaints made in recent years about male members repeatedly flashing the female members of the RAC on mixed days in the Club's Turkish baths, it could perhaps be observed that clubs have long had reason not to trust their male members to behave themselves.[24] Against this, women's clubs provided a prized venue for women to meet one to one, in a single-sex atmosphere to rival that of men.

The merging of single-sex and mixed-sex environments made it all the more important for gay, lesbian and bisexual club members to identify one another, without any room for embarrassing missteps. Just as Clubland slang evolved, so did Polari among London's gay community.

Polari slang evolved from its eighteenth- and early nineteenth century predecessor, Parlyaree. Yet it also encompassed a wide range of other linguistic influences, including Italian, Yiddish and actors' slang.[25] Paul Baker, an authority on the dialect, writes:

> Polari is about drama and Polari speakers were drama queens par excellence. Another feminine stereotype – gossip – is meat and drink to Polari. Polari was essentially a social language, and many speakers lived in densely packed urban areas and had numerous friends, acquaintances, lovers, one-night stands, exes, crushes, stalkers, rivals, enemies and frenemies. They also had a perfect recollection not only of all of their current relationships but of the status of the relationships of all the other people that they knew, and social occasions would be spent updating one another on these relationships *in great detail*.[26]

In other words, Polari speakers were the perfect clubmen, giving a sense of comradeship, conspiracy and immediacy, that *something* was about to happen, to which we happy few within the Club would be witnesses. Above all, they were deeply embedded in a range of social networks.

Victorian attitudes to sexuality grappled with another issue: pederasty, and the age of consent. By the Victorian era, pederasty had come to be embedded in popular gay subculture in several ways. Such ideas predated modern notions of consent, although there were extended debates around consent and maturity in Victorian Britain, rising to thirteen in 1875 and sixteen in 1885. Before then, it had been fixed at twelve since the thirteenth century. Intertwined with this was the relatively modest 'respectable' literature around homosexuality which existed, being drawn from ancient Greece in particular. This led to the identification of pederasty – invariably by the older men involved – as an educational experience for both parties, drawing parallels between a physical and an intellectual apprenticeship. This led to a considerable blurring of boundaries, from happy and fulfilling relationships among consenting men with a large age gap, through to the most obvious forms of sexual exploitation including what would now be regarded as straightforward cases of rape and paedophilia.

It was the relatively respectable cachet of pederasty in the Victorian era that led Oscar Wilde, when cross-examined over his meaning in writing about 'The love that dare not speak its name', to outline it thus:

'The Love that dare not speak its name' in this century is such a great affection of an elder for a younger man as there was between David and Jonathan, such as Plato made the very basis of his philosophy, and such as you find in the sonnets of Michelangelo and Shakespeare. It is that deep, spiritual affection that is as pure as it is perfect. It dictates and pervades great works of art like those of Shakespeare and Michelangelo, and those two letters of mine, such as they are. It is in this century misunderstood, so much misunderstood that it may be described as the 'Love that dare not speak its name,' and on account of it I am placed where I am now. It is beautiful, it is fine, it is the noblest form of affection. There is nothing unnatural about it. It is intellectual, and it repeatedly exists between an elder and a younger man, when the elder man has intellect, and the younger man has all the joy, hope and glamour of life before him. That it should be so the world does not understand. The world mocks at it and sometimes puts one in the pillory for it. (Loud applause, mingled with some hisses.)[27]

How much Wilde was describing pederasty, and how much he was speaking of homosexuality, or indeed simply love with a large age gap, remains a topic of discussion.

The degree to which pederasty was regarded as a viable, respectable interest behind the closed doors of London clubs found expression in the privately published 1881 homoerotic novel *The Sins of the Cities of the Plain*. As with many of the most popular renderings of Clubland – such as Trollope's novels portraying political intrigue in clubs – debate persists as to which proportion was fact and fantasy. Nevertheless, for homosexual writing to find public expression in the Victorian period, it was necessary to dress up the contents as fiction, and the book has numerous hints of being based at least in part on fact. The narrator was a male prostitute who is engaged by:

a secret club, the members of which he assured me would only be too glad of my services at their pederastic seances . . . This club was in a street out of Portland Place, and if you had looked in the London Directory you would simply have found it as the residence of a Mr Inslip – a rather suggestive name, you will think, considering the practices of the members of his club. I afterwards found that no gentleman was admitted to the freedom of this establishment unless he first paid an admission fee of one hundred guineas, besides a handsome annual subscription and liberal payments for refreshments and the procuration of boys, soldiers or youths like myself.[28]

The narrator built up an image of secrecy as he turned up to find 'a club meeting, at least a dozen gentlemen being expected to be present, so after having subscribed my name to a very fearful oath of secrecy, I took my leave of the proprietor with a promise to look in and be introduced to his patrons about 10 p.m.'.[29] The narrator was expected to provide not only sexual services in strictest secrecy, but to excite members by sharing tales of his previous sexual experiences. The book is highly graphic, and such is the physical and emotional ordeal, the narrator wrote, 'it took a good week's rest to make me feel fit to pay my next visit to Inslip's Club'.[30]

Such a lurid account in a pornographic novel should be put into context. Clubs did cater far and wide to servicing their members' many whims, and in some cases this did extend to providing sexual services, or at least turning a blind eye to members' whims. Yet it was far from being the norm, certainly on any institutional basis. Reputational concerns alone meant that where such things happened, they tended to be sporadic and short-lived. In the 1830s, the Cocoa Tree Club on St James's Street maintained an in-house brothel for the members – it was such a badly kept secret that none of the numerous MPs who belonged to the Club would admit to their membership in *Dod's Parliamentary Companion*, for fear that this would be an admission of availing themselves of such services. In the event, an outbreak of venereal disease led to the Club's closure for several months.[31] In their public image, clubs were as averse to any public hint of heterosexual activity as they were to homosexual activity – members might as well have existed only from the waist up.

Furthermore, in response to the *Sins of the Cities of the Plain* image, notions of organised groups, rings and coteries had more than an element of conspiracy theory. Elaborate organisations within Clubland were rare – far more common was the informal personal network or dining society. Additionally, the structuring of so many clubs around adult male membership made notions of rings of pederasts in clubs the stuff of fantasy, barring the possibility of a few rogue gatherings on the fringes. It was considered a remarkable aberration to admit children as Clubland guests in the first place. Typically, clubs only admitted youths as members and guests from the age of seventeen (sometimes not until twenty-one); although the same was not true of junior staff, and instances of members' sexual liaisons with junior staff sometimes occurred.

Additionally, where clubs *did* attempt to construct elaborate secret networks – like the efforts of the Carlton and Reform Clubs to set up a nationwide network of political agents to dabble in the dark arts of electioneering in the 1830s and 1840s – such efforts were piecemeal, and often marked by amateurishness and incompetence.[32] If you were going to mount a competent conspiracy, Clubland was the last place to start, especially as it was marked by constant gossip.

Accordingly, while clubs could attract lurid rumours of covens of perverts performing demeaning acts, the reality was usually markedly more mundane. Gay, lesbian and bisexual members could find their clubs a convenient place to unwind, and to meet like-minded people. The added layers of confidentiality and anonymity, combined with the impeccable reputation of many institutions, provided the perfect cover for members of a wide range of sexualities to meet, socially and sexually. And indeed, with the very real need in Victorian London for queer people to remain discreet, they often made consummate club members.

Chapter Eleven

The Great War and its shadow
(1913–1939)

London's Clubland had reached its height in the twenty years leading up to the First World War. Some 400 'elite' clubs were found on or off Pall Mall and Piccadilly, and assorted major clubs were in every Central London district, including Bloomsbury, Holborn, Kensington and Waterloo. Innumerable thousands of working men's clubs dotted the country, and hundreds of 'elite' clubs worldwide consciously imitated the grand clubs of Pall Mall. The pinnacle of London Clubland was the city's largest ever clubhouse, the Royal Automobile Club (RAC), completed in 1913 for 16,000 members, in celebration of the still-new sport of motoring. To this day, it houses three dining rooms, half a dozen bars, 180 bedrooms, a Turkish bath and an Italianate marble-floored swimming pool. It even once merited its own branch of the Post Office.

Yet this was to prove an Indian summer for British clubs. Although it was not apparent to members at the time, the war would have a shattering effect on these institutions. It was the first time in nearly a century that war had really impacted the shape of Clubland. Not since soldiers returning home from the Napoleonic Wars had set up the United Service Club in 1815 had the whole direction of Clubland been changed by war. True, the nineteenth century was littered with colonial wars the world over, most notably the Crimean War in the 1850s. But as a maritime power, Britain had consistently tried to avoid deploying large numbers of ground troops, and so the number of veterans coming home from any one conflict was sporadic. Even military clubs were as likely to be filled with those whose careers had been spent on policing duties in garrisons as those who had seen combat. London Clubland's exposure to wars remained limited in the so-called 'Pax Britannica' until 1914.

Most obviously, the war effort deprived London clubs of many members. The mobilisation for war was relatively slow in Britain. Nevertheless, club members were well represented among those who signed up. This was particularly true after the introduction of conscription in 1916 – some 11,000 of the RAC's 16,000 members joined the armed forces.[1] This impacted club finances, especially as many clubs still had the practice of temporarily suspending the membership of those placed on the 'abroad list', and so they did not collect any subscriptions from overseas members.

Conscription also made it very difficult to recruit and retain male club servants as the war progressed – those who stayed behind, working in the clubs, tended to be either extremely young, or extremely elderly.[2] This had a knock-on effect, as in the wider economy, of boosting the importance of the female workforce. Already in 1915, the Carlton Club relented on its earlier policies, and began hiring female waiting staff for the first time.[3]

Wartime death tolls were high, especially among those who volunteered in 1914–15, lured by the early promise of a swift war that would 'all be over by Christmas'. The Public Schools Club on Piccadilly closed after 80 per cent of its members were war fatalities.[4] Not all clubs were as severely hit – the Savile Club, with several hundred members, lost just fourteen members and three staff.[5]

Before and after the casualties rolled in, there were numerous high-spirited club efforts. The RAC, which played a regulatory role in the then still new sport of British motoring, shared with the government its register of the names and addresses of 13,000 motor-car owners in Britain at the outbreak of war. It also rapidly cobbled together an expedition of twenty-five drivers to help with the ill-fated defence of Antwerp in Belgium during August 1914. The Club's drivers were eager, but unsurprisingly inexperienced at combat driving.[6]

Although London was the subject of a handful of air raids after 1915, in day and night, the damage caused was limited. Zeppelins flying from the east tended to drop their bombs over the East End before turning around, and Pall Mall was unscathed – the nearest the air raids got to Clubland was Charing Cross. The main effect of these early air raids was psychological, in fomenting a sense of fear and paranoia.

Until the First World War, clubs had embraced a full range of attitudes towards internationalism, from welcoming cosmopolitanism to Blimpish jingoism. A national hysteria of anti-German feeling soon enveloped Clubland as well. This had its roots in the Edwardian period – there had long been a strain of paranoia at creeping German militarism, with Erskine Childers' 1903 novel *The Riddle of the Sands* kicking off a wave of copycat 'invasion literature', portraying fifth columnists and German invasions at every turn.[7] Britain was not short of expatriate Germans (starting with the royal family, still called Saxe-Coburg and Gotha until 1917), for Germany was a world leader in fields as diverse as universities, chemicals and armaments. Many of London's German expatriates in these fields were members of the German Athenaeum, abruptly closed down when war broke out. Even before the war, German expats were routinely accused of being spies – one man found himself accused of espionage on the grounds of hanging a German flag on a flagpole at his home, which was seen as clear evidence of his being an undercover spy.

Numerous clubs proceeded to introduce blanket bans on German or Anglo-German members and guests visiting for the duration of the war. A spirit of xenophobia and paranoia persisted.

In early September 1914, barely a month into hostilities, 144 members of the Royal Automobile Club wrote to the Chairman demanding the removal from the Club's membership of all 'enemy aliens'. This covered German, Italian, Turkish and Austro-Hungarian members, including those descended from these nationalities as well as those who had long since renounced these nationalities in favour of British citizenship. On the evening of 9 September, the lead signatory of the letter, H. C. C. Gittings, was boasting in the Smoking Room of having organised the petition. He was overheard by Sir Tudor Walters MP, a Welsh member of German descent, who was infuriated by Gittings' boasts and confronted him. Walters called him a 'damned scoundrel!' and Gittings punched him in the face. The two men had to be pulled apart by other members, with the Club Secretary intervening.[8]

The RAC responded by forming a sub-committee to look into foreign-born members, and in May 1915 it formally banned all 'enemy aliens' as members or guests.[9] The Travellers Club followed in March 1916, stipulating that an ordinary member had to be 'a British subject'.[10] Anglo-German members, already facing the risk of internment, were expected to keep paying their full subscriptions for the duration of the war, while being banned from setting foot on the premises. Failure to keep paying fees offered a convenient excuse for immediate expulsion. Similar scenes were repeated elsewhere – the Savage Club vowed at the outbreak of war that no 'enemy alien' would set foot in the Club for the rest of the war.[11] The RAC experience was one replicated not only in the smart clubs of Pall Mall, but in local working men's clubs and sports clubs up and down the country.

Meanwhile, at the National Liberal Club, the establishment's pre-war flirtation with pacifism and internationalism made it an object of ridicule. Anti-German polemicist Arnold White complained that 'An official of the National Liberal Club at the beginning of the war publicly expressed the opinion that Germans would always be welcome', dubbing the Club 'the spiritual home of every pro-German crank in the country . . . a temple of luxury and ease where every enemy of England enjoyed the rites of hospitality'.[12]

Clubhouses could be made to atone for their conspicuous sense of luxury by being requisitioned for war work. Unsurprisingly, members in establishments like the RAC were far from enthusiastic about forsaking their luxuries. They began to look at elaborate schemes to prove that their clubs were going above and beyond the call of duty, to head off any risk of being seized. A wing of the RAC's clubhouse at 83 Pall Mall was loaned to the British Red Cross, rent-free, while the Club's country clubhouse at Woodcote Park was loaned as a training ground for the University and Public Schools Brigade, whose privileged recruits were used to rather more lush quarters than most military barracks. In November 1915, the RAC came up with a scheme aspiring to 100,000 members at cut-rate subscriptions, offering serving military officers the status of 'temporary gentlemen'. In this way, they hoped to argue that they were using their facilities to benefit the war effort, offering solace to soldiers on leave. It bought them temporary respite, but it did not save them from seizure altogether.

The National Liberal Club presented an obvious target, located away from Pall Mall and surrounded in Whitehall by the War Office, as well as the Metropole Hotel opposite that had already been requisitioned for office space by the Ministry of Munitions. The secret service operated out of the Whitehall Court mansion flats next door. It was little surprise when the Commissioner of Works commandeered the NLC's clubhouse in September 1916. The Club temporarily moved to the public tearooms of the Westminster Palace Hotel off Parliament Square, while some exceptionally fortunate Canadian officers moved into the Club, having been billeted there.

In January 1917, the RAC followed, receiving a government requisition of their own. The RAC fervently lobbied for a reprieve, appealing up to and including King George V. In the end, an elaborate compromise was devised. In March 1917, the RAC building was rebranded as the home of the recently created Royal Overseas Officers' Club. As before, it extended club facilities to officers on leave; and through a loophole negotiated by the RAC the thousands of existing RAC members were all elected to this 'new' club, so they could continue accessing their own facilities. As the clubhouse was turned into accommodation, some sacrifices were made, with more bedrooms provided and the basement swimming pool covered and converted into a dormitory.[13] These concessions helped RAC members salvage some of their amenities, but the constant throughflow of temporary members on furlough did little for any sense of continuity or club life – the *Evening Dispatch* sniffed at how the Club had become a 'heavily camouflaged resort'.[14]

In total, some 12,122 overseas officers were given temporary membership under the RAC's Royal Overseas Officers' Club incarnation by December 1918 – nearly doubling the size of the RAC membership.[15] By September 1919, 228,125 officers had been given bed and board, and 2,000,000 meals had been served – although this in part reflected the slow rate of demobilisation after the war; and those put up in sumptuous clubland accommodation were often reluctant to relinquish it. These delights were also exclusively reserved for the officer class – enlisted men had clubs of their own, such as the Union Jack Club in Waterloo, which offered rather more spartan pleasures.

There were other losses of amenities across clubs. The Defence of the Realm Act 1914 was to inadvertently have a major effect on the popularity of clubs for the rest of the twentieth century. It was passed just four days after the British entry into the war. One of its objectives was to maximise productivity in factories, by stemming the drinking culture among factory workers. In order to do this, new licensing laws were brought in, initially argued to be a temporary emergency measure. Naturally, these temporary measures were to remain in place for ninety years.

Under these licensing laws, pubs had to shut between 3 p.m. and 6 p.m., to deter all-day drinking, as well as to close up for the night by eleven o'clock. Clubs were conveniently exempted from these restrictions, and they could carry on serving alcohol at all hours. The full exploitation of this loophole would not start to hit clubs until after the Second World War; but already during the First World War, the working men's club and the Pall Mall club were a popular retreat to keep drinking through the day. This was just one example where the shadow of the Great War was even greater than the war itself, persisting for decades after.

The First World War marked a generational shift in club use. Devoted club members who had signed up in the Victorian and Edwardian eras continued to frequent these urban playgrounds. Yet war conditions did little to entice new members. As the Edwardian clubs were already bulging with long waiting lists, it was not immediately apparent that clubs had a problem. Nevertheless, from the 1920s onwards, a noticeable fossilisation of club memberships – and club tastes – began to take place. As the existing clubs were already full, it was not yet apparent that this posed any kind of existential threat. Yet after the First World War, the existing club members began to grow older and older. It was only once large numbers of them started dying of old age, several decades on, that it became apparent that the rot had set in during the 1910s.

Some signs of decline already manifested themselves before the war. There were several fields in which clubs had ceased to innovate – most notably in food. As we have seen, the early to mid-nineteenth century saw club catering dominated by a series of innovative celebrity European chefs, who paired their club roles with a high public profile, penning popular cookery books, all heavily influenced in different ways by the nineteenth century's most influential chef, Antonin Carême.[16] By contrast, the twentieth century saw a revolution in cooking, personified by Georges Auguste Escoffier, which was driven through leading luxury hotels of London like the Savoy and the Ritz.[17] Gradually, clubs became trend-followers rather than trend-setters. This was further exacerbated by the introduction of food rationing in 1918, which particularly impacted the use of meat in clubs – although one member observed, 'at all clubs and restaurants you can always and at any time get an excellent meatless meal – soup, fish, eggs, stuffed onion, etc. The meatless food at the Travellers I consider quite excellent, and I am sure it is equally good at Boodle's.'[18]

The decline of innovation was not limited to food: the Ritz Hotel's distinctive white and gold trim became a fashionable décor for existing clubs looking to renovate their premises, as well as for new clubs like the RAC. As with many styles of décor, it looked perfectly immaculate when pristine and brand new; but it did not age well, so that by the end of the First World War clubs decorated in this style which were in want of a lick of paint were left looking tired and faded: 'just like a hotel' became the mantra of choice, particularly to the larger late Victorian and Edwardian edifices.

As the war ended in November 1918, there was an understandable yearning to return to normality. For club members, this meant everything going back to how it was before the war. It was not to be.

Clubs that had been pressed into war work did not adapt back easily. Since 1916, the National Liberal Club had served as a billet for Canadian troops in London, its 180 bedrooms providing plentiful accommodation. They ran riot around the building, trashing the premises, and a small inconvenience like the war having ended was not going to move them out of the Club anytime soon. The Club's members yearned to return to their clubhouse. In 1919, they held a series of 'farewell dinners', to drop the not so subtle hint that the troops had outstayed their welcome. Nonetheless, a general demobilisation crisis (compounded by the influenza pandemic of 1919–20) meant that the National Liberal Club was not able to repossess its clubhouse until the end of 1920. The troops had actually left in December 1919, with the parting gift of a moose's head for the Club's hospitality; but it did not fully make up for the state in which the soldiers had left the Club, which necessitated a year's closure for renovation.

Many accounts of 1920s history are dominated by the idea of the 'Roaring Twenties', and a credit-fuelled, decade-long party before the 1929 Wall Street Crash, mirroring the experiences of the United States. This was not the British experience of the 1920s. Instead, the decade saw a stream of never-ending major recessions and economic collapses, not to mention the General Strike of 1926. By the time the global recession of 1929 reared its head, it seemed to Britons merely the latest in a fifteen-year run of crippling crises. This mounting hardship started to affect Clubland.

Nor were the existing clubs terribly welcoming to new members, being increasingly set in their ways. Sir Charles Petrie recalled his election to the Carlton Club in 1921:

One of the most frightening experiences in ordinary life is the first visit to a club of which one has just been elected a member. The apologetic explanation of who you are to the Hall Porter; the haunting fear that you have unwittingly taken the chair of the outstanding figure in the club, some man renowned all over the world for his exploits in peace and war; and, above all, the suspicion that by your behaviour you are confirming the servants in their belief that the type of member now being elected is very different from what used to be the case; all these are emotions which no clubman is likely to forget.[19]

Petrie was then aghast when an existing member asked him about the weather, then after a pause observed, 'I see you are astonished at me speaking to you since you are a new Member.' Petrie was so shocked by the sudden intimacy that he did not dare set foot into the Carlton again for several months.[20]

In the inter-war years, clubs had continued their steady stagnation, becoming ever sleepier places – in some cases, quite literally. In 1938, Queen Mary paid a visit to Brooks's, accompanied by her equerry. Not only did Brooks's bar women from joining, but it barred women guests from entering the library. (Quite a few men's clubs barred women from reading areas – in the Savile Club, women were banned from the Smoking Room if a member was reading; presumably the poor members were utterly unable to concentrate on a book if exposed to female company.) Queen Mary nevertheless went in to explore the library. Far from finding anything to excite the senses, she found the Duke of Devonshire sprawled across a sofa, enjoying a nap. He opened one bleary eye, cried out, 'My God, a woman!', before jumping to his feet, clicking his heels and bowing, 'Ma'am!'[21]

Until the First World War, clubonomics had been an arms race – even though clubs opened and closed all the time, the insatiable demand for clubs meant that there was always an incentive to keep building bigger and better clubs, and to throw more money at facilities to overshadow rival clubs.

The disruption and hardship of the 1920s made clubs less viable. Economies started to be made, and this translated to members resigning over poorer quality food and drink. Moreover, as everyday pubs and cafés became more opulent, clubs lost some of their lustre. Members began to wonder why they should bother paying hefty West End club subscriptions when they could find the same sense of fellowship from a local bar, sometimes with even more extravagant facilities. As noted, it was the clubs with shakier finances which were the hardest hit, and which were the first to go. These tended to be the women's clubs and mixed-sex clubs, dozens of which folded in the 1920s and 1930s. The other clubs most vulnerable to mass resignations were the purely social clubs – they had enjoyed greater short-term bar receipts from members who treated them as a value-for-money watering holes; but this engendered little long-term loyalty, and once economies were made, the members fled.

Other existing clubs enjoyed a new lease of life, albeit as scavengers. In 1922, the fifty-nine-year-old Liberal cabinet minister Lewis Harcourt took his own life. It had long been an open secret that Harcourt was a notorious predatory paedophile; but so long as his victims were 'nobodies', this was simply overlooked. However, in 1922 he attempted to molest Edward James, a fourteen-year-old boy at Eton, and when the boy's mother threatened to expose Harcourt to the whole of society, he committed suicide in his dressing room. He left behind a pavlova of a Mayfair townhouse, covered in elaborate gilt doors and with ceiling murals depicting naked cherubs. Despite a prime Brook Street address off Grosvenor Square, no one wanted to have anything to do with a house so suffused in scandal. It went up for auction, where it was sold for a song to the Savile Club (named after its original premises on Savile Row), whose clubhouse it remains to this day, naked cherubs and all – although the dressing room where Harcourt killed himself is now leased out to the Flyfishers' Club.[22]

Even in this unpromising landscape, new clubs were still being established. Some were directly tied to the war. Buck's Club is today known as something of a throwback to the Regency-style clubs, occupying a Georgian townhouse in Mayfair. Yet when it was founded in June 1919, its modest object was as a reunion club for army officers, only with a particular emphasis on American soldiers, so as to put trendy American cocktails at its heart. It took its name from its first proprietor, Captain Herbert Buckmaster, and it is most closely associated with its distinctive champagne and orange juice cocktail, Buck's Fizz.

One of the more intriguing new clubs of the inter-war years was not the creation of a group or a cause, but of some planning decisions by the local council. The Metropolitan Borough of Westminster decided to improve access to Berkeley Square, and so ordered the demolition of one-half of Lansdowne House, a vast mansion off Piccadilly, to build a new road into the square in 1931. The mansion had been the London residence of eighteenth-century prime minister Lord Shelburne, who had drafted the treaty of independence with the United States there. Despite its historic value, it was torn apart (one demolished room was transported brick by brick to New York's Metropolitan Museum of Art, another to the Philadelphia Museum of Art). What was left of the house was given a new façade and renovated in a fashionable Art Deco style – it still resembles the set of a sumptuous Fred Astaire/Ginger Rogers musical – and so the Lansdowne Club was born in 1935.

In its modernity, the mixed-sex Lansdowne captured the zeitgeist of the late Victorian and Edwardian clubs, which had boasted the latest facilities and architecture. Its distinctive Art Deco swimming pool and unusual design set it out as a dynamic club, rather than the increasingly faded clubhouses of London.

Other clubs sought to cater to emerging elites. These included the Labour Party, which grew through the 1910s and 1920s, so that Britain had its first two minority Labour governments in 1924 and 1929–31. A rather bohemian socialist club had already popped up in the heart of one of London's main red-light districts, the 1917 Club on Gerrard Street, with a well-connected membership of writers, intellectuals and trade unionists, before its dissolution amid infighting in 1932. The idea of a more formal Labour-affiliated club sprang up when newly elected Labour MPs in the first Labour government found it difficult to get into existing West End clubs – Liberals and Conservatives alike, who dominated these clubs, formed common cause in keeping them out. Accordingly, a Parliamentary Labour Club was set up in May 1924 to offer Labour MPs accommodation and food, based at 11 Tufton Street in Westminster. Within four years, it had broadened its remit and rebranded, to become a National Labour Club, open to supporters and trade unionists from around the country. Yet from the start, the National Labour Club had a deep tension. On the one hand, it had members who wanted to show that Labour had arrived as a serious party of government, and could hold its own as a club when it came to prestigious surroundings, fine dining and convivial company. On the other hand, it was widely derided by those on the left of the Labour movement who asked what on earth socialists were doing even considering cavorting in such an elitist way. Both viewpoints saw it as part of what Sidney Webb dismissively called Labour's 'aristocratic embrace' in government.[23] The Club limped on through the 1930s, before collapsing.[24]

Long-established clubs tried to compete with the new clubs by modernising their facilities. In 1924, the Carlton Club was completely refaced in Portland stone to a new (if somewhat blander) exterior by Sir Reginald Blomfield; the following year, an adjoining townhouse behind the Club at 7 Carlton Gardens was bought for use as the Ladies' Annexe, to entertain women guests who were still banned from the main Club building itself. The 'Ladies' Annexe' proved to be a popular model in the inter-war years for fending off calls for admitting women into some of the men's clubs, and it was copied by clubs such as the Athenaeum and the Junior Carlton. It was, however, to be an increasingly costly and illogical burden by the post war years, with the added maintenance and rates for an entirely separate building, offering facilities usually regarded as being decidedly 'second rate'.

These Ladies' Annexes flourished, because by the inter-war years the women's clubs started closing down. Erika Rappaport believes 'The expansion of mass catering and entertainment, the declining financial position of the middle and upper classes, and the shifting nature of feminism contributed to [the] ultimate failure' of the women's clubs.[25] In addition, the women's clubs were suffering more than the men's clubs from a generational churn. As noted, with far fewer women controlling household fortunes, the women's clubs had never really been able to 'club together' to defray costs, as the original men's clubs of the eighteenth century had done. Instead, their heavy dependence on a handful of philanthropists meant that by the 1920s and 1930s, many of the women's clubs set up in the 1880s and 1890s found their patronesses were dying. Without them, the women's clubs started dying out, too.

There continued, however, to be new hotel-clubs. Like their Victorian forebears, the new hotels of the inter-war years recognised that there was money to be made in embedding clubs within a larger hotel complex. Park Lane's luxurious Grosvenor House Hotel, opened in 1929, included an entire wing for the new International

Sportsmen's Club, centred around a vast skating rink. To meet London County Council licensing restrictions, the Club needed a separate side entrance onto Upper Grosvenor Street, and was not allowed to connect internally with the hotel – presumably for fear of the male members disappearing upstairs into the mixed-sex bedrooms.

Other clubs came and went in the inter-war years. Future Club Secretary Anthony O'Connor recalled:

> An old friend of mine, Rosa Lewis, who owned the Cavendish [Club] in Jermyn Street and reputedly was an old flame of Edward the Seventh, was always available to provide hospitality for what she called 'evicted' club members. These were young men who because of birth and parental influence had been elected to the various clubs but were not allowed to cash cheques in them. They would be politely informed of this by their club hall porter and Rosa was always the answer when they wanted a night on the town. She seemed to like them and trust them, often giving them money, shelter, wine and a 'kip down' on her well-worn lounge carpet. Rosa was like a goosey kind of mother to these young men.[26]

In the 1930s, Lewis was yet another casualty of competition with non-club places of entertainment.

Paradoxically, just as London clubs were beginning to stagnate, their popular image reached new audiences worldwide. Club fiction remained popular, with 'Clubland heroes' of authors like John Buchan, Sapper and Sax Rohmer. Their heroes were square-jawed 'Establishment' good guys, who naturally belonged to a club, and reflected club mannerisms and their Victorian codes of honour.[27]

The King of Clubland literature was the humourist P. G. Wodehouse. Incredibly prolific, Wodehouse typically wrote a book a year between his first novel in 1903 and his death in 1975. At his peak in the inter-war years, he was penning two a year, and his writings embraced novels, short stories, articles, screenplays, and even classic musicals like *Anything Goes*.

Wodehouse's writing had a soothing quality as well as being very funny. It stemmed from how he managed to cope with personal tragedy on a day-to-day basis, channelling his stress and grief into jocular one-liners that blended verbose, formal English with lightweight slang. This most English of writers actually spent well over half of his life living abroad, starting with 1923, when he moved to France. For his comic tropes, he fell back on institutions which felt comfortable to him: public schools, butlers and, above all, clubs.

Modern readers frequently pick up Wodehouse in much the same spirit as one might read *Don Quixote*, thinking 'That was how people must have behaved back then.' Yet as with Cervantes, the central point of Wodehouse was that his humour came out of anachronism, mixing the manners and habits of a long-vanished world with the everyday trappings of today. (This became ever more apparent as Wodehouse grew older, so that by the late 1960s, the ever-foppish clubman Bingo Little eyes up a Campaign for Nuclear Disarmament demonstration in Trafalgar Square.)[28] In his clubmen, Wodehouse owed much to the Victorian caricature of the 'knut'; a young man-about-town who spends his life in his club.[29] By the time Wodehouse fleshed out this creation, the stereotype was already almost half a century old.

Wodehouse's Clubland never wholly existed. Nevertheless, it evokes the spirit of clubs as he remembered them from his youth in the 1890s, often extending to using outdated 1890s slang which had since become obsolete. Thus, Soho's louche Pelican Club, a hard-drinking establishment with bare-knuckle boxing that only briefly flourished between 1887 and 1892, closing when Wodehouse was only eleven years old, was immortalised in print – his recurring character Galahad Threepwood was invariably introduced as 'The Last of the Pelicans', complete with opaque references to louche activities in the 1890s.[30]

Club slang pervaded Wodehouse, and it was most obvious in his short story collections of assorted club members, from the proverbial *Young Men in Spats* (1936), to the cryptically titled *Eggs, Beans and Crumpets* (1940), referencing male members' habits of referring to one another as 'Old Egg', 'Old Bean', or 'Old Crumpet'.

Even this twee representation of an idealised Clubland was far from being the preserve of male aristocrats. Wodehouse's women were invariably club members, as were his servants – most notably the Junior Ganymede Club became the Club for 'gentlemen's personal gentlemen', whose Rule Eleven stated that each member must record all of their master's peccadilloes in the Club Book for others to read in confidence.[31] As Jeeves explained, 'This not only provides entertaining reading, but serves as a warning to members who may be contemplating taking service with gentlemen who fall short of the ideal.'[32]

Yet the epitome of Wodehouse's Clubland was the ubiquitous Drones Club. Most of his major characters (Bertie Wooster, Freddie Threepwood, Psmith, Uncle Fred) were all members, along with dozens of his minor characters. The Drones Club personified the Wodehousian club, and as an affectionate parody of an already-forty-year-old memory of Clubland it has probably harmed their reputation. There was no one model for the Drones, yet it had elements of several clubs. Wodehouse had fond memories of the Bachelors' Club in his youth, later to be a casualty of the Blitz. Another Blitz victim, the Bath Club of Dover Street, provided clear inspiration for the Drones Club's pool, with its distinctive rings.

Meanwhile, despite Buck's being a relatively new club in the inter-war years, its trendy American cocktail bar was also a feature of the Drones, although Wodehouse would not have had long with which to familiarise himself with it – he moved to France less than four years after it opened.

Wodehouse's own favourite real-life club was the Constitutional Club on Northumberland Avenue – a palatial, terracotta-covered triangular edifice with a striking tower, something of a Conservative Party mirror of the National Liberal Club around the corner. Disguised as the 'Senior Conservative Club', it featured in several of Wodehouse's books, and was the site where his preposterous protagonist Psmith was confronted by an angry member who asked a waiter to have him ejected: 'Beg pardon sir, are you a member of this club?'

> 'I am Psmith,' he said simply.
>
> 'A member, sir?'
>
> '*The* member,' said Psmith. 'Surely you participated in the general rejoicings which ensued when it was announced that I had been elected?'[33]

Wodehouse created an appealing Neverland in his Clubland. Its images endure, and club newcomers today are still quick to ask, 'Which club is the real-life Drones?' The jocular innocence of Wodehouse's clubs helped to paper over the bittersweet reality: that after the First World War, real-life clubs would be in terminal decline for most of the rest of the century.

Chapter Twelve

Clubs at war – the Second World War

(1939–1945)

If the First World War was a hammer blow to memberships of London clubs, the Second World War dealt a fatal blow to their bricks and mortar. Clubs saw a repetition of the previous war's dislocation arising from war work, food shortages, rationing and conscription, only in a more extreme form, as the whole economy mobilised for war, with the added impact of the Blitz engulfing much of Clubland.

Until the bombing of the London Blitz started in September 1940, just over a year from the start of hostilities, clubs were not at the centre of the action. The inter-war trend for clubs to become less friendly continued. During the so-called 'Phoney War' in 1939–40, the British actor David Niven made the decision to leave Hollywood and travel home at his own expense to re-enlist for the war effort – he was the first actor to do so, long before it became fashionable. Upon reaching London, Niven paid a visit to Boodle's, which he had joined a couple of years earlier. With the newspapers full of stories of the Hollywood star who had returned to fight for Britain, Niven described the frosty reception he received in the Saloon of Boodle's, as he sat watching passers-by through the bow window:

I was too occupied to realise that I was myself being examined, with some distaste, by an elderly gentleman with a white walrus moustache. He stood right over me and slapped at me with a newspaper, a sort of fly-removing underhand flick –

'Hhhrrrump!' he said. I looked up at him.

'Hhhrrrump!' he went again and flicked once more.

I wondered if he wanted me to throw him a fish.

He 'hhhrrrumped' and flicked at me for quite a while and finally subsided angrily into a leather chair directly facing mine. There he breathed heavily. And furious, intolerant, upper-class eyes stared out at me malevolently from beneath cotton wool eyebrows.

I tried to concentrate on my magazine but the tension between us was oppressive. At last, he appeared to relax somewhat. He sat back and opened is newspaper.

Suddenly, he sat bolt upright as though he had sat on a nail. He stared appalled at the paper in front of him, then very slowly, like eighteen-inch guns in a warship, his horrified gaze zeroed in on me. His eyes never left my face as he rang the bell beside his chair.

'Bring me a list of members,' he commanded with the voice of doom.

'Very good, m'lord.'

Those terrible orbs bored into me till the members' list was brought to him on a silver tray. Before he opened it he took one last look at his paper, then his finger travelled up and down the pages. The waiter hovered, nervously. Finally, the old man closed the list with a snap, looked at me fully for a minute, then let out a long moaning sound of deep despair – treachery! treachery! it said.

He turned to the waiter and trying to keep his voice steady, said bravely, 'Double brandy – quick!'

'I enjoyed that very much,' said a naval lieutenant-commander, with a pleasant ruddy face and a broad smile. 'That's our oldest member. He hates people sitting in his chair.'[1]

Niven hastily withdrew from the chair and joined the young naval officer for a drink and then lunch. He was prematurely craggy-faced from a hard-living lifestyle, and his name was Ian Fleming.

Fleming was fairly typical of the members who still frequented Clubland during the war. If they were not too elderly or infirm to be in the services, and not on a brief furlough, then they tended to be bored functionaries tied to a desk job. This only accentuated the sense that club members in the Second World War were unusual people, misanthropic misfits, the very opposite of the 'clubbable' image of nineteenth-century club members.

Fleming himself liked to joke that he was 'probably stuck in the Admiralty for the duration'.[2] His James Bond novels of the 1950s and 1960s were the product of excessive boredom in a Clubland fantasist. Clubs, with their grandiose architecture, lend themselves to delusions, and to a greater sense of purpose. Against the backdrop of the war, with its life-and-death struggles, if you took a bored middle manager in naval intelligence with a high libido, roving eye, propensity to fantasy and membership of Boodle's, then that is how you created James Bond.

David Cannadine has argued that Fleming's Bond books are a development of the inter-war 'Clubland heroes' of John Buchan.[3] From M to Hugo Drax, the protagonists and antagonists of Fleming's world were club members, following their codes of behaviour. Cannadine elaborates:

Fleming's novels were, like Buchan's, the product of what Gertrude Himmelfarb has called a 'Tory imagination', preoccupied with physical fitness and individual action, more concerned with success than with sagacity, fascinated by race and class, nation and empire, and pervaded by a sense of 'evil, violence and apocalypse'.[4]

As with the works of P. G. Wodehouse, Fleming's portrayal of Clubland caught the public imagination, only he built his clubs in his own image: snobbish, well-groomed and prone to flights of imagination.

Clubs remained a centre of informal power, with architecture and layouts that encouraged chance meetings, from the main lobbies to the lavatories. Back in 1919, *The Times*' editor Geoffrey Dawson had resigned his editorship under pressure from his then-proprietor Lord Northcliffe, only to be reinstated four years later by the newspaper's new proprietor, Major John Jacob Astor V. Fast-forward to 1941, when both Dawson and Astor were still in post, but their relationship had soured. Astor encountered Dawson at the urinal of the Athenaeum, and coolly informed him that his long-tendered resignation from twenty-two years earlier would now be accepted.[5]

As with the First World War, many clubs tried to enter the spirit of the war effort (and avoid having their buildings requisitioned by the government) through offering extensive temporary memberships to those engaged in war work. At the ever-palatial RAC, for example, 15,000 temporary memberships were given out to civil servants and officers, many of the latter from expatriate officers whose countries had been invaded, including Belgium, France, the Netherlands, Norway and Poland, as well as the United States. These typically covered the length of their assignment in London.[6] This was not without controversy, and clubs like the Army and Navy rued these admissions under sufferance, as a temporary measure to be reversed as early as possible. One member sniffily protested, 'If you now allow people with temporary commissions to join it you will alter the whole character of the Club.'[7]

Clubs like the RAC continued with a range of other well-meaning initiatives to volunteer drivers for military purposes, just as they had done in the First World War. Yet the reality was that warfare had moved on in the quarter-century since then, and such amateurish ventures amounted to little in an increasingly professionalised war effort.

While anti-German sentiment remained, it was not quite as virulent as the widespread xenophobia of the First World War; there was also more understanding of the realities of capture and occupation. In 1941, the Army and Navy Club agreed without debate to waive subscriptions for members captured as prisoners of war. This followed a letter from the wife of a member who had been taken prisoner. There was also much sympathy for members living under Nazi occupation in the only part of the British Isles to be occupied – the Channel Islands, which were captured from May 1940. Members living there found themselves forbidden from sending subscriptions through their banks.[8]

Food rationing hit the clubs very hard. Clubs enjoyed the same exemptions as restaurants, whereby, for a certain price, extra provisions could be purchased and rationing circumvented. However, clubs faced huge financial pressures and ever greater difficulty trying to offer premium cuisine. Accordingly, airmen repairing to the Royal Aero Club found the meat of choice was 'Muscovy duck', bred in a garden in suburban Clapham, and fed on nothing but grass and roots – which was what they tasted like.[9]

The more aristocratic clubs like Boodle's were more insulated: the hall porter boasted in 1939 that with so many wealthy landowners among the membership, 'Chef can still put on a good table because so many of my members bring game from home.'[10] More than ever before, absolutely everything was recycled: one chef described how 'Whole carcasses or sides of venison wrapped in sacking would be dumped unceremoniously in front of the larder', with the finest cuts marinaded, while the trimmings were diced and left under cold water for forty-eight hours to improve their appearance, then recycled in all manner of stews, pies, curries, pasties or casseroles, and the leftovers used for the servants' food.[11] When rationing had fully bitten five years later, and Boodle's had turned to yet more creative alternatives, the Club's Porter tearfully sighed, 'My members don't take to whale steaks at all.'[12]

There was always the black market – a taboo solution, of which a number of clubs availed themselves. The Head Chef at the Orleans Club sniffed that, 'Respectable clubs and establishments frowned on this practice and we were never allowed to buy food other than the legal entitlement', but this noble view was not universally shared in other clubs.[13] The Secretary of the Royal Aero Club sourced half a side of beef, twice a week for £20, through an in-law at the Café Royal, who also kept Winston Churchill plentifully supplied with black market smoked salmon, Tournedos Rossini and Stilton, all delivered to Downing Street. They would distribute their black market supplies to the private members' clubs of London on the same trips that kept the prime minister stocked up with luxury foods. The entire operation arranged deliveries through a black taxicab, with two waiters in the back carrying silver platters.[14] Presumably the policeman outside Number Ten knew better than to ask too many questions.

Rationing and austerity stretched further than food. Cloth napkins gave way to paper. Elaborate servants' liveries were replaced with easier-to-clean dinner jackets. Club documents were reproduced on thinner paper, often simply typewritten rather than printed. Little by little, the creature comforts for which members clubbed together began to be eroded.

The starkest difference from the First World War was how clubs were thrust onto the front line. Far more so than the First War, the Second saw Clubland suffer more than its fair share of casualties from the falling bombs. Clubs responded to air raids in a haphazard way – at first, the RAC used its underground Turkish bath and squash court dressing room as a makeshift air raid shelter, before more solid constructions were built.[15]

On the night of 14 October 1940, the Carlton Club became one of the most dramatic casualties of the Blitz, suffering a direct hit from two bombs in its central lobby. By an eerie coincidence, half the British cabinet were dining in the Club when the bombs fell around eight o'clock that evening (along with an assortment of Tory MPs including future prime minister Harold Macmillan).[16] Remarkably, all the politicians survived, although one servant was killed when hit by a piece of falling masonry. The entire building collapsed in the centre, one wall at a time, like a row of dominoes, leaving the outer walls still standing, an empty shell. Conservative MP Quintin Hogg was seen carrying his father, the 1st Viscount Hailsham, out of the rubble on his shoulders, yelling, 'It is quite alright, father, it is quite alright', and his father replying, 'Yes, I am sure it is.' One eyewitness account from the RAC next door held that, 'They emerged unscathed, though in many cases covered with the century's accumulation of soot which had been released when the building was hit.'[17] Members fumbled through the thick, belching smoke, and more than twenty spluttering incendiary bombs scattered about the Club, as someone asked of the Secretary, 'Where is [Colonel] Willis? Can we do anything to help him?', and another voice cried, 'He has probably gone down below to find out about his staff.'[18] Two hundred and fifty people had been in the Club when the bombs hit. Some members, such as Harold Macmillan and the government's Chief Whip David Margesson, thought that dinnertime was still due, and so nonchalantly walked into the restaurant of the nearby (unrelated) Carlton Hotel on Pall Mall, their hair, faces and clothes still caked with soot. They were at least still able to maintain their routine and boast that they had 'dined at the Carlton' that night.

In the aftermath of the bombing, the Carlton's members were offered hospitality by a range of other clubs. This proved to be remarkably free of political rancour – even Liberal-affiliated clubs like Brooks's and the Reform Club offered the vanquished Carlton a berth By coincidence, the nearby Arthur's Club at 69 St James's Street had gone bankrupt only a few months earlier, in February 1940. By 1943, the Carlton had begun leasing the building. The original plan was to raise the funds to restore the Pall Mall clubhouse, and fundraising drives for this continued for nearly twenty years. Churchill stubbornly insisted after the war, 'They are going to rebuild it.'[19] Yet by the 1960s, Carlton members abandoned any such thoughts and settled for selling the Pall Mall site to a property developer for use as offices, using the income to stave off looming bankruptcy.

The Carlton was not the only club to sustain damage in that night's raid. The Reform Club next door also suffered a firebomb, as did the Union Club on Trafalgar Square. The Travellers Club was also hit that night by high-explosive bombs and incendiaries, its roof and bedrooms destroyed. For much of the rest of the war they would be covered by sheets of asbestos, asphalt and tarpaulin in the attic bedrooms, held down by ropes and forming a makeshift roof.[20]

A few hours after the Carlton's bombs, in the early hours of the morning, the Savage Club had an entire side of its building hit at Carlton House Terrace, just behind the Carlton Club. It was directly opposite the official residence of the foreign secretary. As with the

Carlton, the Savage Club was swiftly offered hospitality by members of other clubs – in this case by their fellow Freemasons in the recently merged East India and Sports Club on St James's Square.[21]

One of the iconic images of the war was the photograph of St Paul's Cathedral standing unharmed, surrounded by plumes of thick smoke from bombs falling all around. The clubs surrounding St Paul's were not so lucky, among them the City Livery Club in the Chapter House of St Paul's churchyard, which was bombed out. Nearby, the City Carlton Club next to the Bank of England was also destroyed. Other Blitz casualties around this time included the Leicester Square-based Green Room Club for actors, the University of London Club in Bloomsbury, the Naval and Military Club on Piccadilly, P. G. Wodehouse's fondly remembered Bachelors' Club in Mayfair and the ladies' Empress Club on Dover Street.

Another casualty was the Royal Aero Club at 119 Piccadilly. In December 1940, it was hit by a high-explosive bomb which demolished the squash court and fractured the skull of a club servant. The First World War air ace-turned-author and editor of *Aeronautics*, Major Oliver Stewart, gave a bemused account of the bombing in his magazine, but he 'found himself in trouble with M.I.5. because . . . the War Office regarded this as disclosure of information to the enemy'.[22]

A casualty of the Blitz in 1941 was another club beloved by P. G. Wodehouse, the Bath Club, which suffered a direct hit on Dover Street, destroying its namesake swimming pool. It had a peripatetic existence for the rest of the decade, its members accepting hospitality from a succession of other clubs. Eventually, in 1950 it merged with the Conservative Club, prompting some bemusement that the Bath and Conservative Club was better known as the 'Lava-Tory'.

The Army and Navy Club, opposite the Carlton on the north side of Pall Mall, initially got away with relatively light damage during a bombing on 16 April 1941. It was less lucky during a heavy air raid on 23 February 1943, when the building suffered extensive damage. No one was killed, but nineteen members and three staff were hospitalised. Existing staff shortages were exacerbated by a mutiny among the cleaners, who decided that clearing up the rubble was more than their job's worth, and they all handed in their notice the morning after the raid. While the Club limped on, the lasting damage was a major factor in the entire building being torn down in the late 1950s, with meaningful repairs being deemed unaffordable amid post-war austerity.[23]

One of the more improbable recoveries was the National Liberal Club, which suffered a direct hit by an incendiary bomb on the night of 11 May 1941. The bomb fell through a skylight and brought the entire central spiral staircase crashing down, with its marble and alabaster pillars. Despite the centre of the building collapsing, the rest of the structure remained unharmed – as Britain's first steel-framed building, it was held up by a series of steel girders running along the outer walls (disguised by decorative tiled pillars around each girder). Members spent the rest of the war ambling around the building in a circuitous route through a tower turret staircase, closing the doors to avoid the draft from the bomb-created open courtyard in the centre. As with the Army and Navy Club, the War Damages Commission was eventually persuaded to foot the repair bill.

The Baby Blitz of January–March 1944 saw a further wave of Clubland bombings, most noticeably at the Royal Automobile Club. A 50 kg bomb on the night of 20 February 1944 blew open the RAC's Great Gallery. Fire raged for several hours, because the Club was seen as a low priority while nearby Downing Street was also on fire. Smoke belched through the rest of the building, which was otherwise unharmed. Indeed, the RAC had been remarkably lucky. Until 1944, some twenty firebombs had already hit the Club throughout the war, but had only caused minor damage or been swiftly extinguished, having landed on locations like the roof, the main hall and the Club's own branch of the Post Office.[24]

Thus, so much of the story of London Clubland in the Second World War was one of bomb damage and deprivation of luxury. There was little dignity in this sorry tale of hardship. As with the First World War, the main effects of the war wouldn't be felt until years (or decades) after hostilities had ceased. Nevertheless, with much of Clubland having been bombed about, it was painfully clear that London's clubs were visibly in decline.

Chapter Thirteen

Stagnation and seediness
(1945–1960)

By the post-war years, Clubland was obviously dying. It was trapped in a vicious cycle of mounting costs and rising prices, while the membership dwindled and aged, with few new cohorts of 'young blood' having joined since the Edwardian era. Half-hearted attempts at modernisation only exacerbated matters, as clubs sought to introduce post-war minimalist furniture and whitewash into their original Regency and Victorian trappings, pleasing no one.

Meanwhile, less than a mile away from London's historic Clubland, the nearby, seedier district of Soho saw a new breed of club crop up: smaller, dingier, grittier, and yet closer in spirit to the eighteenth-century origins of clubs. Establishments like the Colony Room Club and the New Evaristo Club came to epitomise the post-war bohemian spirit found among Soho's creative circles.

This new breed of drinking club was supplemented by *another* new type of club, often on the same streets, which exploited the loopholes of nineteenth-century club licensing legislation, which gave establishments virtual carte blanche if they designated themselves as 'private members' clubs'. Soho's sex clubs evolved by following the London club business model. Nightclub impresario Paul Raymond opened London's first topless bar with moving nude models, evading the censorship restrictions of the day by structuring his business as a club. Through creatively exploiting century-old laws around clubs, Raymond came to redefine attitudes to sexuality at a time when sex was being marketed as a commodity like never before.

The more traditional clubs would have been shocked by these developments, but they had little alternative of their own. They either followed a strategy of managed decline, or, more typically, completely unmanaged decline.

The post-war years saw no immediate improvement over wartime conditions. Not only did rationing continue until the early 1950s, but several types of food rationing actually worsened after the war. Dried eggs were withdrawn from shops in February 1946; bread was rationed for the first time in July 1946; and the rations for bacon, poultry and fresh eggs were all cut. A restriction on the maximum cost of a restaurant meal at five shillings began to be applied to clubs as well. Against this backdrop, and the peak of food shortages caused by the bitterly cold winter of 1946–7, the Reform Club's members formed a dining society in February 1947, the Austerity Club. Its purpose was to dine as opulently as possible, in a private luncheon club within a club, which met once a month to discreetly shun the five-shilling limit, seeking to serve up the best feast that money could buy.[1]

Even though clubs closed with increasing frequency, the wartime legacy did provide a rare burst of colour, in one of the few new clubs to flourish immediately after the war. This was the Special Forces Club, a newcomer to Clubland founded in 1946, as a reunion for members of the wartime Special Operations Executive (SOE), who met in a small house around the back of Harrods that was rather anonymous, even by London club standards. The SOE were innovators, and so were their Clubland equivalents. Female spies

218

were the norm, and so it made sense for the Special Forces Club to be co-ed from the outset, at a time when women's clubs and mixed-sex clubs were closing almost monthly. Accordingly, it provided a welcome home for colourful women like Noreen Riols, who trained SOE agents and had been parachuted into occupied France.[2]

The legacy of the war also had one broadly positive consequence across Clubland. Clubs became more global in their outlook. This found its way through the popularisation of an old idea: the reciprocal club.

Reciprocal clubs had existed since the mid-nineteenth century. The idea was very simple: two clubs in two different countries would reach an agreement, so that if one's members were visiting the other's location, they would enjoy the benefits of effectively being a temporary member of the 'host' club. There was much to gain and little to lose in such arrangements, but they remained relatively rare until the mid-twentieth century.[3] In part, this reflected the relative rarity of overseas travel; the huge lengths of time still required to travel any great distances by land or sea (potentially months in the nineteenth century); and the limited contacts between clubs in different countries.

Sometimes, clubs with a particular focus would be more likely to reciprocate. By the 1900s, the automobile clubs of the world, including London's Royal Automobile Club, Dublin's Royal Irish Automobile Club, Paris's Automobile Club de France and the Automobile Club de Monaco, all corresponded and between them played a crucial regulatory role in the emerging sport of racing ever-faster motor cars. As well as laying down rules, they also organised set-piece races, like the Monte Carlo Car Rally, starting in 1911.

Other clubs were particularly well attuned to the idea of reciprocation. Paris's Cercle de l'Union Interalliée, set in the Hôtel Perrinet de Jars, around the corner from the Élysée Palace, was founded in

1917 as a reunion club for Allied army officers, virtually tailor-made for a string of reciprocal club agreements across America, Belgium, Britain, Italy and Japan. The Travellers Club of Paris off the Champs-Elysée, too, was perfect for reciprocation, like its London namesake.

Yet it was the legacy of the Second World War which prompted London clubs to go on a frenzy of reciprocation in the late 1940s and 1950s. Many members who had served abroad had encountered overseas clubs for the first time. They extensively availed themselves of the facilities while on leave, and when they returned to London after the war they began championing reciprocation. And as decolonisation began to arise in the wake of Indian Independence in 1947 and the 'Winds of Change' from the late 1950s, the reciprocal club seemed a reassuring reminder of imperial trappings, in a Britain still struggling to come to terms with new, post-colonial realities. A member could disappear into a gymkhana club in Bombay, Colombo, Dar es Salaam or Singapore and be waited on by a gaggle of servants, deluding themselves that nothing had changed after colonial independence. These clubs often occupied vast grounds, and so expat Europeans could lose themselves in them for weeks on end.

Many of these global clubs had palatial premises that dwarfed what London's Clubland had to offer. While the London clubs still had imposing buildings to offer overseas visitors, the majority were decidedly threadbare and funereal by the post-war years, suffering from decades of neglect. As this began to impact the London clubs, many realised for the first time that they had failed to invest in maintaining the fabric of their buildings since they had first opened. The process of catch-up proved ruinously expensive, even without the compounding factor of high inflation.

A number of London clubs tried to extricate themselves from this with a very simple solution: demolish their own building. In

1957, the Army and Navy Club led the way by tearing down their historic 1851 edifice on Pall Mall and replacing it with the present brutalist structure. The excuse given was that the old building was far too expensive to heat and maintain, compounded by ongoing structural problems from the wartime bombing. The demolition was a convoluted affair, triggering the resignation of the Club's then-Chairman, Major Martin Gubbins, who pushed heavily for the sale of the building's freehold but neglected to reveal that he had signed a series of agreements with other clubs relating to the sale, and had neglected to tell any of the members. Others were also uncomfortable about the overlap between Major Gubbins' role as Chairman, and his day job as a property developer with a personal financial interest in the redevelopment. A rebel Extraordinary General Meeting was triggered, only for Major Gubbins to jot down his resignation from the Club on a scrap of paper, and silently hand it to the Secretary just before the meeting began, before leaving the building, never to return. By this stage, it was too late, and the Club's Committee felt they had already gone too far down the road to demolition and pressed ahead.[4]

The National Liberal Club *attempted* to follow suit in 1962, going so far as to sign a series of deals agreeing to sell their land for demolition and replacement by a modern new office block, and downsizing to a few converted apartments on Whitehall Court, next to the Farmers' Club. However, the plan was foiled by Westminster City Council refusing planning permission for the demolition in 1965. The Club's Committee was not thrilled to have members strike back in a rogue action to prevent any repeat of the demolition plan. They covertly applied to have the building Listed in 1971. However, this went on to have unintended consequences, especially as the move to a Listing made the Club liable for repairs to the long-neglected and now-Listed building. The repair bill alone would nearly bankrupt the Club in the 1970s and led to the decision to sell the building on in the 1980s rather than continue with the liability.[5]

The Junior Carlton Club was able to follow suit, demolishing its magnificent Victorian clubhouse in 1963, and erecting a distinctly bland office block on the site in 1968, which still stands today. The Club occupied a 'penthouse' on its top two floors, the antique furniture sitting uneasily amid the orange and cyan 1960s décor of the new building. Another conservative club, the Constitutional Club, had already trialled this business model in 1962. Unfortunately for the Junior Carlton Club, they had unwisely followed the advice of their members who lobbied for squash courts in the new building. The rectangular building had enough room for two squash courts at its centre; but that left little room for much else, with the remaining club given over to a series of narrow corridors stretched around the squash courts. Former prime minister Harold Macmillan was asked to open the building and struggled to find something positive to say, before settling on, 'It reminds me of a ship . . . but steady, steady.' Unsurprisingly, the new premises were not a hit with members, and the Club closed in 1977.

Other clubs undertook less drastic, but no less architecturally questionable, decisions. For some time, Boodle's had wrestled with the question of how to accommodate women – at a distance – and how to pay for any modifications. In the end, they sold the large plot of land next to their building to *The Economist* magazine, which in 1964 built Economist Plaza with three towers next to the Club, their headquarters for the next fifty years. The purchase funded the construction of a Ladies' Annex, with an entrance around the back of the Club, to spare the members the distress of encountering someone using the same main entrance who might be covertly in possession of a vagina.

It was not simply with the maintenance of club buildings that clubs attempted to cut corners, but also with staff. As we have seen, clubs benefited in the eighteenth and nineteenth centuries from cheap labour. With large real-term increases in wages from the 1930s onwards, clubs fell even further behind in offering competitive pay. By the post-war years, clubs gained a reputation for miserliness towards wages, compounded by the continued convention against tipping. A knowing reminiscence by a Club Secretary captured a typical conversation around post-war wages rises for staff:

'Iniquitous,' said the members. 'They are serving gentlemen! Surely that should more than compensate for the differences in pay, after all money isn't everything and do we not look after them when they are old?'

'We do indeed', says the Secretary. 'Didn't we give old Bartram £60 a year [approximately £950 a year in 2022] for forty-seven years' service!'

'I think,' says the club accountant, sitting behind a pile of figures, brows furrowed and nose wrinkled, 'that subscriptions will have to go up!'

'Aha, aha!' shouts a member who owns half a county in the Midlands, 'I knew that was coming up. Always subscriptions, always trying to soak us!' He glares at the accountant who replies meekly, 'That is the only answer.'

'Damned nonsense!' comes a Wagnerian bellow from the body of the smoke-filled room, 'damned nonsense! I'll have to resign if subscriptions go up again, bloody staff don't know when they're well off!' ...

One member made me feel like a Shylock when he wrote a despairing letter from Yorkshire. It was so dramatic. I could see himself and his missus running round an empty house in their bare feet and starving to death. Two weeks later I read in the *Tatler* that he had bought a yearling [racehorse] at the Newmarket Sales for £24,000 [some £380,000 today] and his missus had gone for a long month's week-end to the Greek Islands as a guest of Jackie Onassis.

Tax haven refugees in the Channel Isles, Southern Ireland and the Isle of Man shriek in agony if they are what they call, being 'dunned' into paying more for a club in town, while others will confidently tell you that their home address is somewhere east of the North Pole and they should not be liable for payment of a full subscription. Most of these people live in Chelsea, Kensington or Mayfair.[6]

Our gallant Club Secretary went on that when it came to the weekly ritual of counter-signing the staff paycheques, his Club Chairman, an elderly peer who owned 7,000 fertile acres, would stare at the cheques for minutes, comparing them to the cheque stubs from previous weeks, and harrumphed, 'Appalling! Appalling! Is this inflation never going to end? Where is Beever the lounge waiter? I wanted half a bottle this morning, and he wasn't about! Gone to be a bus conductor, My Lord, more money! My God! Surely he was happy here and dammit £10 a week [c.£160 in 2022] should be enough for any club servant?'[7]

Comical though these diatribes could be, the sad truth was that club servants often subsisted in abject poverty. If anything, the poverty of club servants worsened in the mid-twentieth century. Pressure for space meant that servants' rooms were frequently converted into extra bedrooms for members. The result was that as well as being on penurious wages, it was not uncommon for club staff to be homeless, too, lodging at nearby homeless shelters, or on benches in Green Park.

With appallingly low pay, clubs began to look to employees who might accept the lowest wages. Clubs started to comment on growing numbers of immigrant staff. Given that clubs had always had a large proportion of immigrant staff, what was presumably being commented upon was a growing number of visibly non-white staff.[8]

Similarly, one club which replaced waiters with waitresses, on the grounds that they were cheaper – this was before the Equal Pay Act – faced uproar from members. Yet the very same crusty old male members who harumphed about the imposition of women ('We're being disenfranchised') would soon promptly change their tone, congratulating their Club Secretary on a 'bloody good job getting rid of those dirty old sods'.[9]

Where the clubs endured, it was not through the discovery of some great financial secret to viability, but more typically through finding a willing sugar daddy to subsidise their loss-making habits for the time being. The ailing Royal Aero Club, for instance, had the good fortune to be rescued after the Second World War by the 7th Marquess of Londonderry. The marquess was a former secretary of state for air in the 1930s, who remained an avowed flight enthusiast. He offered the Club a peppercorn rent on the run of his Piccadilly mansion, Londonderry House, while he made do with a modest apartment around the back – the Club paid £25 a year in rent, although it also had to pay £10,000 a year in rates on the canny marquess's house. However, the 7th Marquess died in 1949.[10] His son, the 8th Marquess, was a disengaged landlord who died of cirrhosis of the liver just six years later. Charles Graves told a sanitised version of what happened next, that in 1961 the Club had been 'offered £68,000 for the tail end of its lease by a property dealer and duly accepted', upping sticks to a room of the Lansdowne Club with a substantial dowry to do up its new-found corner.[11] The reality was that the alcoholic 8th Marquess had left the family finances in such a state that the 9th Marquess, feeling the pinch of two generations of death duties, felt the cold tug of cash, and sold up, rendering the Club homeless. The Royal Aero Club was not happy in its new clubroom within the Lansdowne Club.

The conspicuous lack of new members resulted in an ever-ageing membership. This brought about a reinforcing conservatism in Clubland tastes. A century earlier, clubs had vied with one another for gastronomic experimentation and distinction. Now the ageing members wanted simple meals, for delicate digestive systems, with everything served 'just the way it used to be'. Post-war gastronomic revolutions and a flourishing internationalisation of London cuisine largely slipped Clubland by. Instead, clubs became synonymous with 'school dinners' – cheap, bland slop, as doled out at many of the leading (and not so leading) public schools. It became self-reinforcing: as with so many other signs of Clubland fossilisation, the defensive mantra became, 'Well, the members certainly seem to like it, just the way it is.'

Another symptom of club fossilisation was in the use of technology – or move away from it. Clubs had once been at the forefront of modern technology, as the first London buildings to accommodate gaslight, electrical light, telegraph wires, telephones and passenger lifts. By contrast, in the post-war era, many were noticeably making a point of refusing to install technology, holding onto their once-innovative Victorian trappings intact. This was a symptom of their decline. Numerous clubs refused to fit even basic features of hospitality. The National Liberal Club, founded by many Quakers, refused to have a bar until 1931. Boodle's held out against a bar until 1957. The Athenaeum did not have one until 1962.[12] Even then, such amenities were often accepted begrudgingly.

Ageing memberships also meant that clubs began to be used in different ways. Families with elderly, infirm, incontinent and senile relatives found it so much easier to offload them onto their clubs – effectively a form of subsidised social care. Never mind that staff in the post-war years had never received any training in caring for the elderly; soon enough, half of Clubland would come to resemble a peculiarly tatty old people's home, where senile relatives were dropped off for the day by their relieved families.

Ageing memberships came to have other consequences. A particular taboo was the prevalence of dementia among Committee members, and club Chairmen in particular. Dementia afflicts one person in fourteen aged over sixty-five, and one in six aged over eighty. When clubs began to be reduced to a demographic almost entirely made up of the elderly, and rules and conventions emphasised seniority, so that only long-term post-holders could reach the top of the tree, then it is scarcely surprising to find that so many club Chairmen since the war have suffered from senility to varying degrees. Needless to say, club staff were rarely if ever in a position to provide the proper care.

The traditional London clubs therefore moved to being institutionally predisposed to a leadership that was losing its faculties. Good governance was the first thing to suffer, and this was certainly an aggravating factor in clubs increasingly falling prey to confidence tricksters and asset-strippers by the 1960s (and beyond). Committee meetings became more meandering, questions grew less sharp, answers even vaguer.

The prevalence of senile dementia among club Chairmen (and, to a lesser extent, Committee members) was also a factor in the huge centralisation of powers around Club Secretaries in the post-war years. In the nineteenth century, the Secretary had a broad managerial role around delivering operational services, in addition to quite literally providing secretarial support to the smooth running of a club. In the twentieth century, the Club Secretary moved more towards becoming a Chief Executive, combined with a concierge and nursemaid, getting to know the foibles of individual members, and gently but discreetly stepping in to correct an increasing number of daily gaffes. At its best, this 'benign dictatorship' was excused as being in the spirit of a P. G. Wodehouse, the affable Secretary cast into the role of a benevolent Jeeves. At its worst, a hopelessly out-of-their-depth Secretary was faced with an impossible task, covering up for a string of fiascos by the Chairman and Committee on a daily basis, leaving little time to run anything.

It was into this picture of stagnation and decline that Anthony Lejeune came. More than any other individual, Lejeune was to define how clubs have been seen for the last five decades. He epitomised all that was worst in Clubland – complacent, nepotistic, self-congratulatory, snobbish and reactionary. And he projected that onto Clubland, which he promoted in this way.

The son of the pioneering film critic C. A. Lejeune, and an 'Establishment' figure through and through with an impeccable Eton and Balliol pedigree, Lejeune might have been born for Clubland. He was to become a member of five clubs, with a particular fondness for the more aristocratic citadels such as White's and Brooks's. When he began frequenting the traditional clubs in the late 1940s, he found them in the doldrums – and he loved them that way. Aside from penning potboiler thrillers, Lejeune filled his days pursuing far-right politics, editing a book by Enoch Powell and broadcasting political tracts in South Africa, supportive of the Apartheid regime. His notion of 'clubbability' peculiarly suited his politics, insofar as it involved not being held to account in any way, shape or form for his prolific hatemongering, and to retire at the end of a day to some wry, witty banter over a bottle with friends. Clubs have always been deeply political institutions, since their earliest beginnings, and the Lejeunian insistence on 'No politics in the club' is usually advanced by those holding the most unsavoury views.

Indeed, as Lejeune recalled of his beloved White's, the single incident during his long membership which attracted most celebration and notoriety was when the firebrand left-wing Labour cabinet minister Aneurin Bevan was invited in for a drink by Air Chief Marshal Sir John Slessor on 23 January 1951. When Bevan was leaving around 11.40 p.m., one White's member, John Fox-Strangways, took 'a flying kick' at Bevan's backside, pushing him down the front steps. Fox-Strangways is often described as a 'young member' in accounts of the incident (and he would have been by the standards of White's in the 1950s), but he was in fact forty-two years old. He ultimately resigned, as did two other White's members who telephoned him across the road in Brooks's, for it emerged that once Bevan had been seen in the bar, an impromptu 'conspiracy' developed over the evening.[13] However, despite the resignations on a point of honour over the adverse publicity drawn, many of the more reactionary members of White's rather approved of what they saw as the 'de-bagging' of Bevan.

In 1969, Lejeune embarked on a decade of work, to write his seminal, influential *The Gentlemen's Clubs of London* (1979).[14] Lejeune's modus operandi was to secure at least one lunch in every London club, taking notes of the well-worn anecdotes told of each club. Unusually for a book on clubs until then, it was also lavishly illustrated, making it very popular in providing the first comprehensive look at beautiful club interiors. The book stands as a love letter to the stagnant, declining clubs of the post-war years; and, indeed, it served as something of a tombstone for them: many of the clubs Lejeune covered in his research in the 1970s, such as the Bath Club, the Devonshire Club, the Public Schools Club and the United Service Club, had already closed down by the time the book's first edition was published. Several more closed their doors shortly after the book's publication.

For all its considerable charm, the book was a travesty. No attempt was made at archival research, or even consulting 'official' club histories. Instead, the staple source was third-hand anecdotes of doubtful provenance, related over boozy lunches. These varied from the slightly inaccurate to the completely wrong. Lejeune's breezy, confident narrative was full of assertions about what made clubs great (or at least, great to *him*.) Almost every word is factually wrong.

The book's illustrations, not to mention Lejeune's ongoing reputation to be maintained in Clubland, ensured that the text was a 'safe', discreet history, which papered over any whiff of recent scandal – even though, as we shall see, the 1960s and 1970s proved to be a boom time for club scandals.

Lejeune's book hugely popularised clubs. It also promoted an idea of clubs in Lejeune's own image: waspish, snobbish, elitist, aristocratic, male, white, Protestant, complacent, tired; the kind of place where members 'prefer a silver salt shaker that does not work, to one which does'.[15] There was no sense that clubs had ever been anything else, or that they could be anything else. The book was omnipresent, running through three major reprints into the mid-1980s, and commanding three-figure prices on the second-hand market. A 2012 edition, largely and clumsily ghosted by a series of research assistants while Lejeune lay on his sick bed, with entire tracts copied and pasted from Wikipedia, produced even more stunning illustrations, in full colour this time, but was even less accurate. The book remains a bible of Clubland misinformation.[16]

The Gentlemen's Clubs of London also led to a major neglect in Clubland being studied as a serious phenomenon. In the 1960s, Anthony Sampson had made a sociological study of clubs;[17] but after Lejeune, all such study ceased until the 1990s and 2000s, with the topic being thought of as insular and complacent. Even today, 'Lejeunists' abound in club literature, taking their self-congratulatory cue from him.

An abiding legacy of Lejeune's snobbery was to promote a certain narrow-mindedness about what constituted 'Clubland'. By the second half of the nineteenth century, clubs were a more fluid idea, encompassing sports clubs and working men's clubs as well as the elite establishments of St James's. Lejeune's obsessive interest in the latter meant that he overlooked the clubs that were most conspicuously flourishing in his lifetime, just as St James's stagnated.

Much of this was down to the reinvention of clubs. This was not happening in fusty old establishments, but in more informal, disreputable clubs based around drinking, gambling, comedy and sex. In other words, they resembled the earlier clubs of the eighteenth century. The home of these clubs was Soho, in the West End.

Soho in the 1950s was a world of its own, a distinct urban village. Paul Willetts describes it:

> While it hosted none of the traditional brand of gentlemen's clubs, Soho did offer clubs catering for most tastes, age groups, income brackets, classes, races and sexual preferences. You could drink, dance and watch cabaret at supper clubs. You could, if you were a homosexual, spend the evening in a club patronised by people who shared your sexual tastes which, in the case of male homosexuals, rendered you open to prosecution. You could go to a drinking club – typically housed in a basement ripe with the sour tang of unwashed socks and unfulfilled ambitions.[18]

As noted, these clubs also exploited the long-standing manner in which private members' clubs were exempted from the licensing laws – particularly the 'temporary' First World War restrictions forcing pubs to close in the afternoon, which remained in place for decades after. The new breed of 'drinking club' in Soho flourished in the post-war era, making the most of this hallowed status. Louche and dissolute, they became known as haunts for nonconformists, artists, writers, prostitutes, pimps and, of course, alcoholics. Many punters fit into two or more of these categories. The drinking clubs came in many shapes and sizes. Jazz musician George Melly recalled, 'There were many different clubs in Soho – some were crooks' clubs, police clubs, jazz clubs, some were even taxi drivers' clubs!'[19]

The ritual of visiting a drinking club was different from visiting either a West End club or even a pub – members would sign in any visitor, 'although ninety-nine percent of signatures are illegible', recalled former club barman Ian Board.[20] Visitors were not allowed to buy drinks.

The most famous of these 'drinking clubs' was the Colony Room Club founded in 1948 at 41 Dean Street, by Muriel Belcher, a Jewish barmaid from Birmingham. Regulars included Francis Bacon (who seemed to take up an almost nightly residence, and remained ever-popular for his generosity in buying drinks), as well as Lucian Freud, Christine Keeler and Jeffrey Bernard. Barry Humphries recalls, 'It provided an atmosphere of delectable depravity for the select company of alcoholics and would-be artists who managed to win the reluctant approval of Muriel Belcher, the gorgon-like proprietress.'[21] Graham Mason notes that Belcher 'realised a lot of homosexuals had spare cash and nowhere to go. The Colony was a bolthole for queers at a time when they needed somewhere to hide.'[22] In the case of the Colony Room, 'Their secret was: "The Slate"', recalls Humphries, 'No one paid. It was the alcoholics' paradise. You merely ran up a slate. Later, much later, came the reckoning, but you never knew how they arrived at the astronomical total, and alkies like to pay more anyway. It's our reward and our punishment.'[23]

Also launched in 1948 was the New Evaristo Club, which still survives, and is now better known to its regulars as Trisha's, after the present proprietress, Trisha Bergazoni. One of the last survivors of 'old Soho', it is reached via an anonymous, unmarked door on Greek Street – questions on what goes on in the flats above are best not asked – and consists of a small barroom and a tiny outdoor smokers' yard. The décor is one of lurid green walls with pictures of Italian popes and gangsters, plus a wine bottle with Mussolini. In a sign of gentrification, it only recently acquired its first male toilet, where a solitary urinal had previously stood.

Another iconic, long-standing drinking club, in an upstairs room above the French House pub on Dean Street, is Gerry's. Like the Colony Room, it could only be reached through an anonymous entrance usually strewn with malodorous rubbish bags. One of its regulars was the actor Tom Baker, best known for playing Doctor Who. He preferred private members' clubs to pubs, because there was less chance that his heavy drinking, vomiting, womanising and high-spirited antics would be seen by the children watching his show. He described a typical day at the height of his fame in 1978; having woken up at 5.15 a.m. in Soho with only a dim recollection of the previous night's carousing, he spent the day acting (or working as 'a paid fantasist' as he memorably put it):

> At teatime I arrived at The Colony Room Club and Francis Bacon bought me a large gin and tonic. The anxieties went away and the conviction grew that I had something to say on any subject. Kenny Clayton played the piano and a bunch of inebriates harmonised to *Home on the Range*. At 5.30p.m., after a vaguely lunatic afternoon, I went back to the Yorkminster [pub, now the French House] in the hope of finding some conversation before bedlam set in. Then I met the beautiful

Moe Jenns and invited her to Madisons in Camden Lock. Dinner and cabaret at 9.00p.m. costs £9. But before that I went to Gerry's Club and met Peter Crouch, the agent, and played pool and lost. Dee Lynch, the manageress, embraced me and that was nice. Then I talked about cancer for a while with a man who had a bad cough. After that, I was introduced by an actor acquaintance to a Welsh school teacher who said he was delighted to meet me. We shook hands and he promptly had a heart attack. Astonishingly enough there were two doctors in the house – well, three if you included me – and the poor man was carried out and put into an ambulance. And then we embarked on a conversation about having heart attacks. After that we went on to Madisons ...

I tottered off back to Gerry's Club and spent most of the evening telling everyone I met there about Peter Crouch. I had several nightcaps and felt relieved that another day had passed. As usual there was someone there with whom to discuss crumpet and the meaning of life. I then popped into Ronnie Scott's Club . . . Then I went back to Gerry's Club for another drink and after I'd cadged a Valium from someone, I went home to my padded cell.[24]

Sometimes, Baker's eccentric club lifestyle caught up with him. Later that year, he sported a highly visible scar after actor Paul Seed's dog had bitten him on the upper lip the night before recording a *Doctor Who* episode.

These clubs flourished in the post-war years, until at least the 1980s. Former Madness singer Suggs bemoans how, 'Many of the afternoon drinking clubs closed down in 1988 when they changed the licensing laws to allow pubs to open all day.'[25] The even more decisive licensing relaxation of 2005 meant that most pubs began to be open all day, striking a death knell. The Colony Room finally closed its doors in 2008.

During this flourishing of clubs, pornography baron Paul Raymond was, somewhat improbably, a key figure. He grew his fortune through running such magazines as *Men Only* and (the distinctly non-club-related) *Club International*, and went on to become a billionaire on the back of his property investments which saw him dubbed 'the King of Soho'; even though *habitués* of the area like Jeffrey Bernard complained that 'Property developers, like Paul Raymond, have ruined Soho.'[26] However, Raymond made his first fortune through the reinvention of the club in the 1950s and 1960s.

Fifties Soho was already the centre of London's sex trade, as well as home to a large throughflow of transient members' clubs, which often lasted only a few months. Raymond's background was as an organiser of the seaside *tableau vivant* – one of the few examples of naked women being allowed onto a stage show, on condition that they did not in any way move. Already, Soho was famed for its Windmill Theatre, where these *tableaux vivants* were a fixture. Raymond wanted to put on more daring, risqué shows without the ever-present risk of arrest on obscenity charges. His solution was to set up a private members' club.

As a club, the Raymond Revuebar was exempt from censorship requirements. It could not outrage public morals, because it was not open to the public. Even though membership could be inexpensively purchased on the door, Raymond took the club arrangements seriously. He put together a committee, chaired by his wife Jean – like most proprietary clubs, there was no democracy, and the company directors appointed whomsoever they liked. Incomplete applications were rejected, in the full knowledge that this was a favourite police entrapment technique for bringing charges on a licensing technicality.[27]

The Raymond Revuebar was more than just a strip club – although its provision of striptease was a major attraction for its patrons. It had a restaurant, casino and theatre. It popularised the strip club as a fashionable innovation – when the Club opened in 1958, Raymond claimed he wanted it to be 'a place where a man can take his wife'.[28] It never became the family-friendly place of his posturings – a door on Walker's Court rather than on the main road of Brewer Street ensured that patrons could queue anonymously. Nevertheless, stars flocked there, including actors John Mills and Peter Sellers. The Club had a thousand members on its opening. It was never reputable, but for a while it became chic.

As the Revuebar became a stunning success in the 1960s and 1970s, Raymond also woke up to the scalability of its business model. He began to open other copycat sex clubs, in the image of his flagship club. And as Raymond grew into a wealthy Soho landowner, he charged ever-more exorbitant rents in the area, to tenants who often ran copycat sex clubs of their own. Raymond's biographer writes that he 'helped to turn the sex industry from an illicit enterprise to a vast rapacious business, into a phenomenon that permeates culture'.[29]

Raymond fought a decades-long battle with the Metropolitan Police, who were by turns corrupt and censorious. His secret weapon was the liberty granted to him by running a private members' club. It is perhaps striking that the sex industry had not appropriated clubs on as big a scale until Raymond's revolution in the 1950s and 1960s. However, once the door had opened it provided – and still provides – the perfect legal cover for activities which could not happen elsewhere. Maintaining a brothel remains illegal in Britain; yet 'clip joints' (where a passer-by is scammed by a pretty lady into buying her drinks, only to be presented with astronomical bills), strip clubs, sex clubs and organised orgies have all been able to flourish over the last seventy years under the purview of private members' clubs. How their members choose to amuse themselves is, in the eyes of the law, nobody's concern. And as the 1960s dawned, London was about to see another innovation in the way that clubs could branch out in new directions, while the palaces of Pall Mall crumbled.

Chapter Fourteen

The Satire Boom, and the 1960s

(1960–1969)

If the late 1950s saw the popularisation of 'Angry Young Men' in British books, plays and music, the early 1960s saw this disenchantment with authority find a new voice, in the 'Satire Boom'. A new generation of comedians lashed out at the anachronistic absurdities of the 'Establishment'. The centre of this anger was found in a new breed of club which operated in Soho, appropriately also named The Establishment. Just as Paul Raymond updated the club for selling sex, so the satirist Peter Cook exploited the club for selling comedy, evading the censorship laws of the day.

Yet The Establishment did not invent this creative new use of a private members' club. Clubs had been using their unique licensing status to get around censorship laws and host topical comedy for decades. Since 1927, the Arts Theatre Club on Great Newport Street in Covent Garden had successfully trialled this business model. Similarly, since 1936, the Players' Theatre Club beneath the arches of Charing Cross station had evaded censorship. Yet neither club maximised the potential of this set-up. The former favoured introducing avant-garde new theatre to the London stage, including *The Iceman Cometh* and *Waiting for Godot*, though it was less geared towards political satire; while the latter favoured relatively tame entertainments around traditional music hall. The odd risqué Gilbert and Sullivan song lyric was the limit of the Players' Theatre Club's satirical ambitions.

In Cambridge in the late 1950s, the young satirist Peter Cook had noted the possibilities offered by the club business model. Cook came from a conventional, well-to-do family of colonial civil servants, and he was perpetually bored, with a whimsical imagination seeking creative new diversions. At university, he took a laconic attitude to his studies, focusing instead on writing comedy. By his final year, he was President of the Footlights, the university's main comedy society. Shuttling back and forth to London's West End, he had already enjoyed some success as a professional writer while still an undergraduate, penning stage sketches for Kenneth Williams. In the autumn of 1960, he would rocket to stardom as one of a quartet of Oxford and Cambridge student comedians from very different backgrounds, who performed the innovative stage show *Beyond the Fringe*. Relatively little of the show was given over to satire, but with its mockery of Second World War tropes and even the current prime minister, it was a turning point in challenging the deferential culture of 1950s Britain.

One of the features that bothered Cook – which had already been an annoyance in his early Kenneth Williams revue sketches – was having to submit the show's scripts for approval to the Lord Chamberlain's office, for potential censorship. Cook recalled some of the absurdity of the Lord Chamberlain's arbitrary censoring decisions: 'I remember him objecting to the angle of the ladder that was brought on in some play at the Royal Court [Theatre]' in Sloane Square, protesting about the suggestive forty-five-degree angle of the ladder's positioning, and stipulating that it had to be either fully upright, or flat on the floor.[1]

Beyond the Fringe took the Edinburgh Festival by storm, and the show transferred to the West End for several years, with the original cast crossing the Atlantic to Broadway after a year. Cook, however, rapidly grew bored of performing the same script every night, and he mulled over how he might be able to regularly perform biting new political satire which would (above all) remain *topical*. The cover of a private members' club, exempt from censorship restrictions, was a logical solution. Cook had already sampled clubs like the New Players' Theatre Club. While the business model was pure London Clubland, the atmosphere he envisaged was more continental, owing more to Bertolt Brecht. Cook would often wryly quip that he drew his inspiration from 'Those Weimar cabaret clubs that did so much to prevent the rise of Hitler.' He later recalled, 'I didn't think it was a risk at all. My dread in my last year at Cambridge was that somebody else would have this very idea to do political cabaret, uncensored by the Lord Chamberlain, and I thought that it was a certainty.'[2]

Cook had little difficulty taking the lease on an abandoned strip club on Greek Street, along with his business partner Nicholas Luard. Satire was all the rage, and prospective members queued up: 'It was financed by people joining it before it opened.'[3] Even before the Club had launched in October 1961, it had 4,500 fully paid-up members. Cook conceded that part of its initial success lay in being in the right place at the right time, with a distinctive identity that captured the youthful zeitgeist of the day. The name certainly helped, tapping into a fashionable identification of a fossilised, all-pervasive 'Establishment' as the cause of British decline.[4] 'It's the only good title I've ever thought of – The Establishment was a very good name.'[5] Cook was perhaps a little modest in this respect, for he had something of a talent for naming things around the more louche side of Clubland. In the 1970s, he would become an habitué of Mayfair's Playboy Club. There was a distinct reluctance among the licensing authorities to give the enterprise the respectability of a club, and so a stipulation of the club premises certificate was that it could not have 'members', but instead needed to have 'cardholders'. It was Peter Cook who coined their promotional motto, 'Beauty is in the Eye of the Cardholder'.[6]

The original intention had been to have the quartet behind the *Beyond the Fringe* revue available for nightly political cabaret at The Establishment, but this was never realised. Of the four comedians, Jonathan Miller was already moving towards a medical practice as a pathologist, and Alan Bennett too preoccupied with an academic career at Oxford, which often necessitated taking an early train back. (When Miller was asked how he could combine medicine with appearing on the West End stage, he would quip, 'My patients can wait. They're already dead.')[7] Peter Cook himself regularly performed in sketches and improvised stand-up comedy into the small hours in various stages of inebriation, but Dudley Moore preferred to contribute at the jazz piano rather than as a comedian, regularly playing until three in the morning.

Instead of the *Beyond the Fringe* cast, a regular in-house line-up of young comic actors was recruited to give the Club its unique atmosphere, including John Bird, John Fortune, Eleanor Bron and Jeremy Geidt. Bron was keen to steer the comedy towards sex and class, rather than political satire.[8] The company developed a distinctive style of working, neither fully scripted, nor fully improvised, but improvising around some pre-prepared jokes.

The Establishment's image was subversive, bordering on what would later be called counter-culture; yet its membership actually resembled the very 'Establishment' it sought to satirise. Early visitors included Conservative journalist Ian Gilmour, Travellers Club staple Patrick Leigh Fermor, waspish theatre critic Kenneth Tynan, the volcanic Randolph Churchill (son of Winston), Warden of Oxford's All Souls College John Sparrow, maverick Conservative peer Lord Boothby, and even the chancellor of the exchequer Reginald Maudling. The smart, well-heeled audience could have come from any Pall Mall club. Despite the occasional smattering of star names in the audience, most members were middle class, and turned up in formal suits and dresses, even though there was no requirement to do so, and they could combine a visit to the Club with dinner in a smart West End restaurant.

On a typical night, the atmosphere was unruly and bohemian, with packed seats – John Bird recalled, 'It was so fashionable, there were no empty seats, ever.'[9] On one evening, it was noted to general astonishment that there were two empty seats at the front, before it was realised that that was because a member had just died of a heart attack.

The Club was not particularly well run – the food was indifferent, and the drinks watered down. Yet it was edgy, avant-garde comedy that drew in crowds. 'Members of the audience got upset from time to time, especially when Lenny Bruce was on', Cook remarked.[10] He had flown in the famously acerbic, foul-mouthed New York comic, to great publicity, for his first British performances during a month's residency. Kenneth Tynan, watching Bruce's Establishment outbursts, thought 'that if *Beyond the Fringe* was a pinprick, Mr Bruce was a bloodbath'.[11]

How audiences dealt with taboo subjects could be unpredictable. When Bruce gave a monologue on smoking and lung cancer, Cook recalled, 'I remember one wonderful evening, a very upper-class couple were there with their daughters, and they sat through every four-letter word in the world, then suddenly Lenny mentioned the word 'cancer', whereupon there's a shout of 'Fiona! Caroline! Deborah! Cancer! Out, out!', and they all stormed out.'[12]

The Establishment also had a well-earned reputation for raucous behaviour. Barry Humphries recalls being booed and jeered as he gave the British debut of his signature character, Mrs Edna Everage (who had not yet been elevated to damehood). Jonathan Miller had a similar debacle on the opening night, the only performance he could recall giving. During one of Lenny Bruce's sets, the Irish actress Siobhán McKenna was so vocal in her outrage that she had to be asked to leave. Cook, as the proprietor, stepped in to handle the matter as tactfully as he could, but she did not care to be asked to move on, or to have it suggested that she was being less than well behaved. McKenna hit Cook with her handbag, yelling, 'These are Irish hands, and they're clean!' The bruised Cook coolly responded from the floor, 'This is an English face, and it's bleeding.'[13]

A symptom of how badly run The Establishment was as a club was that it never fully found its feet in daytime hours. There was an offering of light snacks, a photo gallery and free daytime screenings of French arthouse films of the *Nouvelle Vague*. Though no doubt convivial, none of this added up to compelling or profitable use of West End real estate. Several upstairs rooms were leased out to a hotch-potch of groups including theatre designer Sean Kenny, and photographer Lewis Morley, who maintained a studio on the third floor. It was here in 1963 that Christine Keeler, the former lover of cabinet minister John Profumo, posed for her iconic photos behind a Scandinavian chair in the aftermath of the Profumo scandal, forming one of the indelible images of the 1960s sexual revolution.[14] The new satirical magazine *Private Eye* also moved in – it had launched in October 1961, just as The Establishment opened, but swiftly ran out of money and needed rescuing. Cook and Luard bought a 75 per cent stake in the magazine, and it moved into The Establishment in June 1962. It was not necessarily a happy merger – Eye cartoonist Willie Rushton bemoaned how the Club 'was usually full of the very people it was targeting, all these people roaring with laughter and saying, "That's damn true about old Cyril."'[15]

A further complication was Peter Cook's determination to open a New York equivalent of The Establishment, which only accelerated once he and the cast of *Beyond the Fringe* transferred to Broadway in the autumn of 1962. They set up the Strollers Theatre Club in a disused former nightclub at 154 East 54th Street, and had a grand gala opening on 23 January 1963, flying over the resident cast from The Establishment in London. This proved a serious overextension to the London club, financially and theatrically, depriving the original club of its core cast. There were other casting fiascos back home – an attempt to bring back Lenny Bruce for another month's residency in April 1963 saw him detained overnight at Heathrow and then refused admittance to the UK on the grounds of his 'sick jokes and lavatory humour'.[16] Despite elaborate attempts to see if he could be smuggled in via Ireland, the whole saga cost The Establishment heavily.

Television proved both a blessing and a curse to The Establishment. In November 1962, just over a year after The Establishment had opened, David Frost launched the irreverent, ground-breaking satirical television series *That Was The Week That Was* (or *TW3* for short). Cook had little time for Frost, whom he called 'The Bubonic Plagiarist' for his habit of emulating Cook's stage routines, and he frequently joked that his greatest regret in life was 'saving David Frost from drowning'. Frost nonetheless clung to The Establishment, keen to absorb some of its spirit, and indeed shortly after the release of Christine Keeler's famous nude portrait, Frost posed for his own nude photoshoot in the same upstairs chair at The Establishment, spoofing the Keeler photoshoot.[17] *TW3* became an instant ratings hit, riffing off many of the risqué political satire themes at the Establishment.

In the short run, *TW3* provided excellent publicity for The Establishment, popularising its brand of humour, and carrying it to ever-wider audiences. However, it was also a direct competitor. For thirty-seven of the next fifty-five weeks, viewers could tune in to edgy political satire in the comfort of their own homes, without needing to queue up and then be corralled into a sweaty, cramped, overcrowded and overpriced Soho venue. The Establishment's distinctiveness suffered a blow, for it had always worked better as a form of media than as a club.

Prior to The Establishment opening, Cook had a visit from the notorious Kray twins, the East End gangsters whose reign of terror across the West End was then at its height. They told him, 'It's a very nice place you've got here, with a lot of lighting and a lot of projection equipment and so on. It would be dreadful if "the wrong element" came in and started smashing the place up.' They made their offer: 'We're willing to put people on the door to keep those types of elements out, because we know those elements, and we can keep them out.' Cook, knowing full well that Ronnie and Reggie Kray *were* those very 'elements' themselves, and unwilling to pay into a protection racket, simply said, 'Well, thank you very much, it's very kind of you, but the police are just around the corner, and I'm sure if there's any trouble we'll call them, and they'll do their best.'[18] Cook said he never heard from them again.

That was not the end of the saga, however. During Cook's absence for much of 1962–4 in New York, organised crime moved in on The Establishment. In particular, financial trouble for Cook's business partner Nicholas Luard meant that he sold the Club under pressure from his bank. By late 1963, the new owners were Raymond Nash and Anthony Coutt-Sykes (the 'Coutt' was added for a touch of class), both major figures in London organised crime. The Club effectively came to be run by firearm-wielding gangsters, as a not particularly subtle front for a spiralling number of criminal activities, from gambling to gold smuggling. Cook was offered a 50 per cent stake with the new management when he returned from America in April 1964, but 'I took one look at the club and said No. The whole atmosphere had gone – the place was filled with rather large men, and I didn't think it was salvageable.'[19] This was further compounded by a serious problem – all too familiar in the more traditional clubs as well – with staff stealing from the Club's funds: 'Most of the waiters were lifting all the money,' recalled Willie Rushton.[20]

The result was the gradual, ignominious closure of The Establishment in mid-1964, less than three years after it had first opened to such high hopes. Like its television counterpart *That Was The Week That Was*, it had proved a meteoric but short-lived manifestation of the 'Satire Boom'. Cook consoled himself that 'For two years it was a great place, which I still look back on with tremendous fondness. Those were tremendous times.'[21] Nonetheless, it endured as an icon in popular culture, just as longer-lived but still-doomed Soho clubs like the Colony Room have done. It also had a longer-term effect, in dramatically highlighting the sheer anachronism of the Lord Chamberlain's censorship arrangements. Later in 1964, a Labour government took office, and the following year Roy Jenkins became home secretary. Much ridiculed in Labour circles for his affected accent and his taste for the plusher traditional clubs such as Brooks's, Jenkins was nonetheless one of the architects of 'the permissive society', or as he called it, 'the civilised society'.[22] One of the measures he brought forward in 1967 was the abolition of theatre censorship.

Jenkins, the son of a Welsh miner, cut a somewhat improbable figure in Clubland, yet was one of its keenest citizens. He kept strict hours in his ministerial office, being disciplined about his workload during the day and refusing to work late. Instead, the evening was for meeting friends and lovers – often in Clubland.[23]

247

Yet the Clubland which Jenkins frequented in the 1960s continued its post-war decline – more the much-derided 'Establishment' than The Establishment.

Traditional Clubland remained a more staid arena in the 1960s, resolutely refusing to adapt, save for the occasional addition of a TV room and Tannoy system, incongruously fitted into crumbling clubhouses. Tannoys were cheaper than servants. Harold Macmillan, an affected patrician Tory publisher addicted to Trollope, loved his traditional clubs and frequented no fewer than five during his time as prime minister. As Anthony Sampson observed, 'as he disappears into the Beefsteak or Pratt's or Buck's it is hard to believe that something *isn't* going to happen there'.[24] Yet Macmillan, like all the great 'Clubmen', was every inch the poseur – his country tweeds 'fractionally too new looking', which was studiously 'compensated by having the pocket flap "casual"'.[25] Macmillan personified everything that Peter Cook despised.

Clubs maintained their reputation as a centre of intrigue. When Macmillan abruptly resigned as prime minister in 1963 due to a health scare, the Conservative government was abruptly plunged into a highly public leadership contest, highlighting the secretive nature by which a victor 'emerged', after informal soundings. 'Democratic election – or settled in the clubs around St James's?', asked the *Evening Standard*, the summer before.[26] Clubs and their members, if anything, revelled in this notoriety. It made up for the palpable loss of power and influence felt by Britain in the age of decolonisation.

A stench of death was strong around Clubland; indeed, some of the most notable occurrences in clubs in the 1960s were the deaths of members. American politician Adlai Stevenson collapsed in London's International Sportsmen's Club in July 1965, where he was staying with his mistress. He died of a heart attack later that day.

...airs ...' Imperialism incarnate, in the Royal Bombay Yacht Club, photographed just before its ...lition in 1947. Note the fans, which lined the main rooms of colonial clubs, for Europeans ...d to tropical climates. (*Author's own collection*)

...ownstairs.' The kitchens of the Royal Bombay Yacht Club show how servants' areas are often bare ...nctional, belying the glamour of the public rooms. (*Author's own collection*)

Constance Smedley, Edward[...]
pioneer of the global spread [...]
women's clubs, who founded
the International Association
Lyceum Clubs, headquartere[...]
in London. Armfield Maxwe[...]
*Portrait of Constance Smedley[...]
a Violin* (1918).
(Artepics/Alamy Stock Photo)

The earliest known photograph of a London club member in his club, which shows the Billiard Association Champion of Great Britain, Mohamed Abdul 'Arthur' Vahid, practising at the Nation[...] Liberal Club in 1893. *(Reproduced By kind permission of J. A. Vahid)*

HE NEW MEMBER OF THE ATHENAEUM CLUB WHO ASKED THE WAY
TO THE COCKTAIL BAR

ne set in after the First World War. H. M. Bateman's *The New Member of the Athenaeum Club*
Asked the Way to the Cocktail Bar (1930) spoofs the increasingly crusty attitudes of members, who
nce been experimental and dynamic. *(Reproduced by kind permission of the Athenaeum)*

The Naval & Military Club on Piccadilly was just one of many clubs which were bombed in the B__
pictured here in November 1940. The view is from the iconic gateway signs which gave the Club
moniker, the 'In & Out'. *(Hans Wild/The LIFE Picture Collection/Getty Images)*

... world: the morning room of the Junior Carlton Club, the second-largest clubhouse ever built on ...Mall, prior to its demolition in 1963. *(Reproduced by kind permission of the Carlton Club)*

...p of the Junior Carlton Club's grand staircase, before the 1963 demolition.
...uced by kind permission of the Carlton Club)

'Before …' The Army and Navy Club's 1851 building, photographed in 1896. Dogged by financial difficulties and long-term structural damage from wartime bombing, by the 1950s its management determined to demolish its own building. *(Author's own collection)*

'… After.' The Army and Navy Club completed this Brutalist block in 1963, which stands in place the original above. *(Author's own collection)*

Private Eye spoofs the censorship crackdown on Lenny Bruce performing at The Establishment club in [...] while surrounding Soho went on with its usual business. *(Reproduced by kind permission of Gerald Scarfe)*

[...]sful con-man George Levy Marks – [...] known by his pseudonym 'George [...]abris' – photographed the day he was [...] from the National Liberal Club, 1977, [...] comprehensively asset-stripping the Club [...] his nine-month reign. Ever brazen, he [...] press-released his own departure after he [...]ed. *(Author's own collection)*

"When the committee relaxed the rules during this heat wave, Leggatt, we envisaged a slight loosening of the tie!"

Dress codes, only introduced into London clubs in a post-WW2 bid to maintain 'standards', started to cause friction. 'Jak', *Evening Standard*, 14 July 1983. *(© JAK/Evening Standard)*

Even the most historic clubs constantly redevelop and redesign their buildings. Here, the consummately clubbable Stephen Fry opens a new billiard room in the bowels of the Oxford and Cambridge Club. Martin Rowson, *Mr Stephen Fry Inaugurating the Restored and Renovated Billiard Room (2011). (Reproduced by kind permission of Martin Rowson)*

Meanwhile, in 1966, Sir C. P. Ramaswami Iyer, one-time diwan of the Indian state of Travancore in the 1930s, had been reminiscing with his long-term mistress, the journalist Philippa Burrell, in the National Liberal Club. Looking back upon his eighty-six years, he mulled over a question about his state of health, before observing, 'I've never felt better in my life.' They were to be his last words before he promptly died in his armchair, leaving Burrell speechless.

Instead of grappling with the death spiral of Clubland, committees seemed ever more fixated on a process of fossilisation. An ageing membership would resist change at all costs, even if it meant (as they saw it) going down fighting. Balancing the books came to be seen as a gauche pursuit. This expressed itself in a new-found energy in enforcing ever more elaborate club dress codes, a reliable way of keeping changing dress trends at bay. It also found its voice in the new, gentle fiction of banning commercial activity – even though clubs had originally been founded for that very purpose. Nevertheless, even at the Athenaeum 'members complained that they could hardly hear themselves talk above the noise of lobbying – particularly for university grants'.[27] Appropriately enough, much of the lobbying happened in the Club's lobby.

With traditional clubs rapidly closing down, an increasingly popular solution was for clubs to pool resources, and merge. Typically, the club with the more secure lease – though not necessarily the nicest building – would accommodate the other's membership, once the junior partner closed down. Not all mergers were harmonious, with differences in culture being brought to the fore. Conservative Party treasurer Lord Ashdown attempted to resist the Carlton Club's 1977 merger with the Junior Carlton Club, complaining, 'Damned Junior Carlton is full of estate agents.' The reply was, 'Well, we're full of property developers.'[28] Sometimes, as with both of these cases, the merger would be a lasting one.

The most harmonious was probably that of the Oxford and Cambridge Club with the United University Club, since they were founded for almost identical objectives, with the former having been founded for people languishing on the waiting list for the latter. Even then, there was some tension: just one year before the 1972 merger of the two clubs, the cash-strapped United University Club had admitted non-Oxbridge graduates as members for the first time, to the displeasure of the Oxford and Cambridge Club, into which they merged. Nonetheless, mergers like the Carlton, and the Oxford and Cambridge Club, often succeeded best when there were shared goals.

When shared goals were lacking, then the most successful mergers were more akin to takeovers. The most obvious example would be the East India Club; or the East India, Devonshire Sports and Public Schools Club, to give its full title. It was originally founded in 1849 as the East India United Services Club, for servants of the East India Company who were unable to get into the Oriental Club, then set up as the premier club for servants of the Company. With the dissolution of the East India Company, the Club has become a purely social institution for much of its history, but, as its full name implies, it has absorbed three more clubs. The closure of the Sports Club across St James's Square in 1938 led to the first merger, and the influx of members meant a rising demand for sporting facilities. The closure of the once politically themed Devonshire Club in 1976 had little impact on the composition – by the 1970s, the Devonshire was a purely social club, its one-time Liberal objectives long since superseded by an apathetic Toryism which blended well with the East India's sympathies. However, the 1972 closure of the Public Schools Club had a dramatic effect, opening up new lines of recruitment. Today's 'East India Club' is far more a continuation of the Public Schools Club.

In some cases, mergers would simply be a temporary stepping stone in the long-term dissolution of one or both merged clubs. Where clubs avoided dissolution altogether, it was by continuing as a society which no longer provided club facilities – a fate which befell clubs like the Kennel Club, the London Fencing Club and the Royal Aero Club.

As the London clubs buckled down in a losing war with commerce, the colonial clubs that had been set up by the British abroad moved in several different directions. Many of them had had overwhelmingly (or even exclusively) white European memberships throughout the colonial era – an unsustainable state of affairs as British colonies successively achieved independence by the 1960s, and only a small minority of white Europeans stayed behind. These ageing members, clinging to the last remaining trappings of imperial rule through their clubs, were no recipe for longevity in an organisation. Accordingly, colonial clubs slowly began to admit non-white members, although seeing these members rise up through the ranks to take over the leadership of their clubs could take years or decades.

Thus even though India achieved independence in 1947, it was not until the 1960s that the major Indian clubs began to be run by Indian members. It would be a mistake to imagine that the first wave of Indian members were dedicated reformers. For many, the traditional British way of doing things – however wasteful or illogical – was regarded as synonymous with maintaining high standards. Thus the very same clubs which championed racial integration in 1947 would often hold out against gender integration, with major clubs such as the Calcutta Swimming Club refusing admission to women until 1968. There was also a marked shift in following the lead of London clubs, in seeking to ban business in Indian clubs – even though the country's first clubs, such as the Bengal Club, had been founded by the privateers of the East India Company.

African clubs had a very different experience in the immediate post-colonial years. Nowhere was this more transparent than with the modus operandi of Tiny Rowland, the charismatic but corrupt chief executive of the Lonrho consortium. From the 1960s to the 1990s, Rowland crossed Africa in his private jet, cutting deals with politicians and business leaders. At a time when air travel around Africa was infrequent and unreliable, Rowland's jet allowed him to curry favour with the government ministers he regularly bribed, also loaning his jet for everything from shopping trips to diplomatic missions. Central to Rowland's jet-setting lifestyle was the string of clubs in major cities like Lagos, Salisbury and Cape Town, which formed the backdrop of his negotiations.[29]

Rowland was an outsider, shunned by the establishment. In 1973, he would be exposed as a sanction-buster, and condemned by the Conservative prime minister Edward Heath as 'the unacceptable face of capitalism'. He was not welcome in traditional Clubland; but as he regularly flew back to his London-headquartered company, he made his home in the Clermont Club, one of a new breed of 1960s London clubs, which tried to blend the topicality of The Establishment with the old-world aristocratic charm of the fustiest St James's clubs.

Launched in 1962 by the eccentric millionaire and gambler John Aspinall, the Clermont catered to Aspinall's idea of a buccaneering Georgian club where members recklessly staked everything on one bet. It blended old and new money. The new money came from a wealthy Arab clientele who were encouraged to gamble in a discreet atmosphere. The old money came from aristocrats like the 7th Earl of Lucan (later to achieve notoriety for disappearing on the night his family's nanny was murdered), whom Aspinall paid a retainer to hang around in the club – it gave the place a touch of class to have titled aristocrats on the premises. Aspinall was also far too canny a businessman to leave the Club's lucrative takings to chance: he tampered with the roulette wheels, so they could be fixed at will.

The tycoons who hovered around the Clermont would come to be important in their own way. Aspinall, Birley, Lucan, Rowland, and their old friend James Goldsmith were all fascinated by the phenomenon of British imperial decline, and for various reasons they saw growing British rapprochement towards the European Economic Community (with applications in 1963 and 1967, before accession from 1971) as a threat to British interests. Each was considered a pariah in 'traditional' Clubland, but brooded at the Clermont over grand plans for the rebuilding of British industry, along buccaneering, independent lines, often outside the law. By the mid-1970s, the Clermont Club's tycoons would openly discuss a military coup, to save the country from communism. Half a century on, the children of several of these tycoons would make up several of the leading lights of Brexit, as politicians and donors holding dear the emotive Euroscepticism of their parents. It may be said that many of the key themes and ideas of Brexit were lit fifty years earlier, in the Clermont Club on Berkeley Square.

Despite the rigged gambling under Aspinall, the Clermont Club was hugely fashionable. It occupied a stunning Georgian townhouse at 44 Berkeley Square. Aspinall's flair for publicity was so deft that a spinoff club was set up in the basement by his friend Mark Birley in 1963: Annabel's, named after his wife, socialite Annabel Vane-Tempest-Stewart. To this day, Annabel's remains the only nightclub to have been visited by a British monarch. Yet it has always been run as a private members' club, with an emphasis on aristocracy – or as Birley famously remarked when the Club opened in 1963, it 'must smell of exclusivity and sex'.[30] While several of the louche new gambling clubs of the 1960s were to share The Establishment's fate, Annabel's would endure. In uniting the prestige of traditional aristocracy with the easy acceptance of 'new' money, it would provide a template for how Clubland would rejuvenate its image. But first, London's clubs would hit rock bottom.

Chapter Fifteen

Asset strippers and confidence tricksters
(1960–1980)

What was left of traditional Clubland by the 1960s was in a thoroughly depressing state. Membership deaths due to old age, compressed into a very short span of time, wreaked havoc on club finances. Inflexible and irascible members deterred younger generations from joining. That in turn led to a vicious cycle of hiking up subscriptions, which prompted waves of resignations, which impelled the clubs to further ratchet up the subscription fees. Things only became worse as the 1960s and 1970s saw ever-higher levels of inflation. And as club members sought ways to prolong their increasingly unviable establishments, they fell prey to a range of asset strippers and confidence tricksters, who promised easy solutions without any difficult decisions.

Some clubs wrought the greatest damage on themselves. Seeking to reduce the running costs of their historic buildings, the Army and Navy Club, the Constitutional Club and the Junior Carlton Club had all demolished themselves, replacing their grand clubhouses with anonymous but economical grey office blocks – moves which prompted mass resignations. Other clubs looked to stave off bankruptcy by asset-stripping their art holdings, or by engaging in a range of get-rich-quick schemes.

Clubs, with their diminishing staff numbers leaving valuable assets unguarded, were an increasingly tempting target for smash-and-grab raids. In 1965, the Carlton Club was the victim of a burglary by four masked men, who tied up the night Porter and the Club Secretary, and made off with £1,000 in cash and the Club's finest silverware.[1]

Meanwhile, the lustre of clubs was further tarnished by the profusion of short-lived new 'copycat' clubs, like the Clermont Club in Berkeley Square. The gambling laws were to provide a lifeline for clubs which were willing to exploit them. As early as 1965, Playboy Enterprise's executive Victor Lownes had relocated from Chicago to London to scout out commercial opportunities for replicating the Playboy Clubs he had run in America. The first James Bond film, *Dr. No* (1962), with its introduction to the character first delivering the line 'Bond, James Bond' in his Mayfair gambling club, Les Ambassadeurs, helped popularise these casinos as part of London's chic nightlife. With private members' clubs permitted to carry out the kind of gambling which would be illegal elsewhere, and with a further 1968 liberalisation to the gambling laws, Playboy Clubs set up shop across Mayfair. In 1972, Playboy bought the Clermont Club from John Aspinall, and it became the centrepiece of their London casino operation.

For a while, it seemed as if someone had *finally* found a way to operate clubs profitably; indeed, it was claimed that the new breed of casino clubs like the Playboy Clubs, for all their air of sleaziness, were merely clubs going back to first principles, like the disreputable gambling dens which had bred the first clubs. Playboy were not the only investor in such clubs.[2] The rather more morally censorious Tiny Rowland eyed up a recently re-established Crockford's, named in honour of the nineteenth-century gambling club (though with no direct connection), and his Lonrho consortium saw it as a cash cow.

However, this would not turn out to be tenable for long. While the once-profitable Playboy business empire haemorrhaged money through much of the 1970s, its London casinos consistently drew a hefty profit, sometimes subsidising the rest of the group. This drew the attention of revenue and licensing authorities. By the late 1970s, the Playboy Clubs of London were embroiled in a string of scandals and prosecutions over everything from accusations of sexual harassment against staff to flouting the gambling laws. Terry Lazarus recalls:

> Between 1979–1981, there was an upheaval in London gambling, and several clubs were closed as a result. The main issue was violations of the credit laws. Some clubs were taking checks and allowing players who won to buy them back. This was strictly illegal, as cheques had to be banked within 2 days. There were also marketing issues and other technical violations. The Curzon House Club and other Coral casinos were raided by some 400 police and records seized. The Coral Group, Ladbrokes, Playboy and others lost their licenses to run casinos.[3]

Faced with terrible publicity and mounting legal costs, in 1981, Playboy decided to pull out of the United Kingdom, and their sixteen-year run of casinos ended.[4]

Other clubs had subtler reputational scandals. Through family connections, the 7th Earl of Lucan had long been a member of the heavily aristocratic St James's Club on Piccadilly, which had a membership with a reputation for young Old Etonians who savoured high-stakes card games. When Lucan vanished in November 1974, on the night his family's nanny was brutally bludgeoned to death, the resultant cause célèbre prompted a worldwide manhunt for the now-notorious Lucan, who was variously rumoured to have fled the country or committed suicide. As no body was ever found for Lord Lucan, the St James's Club were in a predicament as to what to do about his membership. After four years of deliberation, the Club's bankruptcy in 1978 spared them from having to reach a decision.[5]

No club was more unfortunate than the scandal-ridden National Liberal Club, which turned to a mysterious self-styled Canadian millionaire, calling himself 'George Marks, His Holiness the Prince de Chabris', who took over the running of the Club, and turned it into a highly profitable enterprise. Only Marks was not all he seemed to be: a bankrupt American financier on the run from his Cayman Island investors, he systematically defrauded the Club, before fleeing to Miami Beach with his ill-gotten gains. Marks' actions can, however, merely be seen as a conspicuous example of the asset stripping that was so common at the time, and was even venerated by press and politicians alike, for breathing new life into moribund old British institutions.[6]

Everybody liked George. He was a fat, jovial, bespectacled, roly-poly marshmallow of a man. Pushing sixty, a trim little moustache and pointed goatee gave him a sinister edge, but his high-pitched, enthusiastic North American accent was thoroughly disarming. He always seemed so very jolly.

And everyone was talking about the mysterious George. There were tales galore speculating about his past – yet no one seemed to really know very much. Amid London's record heatwave of 1976, and the obligatory smell of burned egg and chips in the streets, the tabloids were raving about this mystery moneyman claiming to be from Canada.

Five years earlier, in 1971, George had first arrived in Britain, calling himself 'His Holiness, the Prince de Chabris.' Anyone who queried this was airily told 'it's a Catholic title, I don't use it myself'.

But with the alarming pace of social change of the sixties and seventies, and people increasingly clinging to anything which evoked the Old World, few people ever did query George. Instead, they were charmed by him. 'People keep denying that I'm one of the ten richest men in Canada,' George insisted, 'but nobody ever said I was!'

He was loud, he was brash, he was outgoing, and everything about George screamed money. He toured London in an opulent silver Rolls-Royce, adorned in leather upholstery, and he oozed out of its seats from one merchant bank to the next, brokering deals the whole time. His suits were impeccably cut, though his spherical figure meant he didn't wear them particularly well. And he presided benevolently over Charlton Park, a sprawling seventeenth-century manor house in Kent, becoming its kindly new 'lord of the manor', plunging money into renovations.

Among George's keen new cheerleaders were the members of the National Liberal Club. Never the most well-heeled of club members, they tended to be the political rank-and-file activists of Britain's ailing and eccentric Liberal Party – though in the early 1970s it was experiencing one of its occasional revivals. This was prompted by a by-election triumph in the northern mill town of Rochdale, led by local alderman and paedophile Cyril Smith; another by-election triumph in the Cambridgeshire farming community around Ely, led by the celebrity chef and paedophile Clement Freud; and the party's charismatic leader Jeremy Thorpe, who between attempts to swindle party donors out of money, was then embroiled in a conspiracy to intimidate – and ultimately an attempt to murder – his former gay lover. Smith, Freud and Thorpe were all were keen, active members of the National Liberal Club. The Liberals by the 1970s were certainly an odd bunch – a colourful collection of anarchists, anti-capitalists, aristocratic Whigs, intellectuals, religious nonconformists, sexual adventurers, perverts, trainspotters and urine drinkers, united by a love of civil liberties, and a disdain for the other political parties. And they were perennially broke.

The National Liberal Club was perennially broke, too. Its sprawling eleven floors of Victorian architecture had not seen any serious maintenance since the building had opened ninety years earlier. Only the staircase had had any work done, after a direct hit from a Nazi bomb in the Blitz. The rest of the Club had an air of faded grandeur – 'gloomy' and 'mausoleum' were the most frequently cited words. The Victorian furniture was battered, carpets were threadbare, artworks were chipped, and most of the wall space had been covered in whitewash since the 1950s – even the glazed tiles and the wooden panelling had all been painted white, in an attempt to pander to post-war tastes. The Club was losing £1,000 a week (£10,000 today), and had been running a deficit for decades, raiding ever more assets to survive. They were growing desperate.

So when George turned up in 1973, seeking election to the Club, they welcomed him with open arms. He did not stay around for long. Although he was a frequent presence in the Dining Room, his cheques had a habit of bouncing. Then his 1974 subscription became overdue, so a few months later he quietly resigned. For the time being, he was just another lapsed member. George went back to his business interests, a temporarily forgotten figure.

Matters then grew serious for the Club. Throughout 1974 and 1975, it teetered on the edge of bankruptcy, although no one seemed to believe the grand club would actually go under. Something would come up – it always had. This was all pretty normal in the clubs of 1970s London: dwindling membership, rising land prices, rising staff wages, rising costs of imported food and wine, and crippling inflation all took their toll. Of London's 400 traditional clubs, over 200 had survived into the 1960s. Fewer than fifty would make it into the 1980s.

The National Liberal Club gave every indication of being another casualty in the making. It was profligate on an epic scale. A hundred and eighty staff worked across its sprawling building, in every capacity imaginable. Lunching alone in the Dining Room involved a procession of six servants tending to one member's silver service, while a seventh waiter was dedicated to lighting the member's cigar after lunch. The Club even contained its own barbershop, a second-hand bookshop, a Masonic lodge and a branch of the Post Office. Each of these facilities was (in theory, at least) *strictly* members-only, meaning that much of the Club was empty for most of the day. The rooms were vast, baronial and deserted. Far from seeing this as a problem, as time went by the members started to take pride in this: 'What I just loved about the place was having a whole suite of rooms in central Whitehall, all to myself. I would never belong to a club that's crowded!' confided one member, who clearly failed to grasp the economics of this.[7]

The whole place had the stench of death – not helped by the average age of members, which meant that several actually keeled over and died within the club. Plenty of members had expired in all manner of places – in the Smoking Room, on a lavatory seat, or waiting interminably when the Club's ageing lift got stuck, or even suffering a fatal heart attack *in flagrante* while mounting a waiter in one of the bedrooms. In each case, it had been a matter of considerable embarrassment. The Club's Secretary would have to arrange for the corpse to be shoved into a cupboard for the time being, hoping decomposition – and the accompanying bad smell – wouldn't set in too quickly. The Club's larder was one far from hygienic spot which was perfect for a corpse to while away a few hours, before the Club servants could smuggle the body out, under the cover of darkness. The 1979 *Fawlty Towers* episode 'The Kipper and the Corpse', portraying the darkly comic difficulties of hiding the corpse of a guest, could have been a documentary on life in the National Liberal Club, and – well, it was the seventies.

Matters came to a head in June 1976, when it looked like the Club's time and money had run out. A final notice was issued to members. The Club was dangerously close to bankruptcy, its debts and losses no longer manageable. Furthermore, a series of legal letters from Heritage England and the Crown Commissioners had just lumbered the Club with a ruinous repair bill, worth £400,000 (over £4 million today). Members were faced with a stark choice: close for good, or merge into another club while trying to manage the Club's colossal debts.

That was when George came back. He had a proposition. 'I'm going to make this property profitable,' he declared. Applying his dazzling financial know-how, the 'Prince de Chabris' would import the latest techniques of stock market whizz-kids and turn around the Club's fortunes. George appeared at the Special General Meeting in July 1976 which had been intended to wind up the Club, and dazzled the members with his generous commitments. Nothing too specific was said – though there was talk of restorations, modernisations, investment, better staff conditions, new gym facilities, squash courts, a sauna and even a solarium in the attic.[8] The members – modest, meek, middle-aged men, used to being an overlooked minority – were gobsmacked by all the attention. Whatever de Chabris wanted to do, it sounded bloody marvellous. And they had no choice. They agreed to keep the Club open, and to approve 'the Mr de Chabris plan' – whatever it was. 'He was the last chance,' admitted the Club Secretary, Coss Billson.[9]

And so George met up with the Trustees of the Club, who held its valuable lease from the Crown Estate, and he set out what he had in mind.

The problem with the National Liberal Club was its size. To begin with, it had a ludicrously large number of bedrooms – 160 – and even at its Victorian height, it could never fill more than a fraction of them, for more than a couple of days a week. It had eleven floors of preposterously high-ceilinged rooms, often serving functions that were duplicated and triplicated, and its 4,000 members could never fill them all. Even subletting forty of the bedrooms as scrappy, makeshift offices to a rag-bag of eccentric organisations had not balanced the books. Added to which, the maintenance costs of the creaking Victorian building were ruinous: the heating bills alone exceeded the Club's income. So George's proposal was simple: turn over the Club to him. He would buy the loss-making club for a notional sum, pay off all its debts and then turn it around. In the meantime, they would rent the building from him, for a mere £2,500 a year, while he nobly absorbed the Club's losses.

George would talk to the Crown Commissioners about the Club's lease, and get it extended another hundred years. Then he would sell off most of the Club's bedrooms as luxury penthouse apartments with riverside views over the Thames. He would also turn the Club's middle floors into a conference centre with all the latest facilities. Meanwhile, the Club would be 'consolidated' down to the lower two floors, which would be beautifully restored to the most exacting standards. In the meantime, he would administer the Club and its bedrooms himself, while the Crown Estate negotiations went on for an estimated five years. He promised to sink millions of pounds of his own money into the renovation and turnaround. It all sounded too good to be true. And it was.

Of course, George wasn't the Prince de Chabris. He was plain old George Levy Marks, a struggling, sixty-year-old small-scale property developer from Florida, who had moved to Charlottetown on the east coast of Canada, and then Calgary, where he lost a fortune in the Canadian property bubble of the early 1970s. He had started using the 'de Chabris' title after himself falling prey to a con artist in 1968, who had 'sold' him a title, the Baron de Mornay. George Marks was thrilled, and proudly placed his new title on all his stationery. Rapidly realising that his clients did not care whether or not it was a real title, he set about 'upgrading' himself, and purchased the style of Duc de Vatan, before finally declaring himself to be His Holiness, the Prince de Chabris. 'Just call me George de Chabris, or plain old George,' he cooed to enthralled clients. Armed with a prestigious new identity, redolent of old money, he set about going after some *real* money – in the Cayman Islands.

Details of George's Cayman Islands venture, a 'mutual offshore property fund', remained murky at best. But it was generally agreed by everyone who had had the misfortune to invest in it that the whole thing was a scam. George had learned an important lesson from the con artist who had sold him his title: people are stupider than you might think. And he set about preparing to exploit this, putting together a pot of money for his retirement. Luring investors to a Jamaican yacht, George set about bamboozling them into investing in his fund. He eventually left the Cayman Islands in 1971, pursued by a £700,000 writ (worth £7 million today) from the liquidator in Grand Cayman, who accused him of gross negligence, breach of trust and improper favours. He hoped to lay low in Britain. And for all his showmanship, he was as broke as the National Liberal Club.[10]

In Britain, George purchased Charlton Park, near Bishopsbourne, Kent, from a retired colonel-turned-pop-concert-promoter in 1972. It was a stunning, seventeenth-century mansion, although its maintenance had been ruinously expensive for successive owners.

George needed more than just money, to put himself beyond the reach of the law. He needed respectability. The Liberal Party provided it – particularly through its leader, Jeremy Thorpe, and through the National Liberal Club which Thorpe liked to work out of, much closer to Parliament than the bulk of Clubland.

Thorpe was well aware that he could dole out one major form of patronage: as the leader of a political party, he could propose people for honours. As a young boy in the 1930s, Thorpe had grown up under the spell of his father's good friend, former prime minister David Lloyd George, and he came to idolise Lloyd George's ruthlessness as a politician. Whereas most of Lloyd George's admirers grudgingly conceded that he had a dark side, in being flagrantly corrupt as he sold honours on an industrial scale, Thorpe regarded all this as an example to be followed – and set about doing the same.

And George wanted the biggest honour of them all: a peerage. He had had enough of having his titles denounced as phoney, by pedantic journalists. He wanted a *real* title. As Lord de Chabris, he would surely be untouchable to his creditors. So George set about on his campaign to ingratiate himself with Thorpe.

George began by presenting a £50 cheque to Liberal Party funds. This would be the first and last cheque Thorpe would ever cash from George. A 'party piece' was then set up – George would turn up to Liberal fundraiser dinners at the Club, and give a tub-thumping speech, at the end of which he would brandish a cheque for £1,000 to the Liberal Party. He would finish by asking who in the audience would match his thousand-pound cheque? It was always an impressive performance – but those who saw it over and over again began to notice that it was always the same cheque, looking increasingly creased and dog-eared, and began to wonder if the cheque would ever be cashed?[11]

None of this mattered to Thorpe, an irrepressible snob for whom George's apparent money and title made him just the man to save the National Liberal Club. When it came to handing over the Club to George, Thorpe gave an elaborate luncheon in honour of their new

Canadian benefactor, to introduce him to the Club's Committee. Thorpe rose to celebrate the 'Great families who have given their all to the Liberal cause – the Gladstones, the Lloyd Georges, the Asquiths – and now, the de Chabris!'[12] Members were soon to find out what this meant.

At first, George's changes to the Club seemed innocuous enough. Some were downright progressive. For decades, the Club's Committee had been refusing to admit women as full members – the favourite excuse, as in so many men's clubs, was that women members would mean the need to provide women's bathrooms, and that was regrettably impractical.

In the National Liberal Club, with its vibrant gay scene among members and staff, the real reason was that many members did not want to endanger the carefully cultivated social life they had built up. This was by no means unique in Clubland – an early 1980s attempt to admit women to the Savile Club failed by 49 votes to 51, allegedly because 'The gay membership took a very dim view of this.'[13] Male homosexuality may have been decriminalised in 1967, but nearly a decade on it was still something of a taboo in polite society, with rampant homophobia very much the norm. However, like many other men's clubs, the National Liberal Club had long served as a discreet enclave and hook-up spot for discerning gay men. In addition to the many opportunities for male members to acquaint themselves with their fellow members, a discreet, off-menu service was provided in the Dining Room, with male waiters being available to members for 'after-hours' services. Then for liaison spaces, members were spoilt for choice. They could pop upstairs to one of the club's many bedrooms. They could nip across the rear lawn to the party boat SS *Hispaniola*, moored opposite the club on the Thames, conveniently out of the jurisdiction of the local council and constabulary.[14] Or for the frisson of something more spontaneous and risky, the Club's endless string of Victorian bathrooms afforded numerous opportunities for a rough and ready encounter in a damp alcove. Meanwhile, the Club was not a particularly welcoming space for women, who still had to stalk in through a side entrance, and could only visit certain rooms at certain times of day. As late as the 1950s, female staff taking the minutes of meetings would have to hide behind a screen, out of sight from the members.

There had been some previous attempts at allowing women to enter this male bastion. The most successful was in 1967, when the students of Oxford University Liberal Club nominated one of their number, Hilary Wright, for membership of the National Liberal Club. (She gave her address 'Care of the Oxford Union', to avoid divulging the name of her all-women's college, which would have been a giveaway as to her sex.) Sure enough, the Club wrote back, asking for a clarification that Hilary was actually a man, to which the rather evasive reply was that Wright's membership would be in accordance with the Club's rules. A membership card was promptly sent in the post, and so she turned up one morning, demanding admission, brandishing her membership card. The Porter refused to let her in, but she had taken the precaution of inviting reporters from the *Daily Express* to witness the kerfuffle.[15]

To George, this was all irrelevant. If the Club was to make money, it had to admit women. So when the Committee yet again voted – by an overwhelming margin – to refuse to admit women in July 1976, George simply overruled them, telling them that as the Club's new proprietor, he was putting his foot down. That certainly endeared him to the Club's more radical members.

George did some other good things, too. The Club's servants had all been laid off in anticipation of its closure – only the former Secretary, Coss Billson, stayed on out of a sense of duty, living off his redundancy money while turning up to work for free, as 'Honorary Secretary to the Trustees'. The other Club servants, several of whom were doddering or venal (or both), had all been laid off, and George managed the feat of hiring an entirely new staff from scratch. (Not without some hiccups – chaos in the bar on the first day meant that George needed to buy some goodwill by offering drinks on the house, as a way of apologising for terminally slow service.) With a go-getting recruitment drive, and a blitz of advertising and positive coverage on the BBC evening news, the Club's membership soared, signing up 600 new members within months. The hotel bedrooms suddenly seemed to be booked to capacity. Wasteful use of space was identified and eliminated. The Liberal Party, previously based in a shabby alleyway off the Strand, moved in at George's insistence, and made a part of the Club their national headquarters. George was particularly thrilled at this, as it increased his leverage over the party, in becoming its landlord – he hoped that would help his quest for a peerage. George even gave the Club an indemnity for £10,000 when he took over (although what nobody knew at the time was that he withdrew it again, within days). And while George's refurbishment plans kept being delayed and postponed, he did begin installing thousands of square feet of new carpets throughout the building. It seemed that the Club was entering a renaissance.[16]

Then *The Times* began to take an interest. In a series of articles in October 1976, one of them splashed across the front page, they revealed that 'de Chabris' was a fraud – that he had an assumed identity, and that he was fleeing creditors from the Cayman Islands. The Club reacted in the most English manner possible: it did nothing. Any discussion of Mr de Chabris's financial affairs was barred from meetings, speakers were cut off, their comments unrecorded in the minutes.

Other things started to seem amiss. Coachloads of young Scandinavian tourists, mainly students on gap years, began turning up on Danish package holiday tours, saying they were booked into a hotel advertised as 'One Whitehall Place'. George didn't care much that he was breaching the terms of the Club's lease, which only allowed it to accommodate members. As he saw it, he was turning around a property and making it profitable.[17]

The Club possessed hundreds of paintings, and George would be seen touring the Club, examining each and every one of them. Sooner or later, after closer scrutiny, he would come to the same conclusion: 'That one needs to be sent off for restoration.' Few that were sent off were seen again.

One member staggered back to his bedroom in the Club at five in the morning, after a heavy night out on the town. He was surprised to see a large black juggernaut pulling up in front of the Club, being loaded up with Victorian furniture, complete with several vast antique billiard tables. They were the historic billiard tables installed under Gladstone, that had been used in more recent years for *Pot Black*, the BBC's first ever televised snooker coverage, live from the Club. 'Mr de Chabris said it all has to go,' explained the driver.[18]

George was comprehensively asset stripping the Club. But then, he was only doing what he'd promised to do. Had the desperate Club not agreed to all of this? In agreeing to 'the de Chabris plan', they had agreed to 'consolidate' the Club down to the lower two floors. Anything which was left on the other nine floors was George's property, his to plunder or sell off as he saw fit. Visitors to Charlton Park started commenting on the excellent quality of George's newly acquired silverware, with its distinctive 'NLC' monograms embossed across it.[19]

Saddest of all was the fate of the Club's Gladstone Library – the largest and most comprehensive library ever compiled by any

London club, set across multiple floors and reading rooms, and spanning 35,000 books, 40,000 pamphlets and a unique collection of political ephemera and memorabilia spanning the centuries. George couldn't sell that off, because the library was owned by an independent charitable trust. So he started demanding rent, at the grossly inflated rate of £20,000 a year for their main room – eight times what he was asking the rest of the eleven-storey Club to pay. When they were unable to pay that, he issued them with an eviction notice for non-payment of rent, throwing them out of their purpose built home. He needed the space for his conference centre. They had to arrange a swift bonfire sale of the library's contents to Bristol University, at a month's notice. George took a cut of the proceeds, of course – just as he had taken a £4,000 cut of the Club's wine cellar, which he had sold off for £5,000.

In December 1976 the auditors came in. What they found shocked them.

One of George's first changes had been to merge the National Liberal Club's accounts with those of his own company, Charlton Park Holdings Ltd. George's company barely had any income or assets of its own – but the National Liberal Club did, and it was now trading out of the same shared account. Sixty thousand pounds was missing from the books. Of the £100,000 in income during George's stint, he had kept three-fifths of it for himself.[20]

Even then, the Club did not act immediately. It was all terribly embarrassing, argued the Committee. It would be some years before they started to piece together what had happened, and, even then, the information was spoon-fed to them by inquisitive journalists who had examined leaked club accounts. The Committee and Trustees did not want to pry – particularly as the sordid details only made their own gross negligence all the more obvious. Why had they not vetted George properly? Why had they not noticed all the obvious telltale signs? Why had they sanctioned the asset stripping of the Club? Why had they done nothing for six months after *The Times* had publicly exposed George as a fraud?[21]

Matters were to prove even more complicated. George had siphoned off a lot of the money by operating the Club out of the accounts of Charlton Park Holdings Ltd. The Club was unaware that their own money had been meeting the household bills at George's Kent mansion, plus tax bills, gardeners' wages, even a sports car and the fees for his children at three premier public schools, Westonbirt, Winchester and the King's School, Canterbury.[22]

A quarter of the sum George embezzled came in just one day's transactions, on 17 August 1976. He wrote out a £15,000 cheque, to his own bank account. But he falsified the corresponding stub in the Club's chequebook, so that it gave the recipient as the 'Cash Carpet Company' – giving the impression that the money had been used for carpets. In fact, he then converted the money into a banker's draft at the Trafalgar Square branch of NatWest (thereby concealing the money's origin) and handed that to his solicitors, asking them to pay it into the Williams & Glyn's bank account for Gibraltar Life Assurance Ltd – a company owned by George.[23]

There, the sum made up for a £15,000 shortfall in the accounts, over ground rents George had been collecting on 493 properties across the north of England; ground rents which George's company was contractually obliged to pass on, but which George had been helping himself to. Ever since he'd fled the Cayman Islands, George's life had been a tangle of debts, botched business deals and missing sums used to cover up previous missing sums. The National Liberal Club's funds had got him out of his latest jam.

George also operated other scams which were simpler, but no less effective. Club members were delighted when he unveiled a portrait of Charles Wolfran Cornwall, the eighteenth-century Speaker of the House of Commons, supposedly by Gainsborough. Members were led to believe it was a generous gift from their new benefactor. In fact, George had sold it to the club, for £10,000. And, naturally, it wasn't a Gainsborough at all – the country's leading art experts at Christie's said it was a copy worth 'no more than £1,000' at auction, and that its actual value was a mere £120.[24]

How had this happened under the Club's very nose? Why hadn't anyone noticed anything? The truth was that several people *had* noticed things seriously amiss – but had said nothing. At the centre of it all was Philip Watkins. Watkins in many ways personified the club in the 1970s – pleasant, polite, secretive, a heavily closeted accountant who gave his time generously to the Liberal Party. He had been an Oxford contemporary and occasional lover of Jeremy Thorpe's, and had stood four times as a Liberal candidate in the West Country, in seats with a coveted second place. He was a popular figure within the Club, and while his natural reserve never wholly melted, he was courteous to a fault, and was a passive, sympathetic, agreeable listener.

Watkins was in a hopelessly conflicted position throughout all this. As well as serving on a number of club committees overseeing its finances, he was both the Club's Treasurer and Auditor. He also ran a firm of chartered accountants based in the Club, and so was the Club's tenant. And he was also George's personal accountant – that was how he had brought George to Jeremy Thorpe's attention. And as George's accountant, entering every one of George's transactions into the purchase ledger, he had seen every one of George's moves. He chose to say nothing.[25]

Jeremy Thorpe had troubles of his own around this time. In May 1976, he had been forced to resign as Leader of the Liberal Party, after the publication of an old love letter he had written to his former lover Norman Scott, who had already accused him of trying to have him murdered. Although the more compelling evidence of the murder plot would not emerge for some years, there was now enough in the public domain to prove that Thorpe was a liar when he said he barely knew Scott. Unsurprisingly, Thorpe was rather distracted throughout George's reign, and had hit the bottle in a fairly big way. Nonetheless, the Club remained both Thorpe's refuge of choice, where he could get away with friends, and his favourite platform for press conferences which he gave to insist that he was innocent of all murder allegations. One such conference in the Club library had Thorpe being asked by the BBC's Keith Graves whether he had ever had a homosexual relationship with Scott. Before Thorpe could reply, his wife Marion rose, incensed, and challenged Graves to 'Stand up and say that again!', which he bashfully did. Before Thorpe could then answer, his solicitor John Montgomerie interjected that his client was unable to answer the question. It was the first of many unconvincing performances by Thorpe, so that even though he was finally acquitted on murder conspiracy charges in 1979, he was widely ostracised by a public convinced of his guilt.

Watkins, who had also been installed by Thorpe as the Liberal Party's treasurer, was popular with his fellow members: 'A good man, a kind man, an honest man . . . his problem was that he was just too trusting, and he assumed everyone was as honest as he was', was the verdict of one member who had known him for decades.[26] Members would have queued up to offer similar plaudits. But the Club's staff saw a very different side of Watkins: 'He had his hand in the till . . . He was a crook.'[27]

After the fallout, Watkins continued to hold a string of club offices – until a 1980 *Panorama* exposé on George's time at the Club led him to resign in disgrace. As George's accountant, he had seen each of the dubious transactions, but at no point had he raised any questions in his capacity as the Club's Treasurer. Yet he carried on serving on the club's Committee, and at the time of his early death in 1995 he had worked his way back up to being Vice-Chairman of the Club, in line to be its next Chairman.[28] It was a peculiarly British example of rewarding failure.

It would be unfair to scapegoat Watkins entirely. As with many clubs in the seventies, the National Liberal Club exhibited a breathtaking lack of competence and oversight in allowing this situation to develop. Much blame must go to its Chairman, Sir Leonard Smith, who presided over a series of fiascos from 1972 to 1987. Like Watkins, Sir Leonard had been a treasurer of the Liberal Party under Thorpe, and was no stranger to the seamier side of party political funding. Like Watkins, Sir Leonard had a natural predisposition to secrecy. Unlike the meek Philip Watkins, he could be tyrannical, abrasive and bullying – no one dared cross Sir Leonard.

George may have fooled the National Liberal Club, but one group of people saw through him from the start: the Crown Estate, who owned the freehold of the Club (and many others). Their initial probes into him had concluded that he was a 'man of straw', and they refused to speak to him. George couldn't let the Club know this, and for the nine months that he controlled the Club he went through the motions of assuring members that 'the negotiations are in a very delicate state', and that they would take a few years more. In reality, no negotiations were taking place, because the Crown Estate refused even to see him. The Club was saved from its own gullibility by the Crown's refusal to modify the title deed, which its Trustees were only too keen to see passed on to George.

The Club had another, altogether darker secret at the same time. Watkins had engaged a former Scotland Yard special constable named Mike Wood as House Manager, who served as George's *de facto* deputy. Watkins had first met Wood in a waiting room of the Marylebone magistrates court – Watkins was sitting as a magistrate, and Wood was there to charges of gross indecency with underage boys. The two formed an unlikely rapport. *Private Eye* euphemistically observed at the time, 'Wood remained on more than friendly terms with Philip Watkins, who was extremely abrupt with anyone who dared to criticise his protégé.' George went even further: he had found the two of them having sex in an upstairs lavatory of the Club, and considered both of them to be in his grip thereafter, easy to blackmail and silence.[29]

The Club's staff were terrified of Wood. He was a tall, muscular man who regularly organised demonstrations of physical prowess. Sometimes these would end in farce – he once showed off his mastery of handcuffs on the banister of the club's grand staircase, only to realise he had lost the key, and needed to telephone his old Scotland Yard colleagues to ask them to cut him free.[30]

But Wood was responsible for some particularly unpleasant acts in the club. 'He was a paedophile,' opines one club staffer from the time, who would repeatedly see him leading young boys up to the bedrooms. At least four times, young staff and visitors would be accompanied to Charing Cross Hospital, complaining of having been savagely beaten into submission and buggered by Wood. One staff member recalled Wood breaking down the door of his room in the servants' quarters, and brutally dragging him from his wife's side to rape him in a neighbouring room. It was an intolerable situation.[31]

Outraged staff complained to George, but he dismissed their complaints. With the circling creditors and auditors, he was too busy to notice. He just hoped these things would go away. Wood knew too much, and was unsackable.

Matters with George came to a head in February 1977. The auditors reported back to the Trustees, relaying their concerns about the £60,000 shortfall in the accounts, and several obvious cases of outright fraud.

The Trustees did what they had always done when scandal reared its head at the National Liberal Club. They closed ranks. They refused to tell the Club's Committee, much less its members. They went into secret session, for hours at a time, discussing each of the problems. There was even some confusion as to the legal situation – no one was entirely sure whether George had bought the Club, or not. He was certainly being treated as its owner by the Trustees, who had been keen to pass on the lease as soon as possible (though had never finalised the documents), and he was liable for its bills – but red-ink letters were notifying the Club that he hadn't been paying the bills. Of course, the Trustees had all known since reading the front page of *The Times* the previous October that George was an imposter and a sham; but back then they thought at least he was still rich.

They pondered what to do, and how to avoid the blame for the fiasco. It has been they, after all, who had been so gullible. 'At least you knew where you were with George – he was a good, honest-to-God, old-fashioned crook. That other mob were the real nightmare,' recalls one former staffer.[32]

What George had done was no different from what many businessmen and entrepreneurs did in the seventies. It was completely illegal, but this was the age of the asset stripper, when men like Jim Slater had become celebrities and were lauded for their financial nous in taking fusty, failing old industries – like the clubs of London – and creating new wealth by unleashing a stream of money from them. Admittedly, they hadn't created any new wealth at all – all they had done was asset stripped the company to enrich themselves, destroying the company's viability in the process and retiring on the proceeds. But it was all the rage. The conventional wisdom that this was a new form of capitalism that left companies leaner and fitter – in much the same way as the Charge of the Light Brigade left the said brigade a good deal lighter afterwards. It had never occurred to the Trustees of the Club that this might not be a good thing – until it was too late. George had flogged the Club's assets and pocketed the proceeds. Paintings, statues, silverware, vintage wines, library – all were sold off to enrich George. And as for Mike Wood's reign of terror, George didn't see that as his business. He was too busy planning his retirement.

Finally, the Trustees had little choice but to confront George. On 24 March 1977, he was shown the incriminating ledgers and told his services were no longer required. He tried to brazen it out as best he could, protesting his innocence. But he was given no other option and was told to leave immediately.

George did what any other con artist would have done in that position. He emptied out the Charlton Park Holdings Ltd account of all funds that day – including some £19,000 of the Club's money in it – and even emptied out the cash till on the front desk on the way out, purloining another £800.[33] For a further flourish, he even press-released his departure, presenting himself as the spurned benefactor for good measure. George never did things by half-measure.

Within days of his sacking in March 1977, George made a midnight flight from his Charlton Park mansion, with one local resident remembering 'the vans removing his (and probably others') possessions [and] disturbed the sleep of people in the village as they left', and this being the most interesting thing to happen in living memory in this sleepy stretch of Kent countryside.[34]

The National Liberal Club made little effort to pursue him. Scotland Yard had gathered a hefty file on George and were all set to press charges – but first they waited for the outcome of Jeremy Thorpe's murder conspiracy trial in 1979. By all accounts, they wanted to know whether the Liberals had suffered enough first, before proceeding with another prosecution. Eventually, the Club's Trustees implored Scotland Yard not to press charges. They preferred to reach a private settlement, resolving matters discreetly. Their solicitors ultimately reached an agreement with George's lawyers, whereby they would let him keep half the money he had absconded with if he paid back the other half in instalments. They were grateful to get that much. Philip Watkins – nervous at George's threats to expose his private life – had been the driving force behind letting George keep half the money.

George would settle in Florida, buying a vast Miami Beach mansion at Coral Gables, living out a prosperous retirement with the National Liberal Club's money, until his death in 2001 at the age of eighty-five. He got away with it. But there was one coda to this story.

By 1980, the journalist Martin Young of the BBC's *Panorama* had used a leaked set of NLC accounts to finally piece together George's fraud. Young tracked down George to Miami Beach, and flew out there to confront him, with a camera crew in tow.

Their first meeting was not edifying. Young rang the bell on George's mansion, only for George to appear at an upstairs window. When Young announced why he was there, George responded by yelling, 'Fuck off!' Young tried calling several times a day, both on the telephone and in person, only to be told 'Fuck off!' each time. George even took to answering the phone in Spanish, the second language of Miami, to avoid having to talk to Young. So Young promptly recruited a Spanish-speaking colleague to ring up the de Chabris household. The only result of that was learning what 'Fuck off!' was in Spanish. Young even tried camping out on George's lawn, refusing to go away until he had an interview. Eventually, Young managed to outsmart George. He sent him a letter warning him that he had tipped off the entire London press pack as to where George lived, and that they would all be heading over to hound him – unless George offered him an exclusive. George agreed to give him an interview, provided they could talk in advance. As he left this preparatory chat, Young smiled, 'Don't worry, Mr de Chabris, this afternoon the questions will be the same.' George grinned, 'Don't you worry, Mr Young, the answers will be quite different!' Both men were enjoying themselves, and Young mused that 'Conning a con-man is such a delight.'[35]

That afternoon, they met in Young's hotel room, filming a spirited debate. George gave no ground, and was charm personified. Chuckling through every allegation, grinning at every receipt that was produced, he said he could explain everything. As the overvalued painting of Mr Speaker Cornwall was brought up, he gently batted it aside: 'I don't care what anybody says about the value of paintings, I'm a pretty good expert. And some kid over at Sotheby's [sic] can tell you it's only worth a thousand pounds, that doesn't cut any ice with me.' Young pressed on, insisting that de Chabris had sold it for £10,000 only ten days after the valuation for a fraction of that sum: 'You're defrauding your own company!' George was humiliated on television, for all to see. *Panorama* even hired actors to scoot around London in a silver Rolls-Royce, emulating George's transactions. The BBC had exposed him, when the National Liberal Club had not.

One of George's more revealing answers came when he was asked about the £15,000 cheque stub that he had falsified, writing that the money had gone to the 'Cash Carpet Company' when he had actually pocketed it. It was pointed out that no such company existed. George suggested that he was going to use the money to set one up, which would have produced all the carpets. He had been in the process of setting it up, he insisted. But what about the paperwork for such a company? He had no contracts, no articles of association, no memoranda, no receipts – could he provide a single scrap of evidence to show that the Cash Carpet Company ever existed, or was ever likely to exist?

George smiled. 'No, but I had the money.'[36] He certainly did.

Chapter Sixteen

The strange rebirth of Clubland
(1985–2022)

By the early 1980s, Clubland was in terminal decline, and even the most prestigious London clubs came within an inch of bankruptcy. While the National Liberal Club had suffered a particularly public humiliation in the press, it was far from being the only club to hit rock-bottom. It was therefore to general surprise (bordering on incredulity) that the next thirty years saw a recovery in Clubland's fortunes, and an expansion of London clubs to their largest numbers since the 1920s. Worldwide, clubs have ended up being unprecedented in their popularity.

By the early 1980s, the idea of a successful London club had been several lifetimes ago, and much newspaper coverage of the 1960s and 1970s had alluded to the weary inevitability of it only being a matter of time before the last of these arcane institutions were snuffed out entirely. For all their retained charm, the same problems of ageing membership and utterly dysfunctional economics persisted, compounded by an unflattering image. When Lord Carrington was foreign secretary in the 1980s, he was asked why he didn't use the Carlton more, preferring the atmosphere of White's: 'Because it's full of the sort of people I go to my club to avoid.'[1] Food continued to be legendarily bad across Clubland, despite the odd flirtation with 'Nouvelle Cuisine': in Belgravia, the Irish Club was nearly closed down in 1988 after failing a raft of food health and safety tests.[2] The reaction across several other clubs was 'There but for the grace of God go we.'

These increasingly anachronistic clubs were kept going by old retainers and oddballs, like The Resident Member. A century earlier, it had been quite common for people of limited means to lodge at their club for a few years, and The Resident Member was typically young, broke, and 'on the make'. By the late twentieth century, The Resident Member was typically very elderly, very eccentric, very rich, and long since retired – clubs were no longer affordable places to live, and one had to be decidedly unconventional and of independent means to end one's days in a club. For over thirty years from 1965 to his death in 1998, Monsignor Alfred Gilbey lived at the Travellers Club, and insisted on converting a boot room into a private oratory (which has been retained after his death, as an oddity). In his black cloaks and broad hats, he cut a dashing if unconventional figure.[3] By the 2000s, Colin Merton moved into the Savile Club in his retirement. He was primarily remembered as a perennial candidate for the United Kingdom Independence Party in local elections, with a rather disarming style of campaigning: 'Would you like a UKIP leaflet?', and upon being met by an awkward 'Erm …', would answer, 'No? Oh well, can't say I blame you. But good day to you nonetheless.' He almost invariably lost his deposit.[4] It was all terribly charming, but it was no basis for running a club as a business.

Against this backdrop of stagnation came a wave of new clubs. This did not precisely start in the mid-1980s; for new clubs never stopped being set up, as with the fashionable Clermont Club of the 1960s. In the 1970s, the European Movement ran the 'Stay' campaign of the 1975 EEC referendum, and maintained its offices in the National Liberal Club thereafter, where they ran their own Europe House Club on the ground floor, for pan-European idealists. In 1981, a set of elegant if cramped late Georgian rooms off St Martin's Lane was set up as what is now called the Brydges Place Club, originally as a venue for 'out' gay members, which would be more openly accepting than the traditional clubs, all the while being less celebrity-laden than the louder, loucher club life of nearby Soho. The Club, originally called Two Brydges, was named after its somewhat eccentric Brydges Place address, a urine-strewn alleyway along the side of the Coliseum Theatre, barely half a metre wide at its narrowest point, giving a conspiratorial feel to visits.

None of these new clubs were going to set the world alight, however. What was about to change was the wave of commercial new clubs, touted as 'anti-clubs', which were seen as a reaction to the stuffiness of traditional Clubland. The first of these was the Groucho Club on Dean Street in Soho, founded in 1985 by a group of publishers including Liz Calder, Carmen Callil, Michael Sissons and Ed Victor. Calder recalls:

> It is difficult to imagine London in 1982. If you were a woman, there was nowhere you could go to meet a friend over a glass of wine or coffee, other than grim cafés, seedy wine bars or noisome pubs where you couldn't get served. This made me wonder why it was that men had so many splendidly accommodating clubs where they could meet their friends and colleagues, while we were left outside with our noses pressed to the windows.[5]

The Club shunned jacket and tie dress codes, positively welcomed business, and targeted members in London's burgeoning creative arts industries, who were often far from impressed by the shape of Clubland in the 1980s, yet were keen to engage in all the socialising activities typically found in Clubland, and had a lot more cash to flash than the impecunious members of traditional clubs. Actor-writer Stephen Fry, a keen Clubman who was already a millionaire in his twenties, thanks to his penning the revised and revived hit West End musical *Me and My Girl*, was a founder member and wrote the Club's rules.

The Groucho never slept. From business breakfasts over croissants and orange juice, to all-night boozy benders in the Club's multiple bars, it was a hive of activity, fuelled by a heady cocktail of sociability, business, adrenaline and cocaine. Drug-taking was endemic at the Groucho in the eighties and nineties. One of the rules written by Fry explicitly forbade drug-taking on the premises (then an unusual stipulation in club rules), yet Fry was deep in the throes of a cocaine addiction of his own at the time, and frequently indulged on the premises. The emphasis was instead upon discretion in the members' vices. A traumatised looking Fry once emerged from the gentlemen's lavatories, exclaiming, 'Good God, somebody is urinating in the cocaine room!' Fry argued that the Groucho had its own blend of challenges – although some will sound familiar to readers:

> The daily management of a club like the Groucho presents all kinds of unique problems. How to deal with the notorious Soho bohemian Dan Farson drunkenly pulling rough trade up the stairs to the bedrooms? Vomit in unexpected places. Indiscreet snorters ruining it for the rest of us by tapping out lines on the dining table. Out-of-control revellers who think the place is open to all trying to pile in after pub hours (the club is licensed to serve drinks until two in the morning).[6]

Although the Groucho made much of being an 'anti-club', it was in fact an obvious example of clubs going back to their roots. It arguably shared much more in common with the raucous, racy clubs of the eighteenth century than the stultifying premises that many of those same clubs had become by the twentieth century. Like the earliest clubs, the Groucho was run for profit by a private landlord. It also kept long hours, positively courted fashion and gossip, and welcomed rather than resisted members hustling for business on the premises. Like the earliest clubs, it was helped more than hindered by a dissolute, debauched reputation that only seemed to add to its mystique. And like the earliest clubs, it shunned the inclusivity of late Victorian clubs and unabashedly catered to the elite; only in this case a business rather than an aristocratic elite.

The runaway profitability of the Groucho Club in its early years did not pass unnoticed. Several major new clubs sought to replicate its approach, combining the best in 'old' and 'new' clubs, to appeal to a large new demographic of members who would never have dreamed of belonging to a club, but who were lured by the fashionable lustre of these newer institutions. In 1992, Black's opened in an old Georgian house on Dean Street, close to the Groucho – its name was a riposte to White's. In 1995, the first Soho House opened a few streets along, in Greek Street. In 1998, Home House on Portman Square followed. Over the next twenty years, another sixty 'new' London clubs would follow. Some, like the oenophiliac 67 Pall Mall, were located in Clubland's traditional heartlands. Most popped up in the parts of the capital where the most profitable industries worked – bankers in the City of London, creative industries in Covent Garden and Soho, hedge funds and mercenaries in Mayfair. All would find a flurry of new clubs catering specifically for them. The subscriptions for these new clubs were (and remain) typically far more expensive than that of many 'traditional' clubs, while their entry fees can be eye-watering.

It was not lost on the proprietors of these successful new establishments that the club business model was scalable, and it could be replicated in a great many cities worldwide. The flourishing of the ClubCorp chain of over 200 city clubs, golf clubs and country clubs in the United States showed a template for what could be done globally.[7] The launch of the Groucho Club in 1985 heralded a wave of new clubs in the 1990s and 2000s, often run as highly profitable chains, aimed at a younger, trendier membership. Home House started to open other branches. Mark Birley was a successful impresario who had been operating new clubs for the super-rich since he opened Annabel's on Berkeley Square in 1963, and then several further clubs beginning with Mark's Club off the square in 1973; soon, they grew into a whole Birley Group.

When Mark Birley died in 2007, he disinherited his son Robin of his club empire over a long-running family feud; but this did not dissuade Robin Birley from making clubs his business, and he set up a London club empire of his own. In much the same way that the old Clermont Club had Annabel's nightclub located in the basement in the Swinging Sixties, 5 Hertford Street is a Birley club off Shepherd Market with a louche reputation and a basement nightclub of its own, Loulou's. One regular habitué, noting how the likes of Nigel Farage, Arron Banks, Michael Gove, Priti Patel, Andrew Roberts, Harry Cole and Boris Johnson frequent it, says, 'It's the Brexit sex dungeon.'[8] It was here, over champagne in the nightclub, that Brexit trade deals were brokered, rather than in the more conventional Pall Mall clubs. It was also here that foreign secretary Liz Truss got into hot water for holding a £3,000 diplomatic meal despite the concerns of her civil servants, as well as holding a series of informal, get-to-know-you drinks receptions with backbench Tory MPs, billed as 'Fizz with Liz'.[9] To understand Robin Birley's clubs is to understand Brexit.

The new lease of life from the 'new' clubs has not been a magic wand for the revival of clubs. Plenty of traditional London clubs have continued to close in the last decade, including the Irish Club and Royal Anglo-Belgian Club in 2012, both the St Stephen's Club and Commonwealth Club in 2013, New Cavendish Club in 2014 and the Naval Club in 2021. Nor have the 'new' clubs been immune. If anything, they are far riskier enterprises, for a club is only excitingly 'new' and buzzy in its first two or three years, and must wait several decades to be 'established'; and so for several decades in between it often lacks a clear identity of being one or the other. Plenty of 'new' London clubs have closed in the last four years – even before the Covid-19 pandemic took its toll – including the Chess Club, London Capital Club and Grace Belgravia in 2018, KPMG Number Twenty and the Hospital Club in 2019, Library, the Devonshire Club, Milk & Honey, AllBright Fitzrovia and the Conduit Club all closed their doors in 2020, as did the Fox Club in 2021. All this underlines how clubs are a highly speculative enterprise.

Other groups of London clubs have been rather more international in outlook. Soho House opened branches in other areas of London such as Shoreditch and Notting Hill. Soho House rather ambitiously aimed for a more global reach, attracting venture capital investment to start up in a variety of cities. Some of these cities were almost built for clubs – New York's multiple Soho House branches in up-and-coming areas like the Meatpacking District rapidly found their own niche in New York's established Clubland scene, the second-largest in the world after London. Other cities required a little more creative work – a sumptuous building in Istanbul, formerly owned by the US government, needed to be comprehensively swept for bugging devices before it could be converted into Turkey's first Soho House. At the time of writing, there are twenty-eight Soho Houses across eight countries.

The 1980s economic boom around the City of London created a significant new class, who flocked to these new clubs: 'Yuppies', young urban professionals with a significant disposable income. As they looked for fashionable places to spend their leisure time, the clubs of London seemed an obvious option. While the growing roster of new 'anti-clubs' explicitly catered for this market, the traditional clubs of London *also* benefited from this move. The 'anti-clubs' acted as something of a gateway, drawing a whole new generation's attention to this hidden world of private members' clubs, which had not been seen as the domain of 'Bright Young Things' in well over half a century. Suddenly, the established clubs saw an influx of members who had been born after the Second World War. John Martin Robinson notes the growth of the Travellers Club by 24 per cent in the late 1980s, from 994 members in 1985, to 1,241 in 1990, and how:

> There were suddenly rich young men – commercial lawyers, merchant bankers, 'consultants', hedge fund managers, 'businessmen', who for the first time since the 1950s wanted to live in large Georgian houses and join old-established Gentlemen's Clubs, and could afford to do so. Many of them were 'Young Fogeys', a phrase coined by Alan Watkins to describe brogue-wearing, short-haired, pin-striped or tweedy young reactionaries he came across in the purlieus of the *Spectator*, the Inns of Court, and the *Daily Telegraph*. Such people were drawn to St James's as their spiritual home.[10]

As noted, the young Stephen Fry did not just frequent the Groucho, he was a gregarious Clubman, revelling in membership of some half-dozen 'traditional' clubs. Above all, he prized the annual August exchange between many London clubs in the 1980s, and how membership of the (then still men-only) Oxford and Cambridge Club was a ticket to a dozen more of the fustiest London clubs, normally well beyond the reach of a young twenty-something in Thatcher's Britain.

In August 1984, Fry thought it would be fun to take his friend, the avant-garde left-wing stand-up comedian Ben Elton, to the Carlton Club. Fry acknowledges a 'self-conscious awareness of the ridiculous nature of what we were doing and the ludicrous figures that we cut. Two Jewish comics pretending to be *flâneurs* of the old school.'[11] The pair confidently bounded in, Fry noting the Porter's evidently sniffy disapproval of Elton's suit. 'Ben was, as he knew one had to be in such places, dressed in a suit and tie, but there are suits and ties and there are ways of wearing suits and ties. My charcoal tailor-made three-piece, New and Lingwood shirt with faintly distressed silk Cherubs tie looked as if they belonged, whereas Ben's Mr Byrite appearance suggested (and I mean this warmly and lovingly) a bus-driver reluctantly togged up for his sister's wedding.'[12]

They headed upstairs, where Elton exploded in alarm at the bust of the prime minister on the main staircase. (A staircase which, ironically, she would not have been allowed to climb, since the Carlton banned women from using the staircase, ostensibly as members were not to be trusted not to look up women's skirts.) 'That's Thatch!' Elton cried. 'Of course it is. This is the Carlton Club after all,' replied Fry.[13]

Sitting in the Carlton's first-floor Dining Room, resplendent in red wallpaper with Neville Chamberlain's portrait staring down at them, Fry and Elton idly fantasised about going grouse shooting, before coming down to business: Elton offered Fry a role specifically written for him, Lord Melchett in the new series of *Blackadder*. Meanwhile, two tables away, Elton's broad, working-class vowels prompted the ire of their neighbouring diner, who scowled disapprovingly at them: 'the blotched, jowly and furious countenance of the Lord Chancellor, Quintin Hogg, now Lord Hailsham', with a 'mixed expression of outrage, disbelief and reluctant desire to know more'.[14]

Scenes like this began to be played out all across Clubland, as generations with very different values clashed. However, with the 1990s and 2000s seeing many clubs returning to profitability, there was a growing realisation that this sort of diversification of members of different ages, unheard of for decades, was actually essential to the survival of clubs.

There is another side to some clubs, old and new, which has made them even more of a flourishing *demi-monde* in recent years: espionage. There has never been a time when clubs have *not* attracted a range of spies, foreign and domestic; one thinks of Guy Burgess at the Reform Club in the 1950s, prior to his defection to the Soviet Union. Some clubs, most obviously the Travellers, with its many diplomatic members, have such an accepted proportion of members involved in diplomacy that they have their own informal etiquette for accommodating members involved in the intelligence community. But in recent years, London's 'hidden economy' around libel tourism, wealth concealment, money laundering, business intelligence and mercenaries – usually hidden behind the brass-plate respectability of Mayfair offices – has made it a magnet for oligarchs and spies from a range of countries, particularly China and Russia.[15] Against this backdrop, clubs, with their combination of glamour, secrecy and powerful connections, have been impossible to resist for those involved in espionage, whether as full-time agents, or simply as 'compromised' intelligence assets who may share the odd scrap of gossip or insight over a heavy meal. I should know; I was once the target of an explicit approach to spy for the Chinese government, casually dropped into conversation over lunch at a leading London club (not my own), and backed up by the offer of some lucrative financial inducements, and some all-expenses-paid junkets to Hong Kong. I politely declined, and ensured that the treasonable approach was promptly shared with the proper authorities. Clubs are perfectly laid out for such conversations to happen on the premises, whether in the dining room, the bar, or out on a smoking terrace. Several clubs, old and new, face persistent and ongoing problems with members and guests who are plainly regarded as spies, whether directly state-sponsored, or outsourced via private firms. Because of the standard of evidence required for remedial action, it is rare that any is taken by committees.

Clubs have a tendency to self-congratulation, and a number of the established clubs will swear blind that their recent revival was the product of careful management, and a vindication of long-standing rules. In many cases, however, large-scale social change was something which happened to them, rather than at their instigation – and club committees were often downright resistant to change.

As anyone who has been near a club committee can testify, the default mode is inertia. This has loomed large over the twentieth-century stagnation of Clubland, and nowhere is it more apparent than in the slow pace of men-only clubs admitting women. The root cause – beyond wider cultural factors ranging from an innate mild conservatism of outlook to outright bigotry – is the way most club rules are structured. For a major change such as a men-only club admitting women, it invariably comes under the standard clause of nineteenth-century club rules, that the change requires at least 60 per cent (and in some cases, anything from 67 to 75 per cent) assent of all member present and voting at an Annual General Meeting. This can make necessary change nigh-on impossible to enact, even when the Committee and management who balance the books can see the inevitable necessity of a reform, and even when over half of members favour the change.

This phenomenon can be seen at play in how successive clubs voted to admit women (or didn't). The closure of so many clubs, having also disproportionately hit the women's clubs, only increased the pressure on men's clubs to consider admitting women. While this had been the case since at least the 1930s, the growing financial pressures on traditional men's clubs led to increased desperation to recruit members. The very first of the previously men-only clubs to admit women as full members was the Authors' Club in 1971. This was slightly complicated by the Authors' Club's diminished circumstances. By 1971, it was relegated to subletting a room from the National Liberal Club, which itself continued to refuse women as full members – its first women members had been elected in 1968, but as 'Associate Members', barred from the inner sanctum of the Smoking Room. The NLC therefore forced the Authors' Club to accept that while their male members could use the Smoking Room, their female members could not – a state of affairs which led the Authors' Club to leave in 1976, not to return for another forty years.

The Authors' Club's admission of women was followed by the Alpine Club of South Audley Street, in 1975. They had operated since 1857, and their strong resistance to female mountaineers had prompted the creation of a separate Ladies' Alpine Club exactly fifty years later. By 1975, both clubs were ailing, and the rules were amended to allow a merger. The National Liberal Club followed a year later.

In 1980, the Reform Club followed, in having a majority of members vote in a ballot for the admission of women, by a ratio of two-to-one. But the matter was referred to that year's Annual General Meeting, which vetoed the measure. Only extreme diplomacy resulted in the measure going ahead the following year.[16]

The Oxford and Cambridge Club followed in 1996, but only after years of a concerted campaign, including a narrowly missed

AGM vote in 1995. A majority of members voted to admit women, but the Club fell back on the 'inertia rule' requiring two-thirds support, to block the measure. A wave of protest resignations was led by the eminent psephologist Dr David Butler, a member for the previous forty-three years, who used his platform as a columnist for *The Times* to publicise his resignation by securing publication of his letter in the newspaper, arguing:

> One does not lightly give up association with so comfortable and civilised an institution, but the action – or inaction – of the club committee has made it impossible for a self-respecting Oxford don to remain involved with a body that remains so flagrantly impervious to the will of its members or the norms of contemporary British society . . . In 1995 it no longer seems civilised to remain a member of an institution in which the responsible general committee seems determined to retain every existing barrier to the equal treatment of women.[17]

A couple of weeks later, Butler expressed astonishment at how his 'open letter from an unimportant don resigning from a relatively unimportant institution' had 'thrust upon me a strange, if very transitory, prominence . . . simply because I ventured to say publicly that, even to a moderate, middle-of-the-road character, it was distasteful to continue association' with a club 'which excluded almost half the members of those universities'.[18] The action finally shamed the Club into pushing through the admission of women a year after the botched AGM vote.[19]

The Carlton Club's ongoing political role (it still has a Political Committee which is a major donor to the Conservative Party, as well as hosting other Tory donor groups such as the United and Cecil Club, and the Leader's Group)[20] means that it was subject to more public pressure than most men-only clubs. For a number of MPs and peers who were members, 'How can you justify major decisions being taken in a men-only club?' continued to be an oft-posed question. Already, the ban on women became more incongruous when Margaret Thatcher became the Conservatives' first female leader in 1975, and was promptly elected to the customary Honorary Membership of the Carlton offered to all Tory leaders – yet the Club continued to exclude other women as full members. In 1998, matters came to a head when Conservative leader William Hague gave his backing to an attempt to admit women. While the vote passed at the 19 May 1998 AGM by 108 votes to 92, it still fell short of the 67 per cent threshold.[21] Hague tried again in 2000 at an Extraordinary General Meeting on an even higher turnout, and the motion was again carried by 289 to 166 votes – 63.5 per cent in favour, but still short of the 67 per cent needed.[22] The matter rumbled on when Hague's successor as Tory leader, Iain Duncan Smith, became the first Conservative leader in the Carlton's history to refuse an Honorary Membership when he was elected in 2001 (although he tended not to mention that he remained a member of the men-only Beefsteak Club).[23] Michael Howard, the following Tory leader, was already a member of the Carlton; but his successor David Cameron, elected Tory leader in 2005, was not.

Paradoxically, David Cameron was something of a pseudo-aristocratic throwback to the shire Tories of the 1950s (though he was only a *second*-generation Old Etonian, snobs would sniff), and was very attached to his membership of White's, where his father had been Chairman, and which Cameron Junior continued to frequent while he was Leader of the Opposition. For the first few years of his Tory leadership, Cameron attempted to ignore the incongruity of posing as a dynamic exemplar of the new touchy-feely, 'green' liberal Toryism while unwinding in the High Temple of reactionary aristocratic Toryism, which not only refused to admit women members, but even refused women visitors as well. (To this date, after the death of Elisabetta Bianco, the only women to have set foot in the Club are Queen Elizabeth II, several servants and staff, and a pair of pranksters who bluffed their way in as part of a 2018 stunt – Gemma Perlin got as far as the Porter's Lodge after trying to be smuggled in in a large trunk, and Jess-Luisa Flynn smuggled her way into the Coffee Room by cross-dressing as a male construction worker.)[24] In particular, Cameron followed Iain Duncan Smith in refusing Honorary Life Membership of the Carlton Club, citing their non-admission of women. Eventually, the Carlton finally admitted women as full members in 2008, with long-standing MP Ann Widdecombe becoming the first woman elected. Meanwhile, in 2009, after several years of fielding questions about his White's membership, Cameron resigned from White's, letting it be known that it was in disgust at their being a men-only club. Perhaps, after two decades of membership, he had never noticed before.

Fast-forward to 2017, less than a year after his resignation as prime minister, and to nobody's great surprise it emerged that on leaving office, Cameron had promptly rejoined White's.

Obstruction of women members was most recently seen in the East India Club. After years of debating the issue, they held an informal straw poll in June 2021, which showed 68 per cent support for admitting women as members. They proceeded that November with an Extraordinary General Meeting, where 73 per cent of members voted to admit women. However, as the rules stipulated that a 75 per cent threshold was needed for a rule change, the move was still vetoed, and at the time of writing women remain excluded from membership.[25]

The Travellers Club remains far more avowedly opposed to admitting women – an informal email poll conducted by its

Chairman Anthony Layden in 2014 found that members backed the continued exclusion of women by 114 votes to 76. Layden found himself being attacked by members for even asking the question in the first place, as he was told, 'it was wrong even to consult members on the question', and it was opined by another member, 'I consider the consultation as unnecessary as the concept is undesirable. It is divisive, poorly-timed, and unsettling.'[26] The same stock excuses continue – that it would mean installing women's lavatories for which the funds simply could not possibly be found, and that there is no demand for women to join – perhaps, it offered full and equitable membership, women will not want it', sniffed Richard Hough of the Garrick Club in 1986.[27]

These obstructionist arguments sound all too familiar. While my own club, the National Liberal, admitted women as members forty years earlier, exactly the same arguments were being aired in the 2010s in a rearguard action to try and prevent any relaxation of the dress code – a dress code that had only been imposed in 1979, without any vote of the members, by the small reactionary ruling clique that had overseen the George de Chabris scandal of the seventies and who were desperate to show progress towards respectability. Typical assertions would be: 'This has all been gone into before' (it hadn't); 'This was all looked at very recently' (if one accepted 'recently' meant a stitched-up review held fifteen years earlier); and of course, the old favourite, 'The matter has been settled for good, and that's that, so it can serve no purpose reigniting such a divisive matter.' In reality, what usually lurked behind such bluster was fear of losing a vote, and so using any amount of procedural chicanery to try and avoid matters ever being put to members.[28]

Returning to Clubland sniping around the admission of women, one of the more explosive cases in recent years has been that of the Garrick Club, where all these arguments were deployed. In many ways, the Garrick Club is a fairly typical example of obstructionism: at the last members' vote on the issue in 2015, a bare majority of 50.5 per cent of members voted for admitting women, but it was still well short of the two-thirds vote required.[29] This followed an earlier 2011 attempt by *Downton Abbey* actor Hugh Bonneville to propose actress Joanna Lumley for the Garrick – Bonneville reckoned that Lumley's status as something of a national treasure would make her hard to turn down, but the Club simply refused to process the application.[30] Matters escalated, however, in 2020 when lingerie entrepreneur Emily Bendell was rejected for membership, and initiated legal proceedings against the Club.[31] Bendell subsequently dropped her lawsuit, however, preferring to back a campaign which saw 100 QCs signing a petition.[32]

The Garrick is far from being the only men-only club remaining in London, but Bendell selected it in part due to its prominence as a centre of political, judicial and media power, especially with its concentration of barristers and judges.[33] (A barrister once confided to me of a case in which it proved very difficult to appoint a neutral judge, as the defendant was a member of the Garrick, and so many judges are also Garrick Club members. In the end, the only way to break the deadlock was to appoint a female judge who had been excluded from Garrick membership.) A flurry of other clubs continue to exclude women to this day: the Beefsteak, Boodle's, Brooks's, Buck's, the East India, the Flyfishers', the Garrick, the Langham, the London Sketch Club, the Portland, Pratt's, the Savage, the Savile, the Travellers, the Turf and White's.

In the background of the various disputes on women's admission was the 2010 Equality Act. Government minister Harriet Harman, in drafting the legislation, confirmed that her original intention had been to outlaw male-only social clubs; but that she saw no way of doing this without also outlawing single-sex sports clubs, and so the final legislation backtracked considerably. However, what it did across Clubland was to outlaw single-sex spaces. Clubs today can exclude women (or men) entirely, but they can no longer allow women to access only part of the building. Clubs like the East India were rapidly bounced into change – the Smoking Room, which was men-only until 2011, suddenly had to admit women guests; while the Ladies' Bar, which members could only enter if accompanied by a female guest, was turned into a mixed-sex bar. The East India Club, with its 5,000 members, had no choice but to comply with the law – they were too big to get away with any breach of the law. Smaller clubs with far fewer members attract much less attention, and a handful (typically outside of London) continue to discreetly flout the law, largely unnoticed.

Men-only clubs have also had to wrangle with more nuanced issues around gender. In 2017, the Savile Club generated interest when an existing member transitioned from a man to a woman, making her the first female member in the Club's history.[34] She was ultimately permitted to stay on, on the grounds that when she had joined she had been a man. While the case made headlines worldwide, it was far from being the first of its kind.[35] Forty-five years earlier, in 1972, renowned travel writer Jan Morris transitioned from James Morris and was a member of the men-only St James's Club on Piccadilly. One of London's more socially conservative clubs, its somewhat flustered Committee was still trying to make sense of transgender issues when the Club went bankrupt in 1978.[36] Morris was, however, excluded from joining Brooks's when the St James's Club membership merged into it. Morris was also expelled from her other club, the Travellers, although a decade later the Travellers Club introduced a system of 'nominated ladies' who became 'Lady Card Holders', whose membership was tied to a proposing male member, and they were allowed to use some rooms unaccompanied, but not two of the Club's principal gathering points, the Smoking Room and the Bar. Jan Morris eventually returned to the Travellers under this somewhat demeaning banner, noting, 'To cap this social reincarnation, I was taken to dinner at the Ladies' end of the Travellers Club dining room, one of my favourite rooms.'[37]

As clubs faced more specialised challenges, they sought to professionalise across the board. For decades, an informal network had existed among Club Secretaries discreetly lunching with one another, and sharing common problems including legal wrangles, members' behaviour and staff recruitment. Over time, this network became formalised in the post-war years, into the Association of London Clubs (ALC), the principal trade body of the major clubs for the last six decades. Almost all the historic London clubs now belong to the ALC (although this has not always been the case), as well as a number of membership organisations that offer some club-like facilities, like the Royal Society of Medicine. Although they would deny it, the ALC effectively operate as a cartel for London clubs. They exchange annual subscription figures, as well as salary figures that are used to benchmark income and expenditure across London's club sector. They also commission joint legal advice on topics of shared interest, such as tax liabilities, and they serve as something of a labour exchange for clubs, advertising posts and discreetly recommending the engagement of former employees in other clubs who are a known quantity.

If this cartel approach to club subscriptions seems overly cynical, it may be preferable to the alternative. Among the newer clubs, which seldom participate in the ALC, subscriptions remain a closely guarded secret – even from their own members. Without a widely circulated set of rates, the management of these proprietary clubs can be free to name their own price, gouging it up accordingly, depending on the estimated means of each member. Members are thus left irate when a press leak gives their club's subscription as £1,800, wondering why they have been paying £5,000 all these years. Members may not be aware of it, but they can be better off for belonging to an ALC club.

Senior club management has not been the only group seeking to create formal ties across Clubland. The booming contingent of younger members in the historical clubs started to notice that while they were often a minority in their own clubs, they had much in common with the younger members of other clubs. Being younger, they also had fewer excuses and contacts than older members to nose around the grand premises of other clubs. Accordingly, in 2005, a group of twenty-somethings and thirty-somethings led by James Scott of the Carlton Club formed the Inter-Club Younger Members' Group. I have an interest to declare, as one of the founder members of the group, which held one of its first events in the National Liberal Club – not a great success, with hindsight, as an Oktoberfest where the only German feature (apart from some indifferent chipolatas doubling for *Wurst*) was a solitary member wearing an Alpine hat. From this unpromising beginning, however, Inter-Club (as it became known for short) soon grew into a flurry of social events in which each club sought to outdo the other.

The spirit of curiosity which marks Inter-Club is distinctive. On the one hand, it provides a fun way for curious members to peer around rival clubs, and 'see how the other half lives'. For many, it is their first glimpse of another club, and there soon grows a 'Gotta Catch 'Em All' compulsion to collect clubs like trading cards. On the other hand, no one wants to admit that they made a poor choice in joining their current club – they want some level of validation that their own club is by far the nicest, and that everyone else's has something seriously wrong with it. This attitude is all the more perverse, as in the more traditional clubs contacts are everything. Very few people objectively consider all the factors on offer across all clubs before making an informed decision on which club to join; instead, they just join the first club they can get into, where they know a member (or, just as likely, were talked into joining after a drunken dinner where they signed an application form over the cheese and biscuits washed down with a pint of port).

For all its enjoyable parties, I found myself growing bored with Inter-Club after a while, as it very obviously morphed into a young conservatives' dating circle. I have made many abiding long-term friendships through Inter-Club; but a large slice of the members *are* chinless wonders in investment banking or management consultancy in search of a socially 'suitable' spouse, with an abundance of Charleses and Vanessas and Henrys and Felicias.

Behaviour is not a high point of Inter-Club. Members are liable to run riot in the luxurious surroundings of a club which is not their own, where they won't be recognised. At one event I compered, a couple were caught *in flagrante delicto* in an alcove of the Reform Club's main atrium. What upset the Reform Club hosts most of all was that it was not the first time this had happened with Inter-Club.

However, if there is a defence of Inter-Club's high jinks, it is that they are largely victimless crimes. My good friend Tom Whitehead, then an up-and-coming young barrister, was on the National Liberal Club's victorious quiz team in the first Inter-Club quiz, which was hosted by the Carlton Club. In a rush of blood to the head, Whitehead celebrated by making off with a large wooden bust of Benjamin Disraeli from the Carlton bar, somehow concealing the thing under his coat. He woke up in the small hours, heavily hungover, with Disraeli sharing his pillow. He nimbly crept back first thing the next morning, using the jangling milk delivery float as cover to deposit the bust on the club's stone front steps, unharmed. I am told the bust is now glued to its table in the bar, to prevent a repeat of the incident.*

Younger members did not have a monopoly on high jinks. Clubs in general have had their own fair share of scandals in recent years, even though they often go to considerable lengths to cover things up.

During the 2009 MPs' expenses scandal, Conservative MP John Maples drew flak for paying his Royal Automobile Club accommodation bills using his parliamentary expenses.[38] The story was clearly irresistible – an MP billed the taxpayer £100 a night at London's most expensive club, then costing £1,175 a year, plus a £2,600 joining fee. On closer examination, the story was rather more mundane. There was no suggestion Maples had ever billed the taxpayer for either his subscription or his joining fee. Instead, as he was in the middle of moving house, he spent a month billing for an overnight room that was significantly cheaper than most other Westminster hotels.

A more eye-catching scandal involved a botched plot to blackmail cabinet-level minister Robert Halfon. Halfon, who resembles a hard-boiled egg, is not your typical lothario – politicians seldom are – but for six months in 2015 he had gone behind his partner's back to use the East India Club as an inexpensive rendezvous for liaisons with a Conservative Party activist then heading up the party's youth wing. He had also claimed his club bedroom on parliamentary expenses, racking up some £30,000 in costs from 2010 to 2014; although in an admirable display of accounting ethics, he argued that no substantive instances of nookie had occurred on the nights

---

* The following year a member of the National Liberal Club's team, Jonathan Isaby, put a reference to the incident in his *Telegraph* gossip column, along with a tip-off he'd received that with the NLC hosting that year's tournament, the Carlton quiz team intended to steal a Gladstone bust in revenge. The combination of hawk-eyed NLC porters and the sheer weight of the large marble busts proved a deterrent.

that were funded by the taxpayer. Although Halfon initially denied the affair, he eventually admitted to it after he began suspecting a friend of his lover's, a subsequently disgraced campaigns organiser, was planning to photograph the pair emerging from their Clubland trysts, setting up a camera tripod in St James's Square.[39]

The East India Club also made headlines over a staff member in the accounts department who managed to embezzle £500,000 over a five-year period before being noticed.[40] The Club later sued its own bank, over an alleged lack of warnings given. While it was the East India which suffered the ignominy of the headlines, this remains a much wider problem. In truth, endemic secrecy over club finances has made them a haven for malfeasance over the years, and there are few clubs which have not been defrauded by staff or committee members at some point in their long histories. The East India Club merely had the misfortune to have experienced this in the full glare of publicity.

There were other, more improbable ways in which the secrecy of clubs lent itself to fraudsters. Police from the Met's 'Operation Bumblebee' turned up at the Travellers Club between September 1996 and January 1997, producing batches of stolen books worth £185,000, all containing the Club's bookplate. Through a long-standing arrangement, the Club's own librarian had been assisted by part-time librarians from the London Library, who helped curate their valuable collection. It turned out that one of the London Library's associate librarians, Bridget Griffin, who had been hired in 1992 with impeccable credentials, was alleged to have been responsible for the Travellers Club thefts. Griffin had a drug habit, which police say she fed through the sale of rare antiquarian books. She had been diligently removing the corresponding index cards in the library card catalogue, so that during periodic stock-taking it would not be noticeable that anything had gone missing. However, she had left the bookplates in, and so the flooding of the antiquarian book market with Travellers Club books began to arouse suspicion.[41]

Clubs today are in a strange, transitional phase. They have inherited hundreds of years of custom and tradition, often without realising it. They operate a unique business model which can be highly profitable in the short term, but which has the odds stacked against it in the long term. They go through cycles, often without noticing it. There is a stark divide between those clubs which embrace their fusty image, and those which try to be more entrepreneurial (scandalous even), often without realising that they are two sides of the same coin. Across the board, their most treasured asset is their reputation – but how they handle (or mishandle) that can have deep repercussions for whether people want to join or remain in these quirky institutions. Yet as an international, globalised brand, clubs seem to have never been so numerous; and in their spiritual home of London, a wave of 'new' clubs has been on the way up. Those traditional clubs that have adjusted are those which have updated some of their business practices – from event hire to HR – while retaining a strong sense of their core identity.

Epilogue

When I wrote *Club Government* four years ago, I remarked that clubs 'have gradually been marginalised into irrelevance – a venue for hire, nothing more, nothing less'.[1] I have now changed my mind.

Originally, I was referring to the way that clubs had gone from being highly significant political headquarters where decisions were made, to mere function rooms for press conferences. What I did not fully take into account was the continued 'soft power' of Clubland's demi-monde.

The Cambridge Analytica scandal of 2018 was a reminder of this. Several operatives of this dubious agency were university acquaintances of mine. Their work often involved flying into cities that were completely unknown to them, when touting for business. Naturally, they often worked out of clubs – whether it was entertaining clients in London clubs, or impressing potential clients with their local reciprocal club when dropping into town, exuding power and discretion. They were not alone. All manner of arms dealers, mercenaries and spies (both state-sponsored and industrial) operate out of private members' clubs today, with Mayfair being a hive of such activity. And the informal government conversations

– Sir Humphrey's 'quiet chats' with civil service colleagues over an after-hours drink in *Yes, Minister* – are alive and well. This does not make clubs endemically shadowy or corrupt; but it does illustrate in the modern world how the privacy which is so central to them is open to abuse.

That privacy has another, deeply appealing side. People can be themselves. Or at least, they *should* be themselves in their club, for there is nothing more unbearable than a room full of cosplaying, strutting peacocks, putting on an act. When clubs have fallen into often terminal decline in the twentieth century, it has been when they have embraced that parody, from dress codes to harrumphing over the iniquity of a wicked world outside.

This was not what clubs looked like when they were successful. In the eighteenth and nineteenth centuries, clubs could be edgy, daring and innovative. Everything we now regard as outdated was state-of-the-art at the time. The buildings were brand new, designed and decorated to the latest fashions. The food and drink were at the cutting edge of what money could buy. Clubhouses were the first buildings in London to have telegraph wires, telephones, gas light, electrical light and passenger lifts. Until the First World War drew clubonomics the first of several hammer blows, clubs were continuously *innovating*. And while individual clubs would scramble for prestige and snobbery, the appetite for clubs was so insatiable that Clubland as a whole grew noticeably more inclusive as the nineteenth century wore on, and clubs grew more diverse, reflecting London as a city. Indeed, it was the privacy of clubs that allowed subcultures to thrive within them, embracing a broad range of different genders, races, religions, proclivities and outlooks within Clubland. By the 1890s, there was at least one club for everyone; whether they wanted to join or not was another matter.

It was after the First World War that clubs started to fossilise. Our image of London clubs is still monopolised by that long, slow decline: empty rooms, ageing members, awful food, and an unfriendly, unsociable atmosphere of hostility permeating. This was what clubs looked like when they were failing. And fail they did, with over 90 per cent of London's historic 400 clubs going bankrupt, typically in the mid-twentieth century. That they have had a rebirth in the last few decades is down to putting this fusty image behind them, and rediscovering what it means to innovate.

Clubs are usually thought of as being enduringly British; and the world over, clubs often emulate British mannerisms and affectations as a sign of quality. Yet clubs were not British in origin, and they have long since outgrown Britain. What the British did was to popularise clubs, and to endow Victorian London as the capital of an empire with clubs at its heart.

Clubs have grown central to how the British do leisure: cricket clubs, football clubs, working men's clubs, gyms, public libraries, even sex clubs; all had their roots in the business model of a private members' club. To this day, some are still run directly as private members' clubs. People can quite literally work, rest and play in a club environment – the semi-official status of a club also lends itself to a blurring of lines, with much work undertaken within them when it needs to be of an informal, or discreet character. And the very setting of a club carries with it its own rules, norms and customs that regulate behaviour.

Perversely, despite not being particularly cost effective for the clubs themselves or their members, these establishments endure; or at least *some* of them endure. The turnover continues to be relatively high, among old and new clubs alike; but where there is affection, and where there is a strong, almost irrational tie to the *culture* of a particular club, there is a glimmer of hope that it will survive the harsh, long-term trends of clubonomics.

In recent years, clubs have globalised into brands, both as historic individual clubs with grand reputations, and with modern international chains of new clubs, like Home House and Soho House. Large chains offer economies of scale, but they also come with higher risks around borrowing and exposure – one unsuccessful club can be a drain on the rest of the chain. There is also the 'danger zone' of falling somewhere between old and new clubs. It is one thing to be an established, historic clubs with its own well-defined identity and traditions; or to be a buzzing, vibrant new club reinventing the club model. But between the first three years of a new club being 'the latest thing', and the roughly fifty-year mark before a club starts to be regarded as an institution, it is neither – just another business, struggling to trade.

What is the future for clubs? Most books that have asked this question tended to come up with gloomy answers. I am not so pessimistic. The British-style club exported around the world is very distinctive in its form. Yet throughout the ages worldwide, people have needed to come together for regular social contact with a group of friends, from the Roman-era bathhouse to the modern-day Mumbai bar. People will invariably invent *something* not so far removed from a club, because it meets a very human social need. And that is why clubs (or club-like organisations) are likely to endure in some form. For all their shocks, scandals, disappointments, secrets and affectations, they are supremely human.

Acknowledgements

I should firstly like to reiterate my thanks to everyone who was thanked in my last book, *Club Government* – I would not have been able to write this book if I had not spent the last twelve years researching club history, building on the knowledge from that last project, and increasingly living a very large share of my life in clubs. It has often enabled me to gain a unique 'insider' perspective – and for that I thank my fellow club members – even if, as a Swiss immigrant for whom English is not his first language, I have never tried to forget something of the sense of being an 'outsider' in this strange world.

I would like to thank for permission to quote Jennie De Protani at the Athenaeum Club archives; the London Metropolitan Archives holding the archives of Brooks's, the Carlton Club and the Junior Carlton Club, for whom I must thank Lord Lexden; Charles Gillett at the National Liberal Club archive; and Simon Blundell at the Reform Club.

While I had planned a version of this book as long ago as 2013, first sketching out the ideas on the back of an envelope on a flight home from Athens, the project would never have got off the ground without my superb agent, Tom Cull, whose wise advice and relentless energy have made it possible. Nor would it have happened without the confidence of Duncan Proudfoot at Little, Brown, who commissioned it after seeing it had the potential to be something very different from the more conventionally 'safe', self-congratulatory Clubland histories. And Zoe Bohm, Richard Collins, Ben McConnell, Nicole Patterson, Rebecca Sheppard and the whole team at Little, Brown deserve huge thanks for steering the project through to completion.

The book has greatly benefited from suggestions made by Lewis Baston, Luke Blaxill, Judy Brown, Benjamin D. Cohen, Grace Gay, Brendan Mackie, Pavan Malhotra, Amy Milne-Smith, Joe Mordaunt Crook, Brian Staley, Tiva Montalbano, Jonathan Orr-Ewing, Dinyar Patel, Erika Rappaport, Dorab Sopariwala and Peter Urbach. Huge thanks are also owed to Genevieve Jenner, a splendid writer who read the manuscript, and also once spoke some of the truest words ever said about me. ('You judge all architecture by its proximity to scandal.') My flatmate John Harper was not only the source of many late-night discussions, but also endured my somewhat eccentric writing hours with good grace. The late Bryan Magee was also a fountain of inquisitiveness and ideas, encouraging his pet theme of 'suburban biographers'; and as most of the book was written at home in Muswell Hill during the Covid-19 pandemic, surrounded by over a decade's worth of sources and materials acquired, I keenly felt his advice.

I also owe thanks to Mary Fitzgerald, Peter Geoghegan and the team at openDemocracy for their confidence in my journalism, and for providing me with such an understanding and supportive base in the months of write-up. And in my spare time, I owe a great deal to the colleagues, members and friends at the National Liberal Club, so ably led by Tim McNally and Karin Rehacek, where I have served as Librarian since 2013.

ACKNOWLEDGEMENTS

And, weirdly, I have to thank David Attenborough, even though we've never met, and he has no idea who I am – his *The Private Life of Plants* provided the inspiration for the subtitle; to which a certain fondness for the films of Alexander Korda made me only more receptive.

Every effort has been made to track down the various rights holders concerned when material has been reproduced, but if there has been any oversight, please do not hesitate to contact me. As ever, all errors, omissions, and outright howlers remain my own.

Seth Alexander Thévoz
Muswell Hill, London
January 2022

Endnotes

Introduction
1   David Palfreyman, *London's Pall Mall Clubs* (Oxford: privately published, 2019), p. 43.
2   Seth Alexander Thévoz, *Club Government: How the Early Victorian World Was Ruled from London Clubs* (London: I. B. Tauris/Bloomsbury, 2018), p. 1.
3   David Niven, *The Moon's a Balloon* (London: Hamish Hamilton, 1971), p. 207.
4   Diana Kendall, *Members Only: Elite Clubs and the Process of Exclusion* (Lanham, Maryland: Rowland & Littlefield, 2008).

Prologue
1   Donald Sinden, 'Foreword', in Kalman A. Burmin and John Baskett, *Brief Lives: Sitters and Artists in the Garrick Club Collection* (London: Garrick Club, 2003), p. ii.
2   Nimrod Kamer, *The Social Climber's Handbook: A Shameless Guide* (Amsterdam: BIS, 2018), p. 19. An absurdist comic, Kamer has successfully penetrated a range of London clubs, not to mention Donald Trump's Mar-a-Lago.
3   Ibid., p. 19.
4   Arthur Griffiths, *Clubs and Clubmen* (London: Hutchinson, 1907), p. 172.
5   Anthony O'Connor, *Clubland: The Wrong Side of the Right People* (London: Martin Brian & O'Keefe, 1976), p. 12.
6   Griffiths, *Clubs and Clubmen* (1907), p. 210.
7   O'Connor, *Clubland* (1976), p. 35.
8   John Darnton, 'A Blessed Haunted Plot, This England', *New York Times*, 21 April 1994, p. 8.
9   Graham Binns, Hugh Massingberd and Sheila Markham, *A House of the First Class: The Travellers Club and Its Members* (London: Travellers Club, 2003), p. 41; John Martin Robinson, *The Travellers Club: A Bicentennial History, 1819–2019* (Marlborough: Libanus Press-Travellers Club, 2018), p. 183.
10   Ibid., p. 62.
11   O'Connor, *Clubland* (1976), p. 55.

Chapter 1
1   Joseph Hatton, *Club-Land, London and Provincial* (London: Vertue), p. 9.
2   Charles Graves, *Leather Armchairs: The Chivas Regal Book of London Clubs* (London: Cassell, 1963), p. xv.
3   Fern Riddell, *Sex Lessons from History* (London: Hodder & Stoughton, 2021), pp. 68–70.
4   Louis C. Jackson, *The United Service Club and its Founder* (London: Sanders Phillips, 1931), p. 7.

5   W. B. Boulton, *The History of White's, with the Betting Book from 1743 to 1878 and a List of Members from 1736 to 1892*, Vol. I (London: Algernon Bourke, 1892), p. 15.

6   Original rules reproduced in Anthony Lejeune, *White's: The First Three Hundred Years* (London: A&C Black, 1993), pp. 25-6.

7   See the seminal Leonore Davidoff and Catherine Hall, *Family Fortunes: Men and Women of the English Middle Class, 1780-1850* (London: Hutchinson, 1987).

8   Percy Colson, *White's, 1693-1950* (London: Heinemann, 1951), p. 51.

9   Peter Clark, *British Clubs and Societies, 1580-1800* (Oxford: Oxford University Press, 2000), pp. 1-59.

10   Ibid., p. 19.

11   Colson, *White's* (1951), pp. 13-14; Brian Cowan, 'Pasqua Rosée', *Dictionary of National Biography* (2006), https://doi.org/10.1093/ref:odnb/92862.

12   See Godfrey Spence, *The Port Companion: A Connoisseur's Guide* (Hove: Apple, 1997), pp. 18-26; Richard Mayson, *Port and the Douro* (Oxford: Infinite Ideas, 2013), pp. 1-52; John Delaforce, *The Factory House at Oporto: Its Historic Role in the Port Wine Trade* (London: Christie's, 1990), pp. 109-11.

13   Roy Strong, *Feast: A History of Grand Eating* (London: Jonathan Cape, 2002), pp. 262-7.

14   Boulton, *History of White's*, Vol. I (1892), pp. 16-8.

15   Quoted in ibid., pp. 33-4.

16   Ibid., p. 34.

17   Lejeune, *White's* (1993), p. 26.

18   Quoted in William Dalrymple, *The Anarchy: The Relentless Rise of the East India Company* (London: Bloomsbury, 2019), p. 235.

19   I am grateful to Brendan Mackie for having shared with me a draft chapter of his forthcoming PhD thesis at the University of California, Berkeley, on the evolution of English clubs in the eighteenth century.

20   David Hancock, 'The Founding Twenty-Five', in Marcus Binney and David Mann (eds), *Boodle's: Celebrating 250 Years, 1762-2012* (Marlborough: Libanus Press, 2012), pp. 13-22.

21   Roger Fulford, *Boodle's, 1762-1962* (London: Boodle's, 1962), p. 7.

22   John Joliffe, 'The Birth of Brooks's', Philip Ziegler and Desmond Seward (eds), *Brooks's: A Social History* (London: Constable, 1991), p. 25.

Chapter 2

1   Lejeune, *White's* (1993), p. 3.

2   J. H. Plumb, 'The World of Brooks's', in Ziegler and Seward (eds), *Brooks's* (1991), p. 21.

3   Ellen Moers, *The Dandy: Brummell to Beerbohm* (New York: Viking Press, 1960).

4   Lucy Inglis, *Georgian London: Into the Streets* (London: Viking, 2013), p. 109.

5   Plumb, 'World of Brooks's', in Ziegler and Seward (eds), *Brooks's* (1991), p. 21.

6   Joliffe, 'Birth of Brooks's', in Ziegler and Seward (eds), *Brooks's* (1991), p. 25.

7   Inglis, *Georgian London* (2013), p. 109.

8   Griffiths, *Clubs and Clubmen* (1907), pp. 179-80.

9   See Brooks's archive, London Metropolitan Archives. See also Thomas Heneage, 'The Eating Room at the Time of William Brooks', in J. Mordaunt Crook and Charles Sebag-Montefiore (eds), *Brooks's 1764-2014: The Story of a Whig Club* (London: Brooks's, 2013), pp. 82-93.

10   Stephen Potter, 'Confessions of a Clubman', *Holiday*, Vol. 19, No. 4 (April 1956), p. 154.

11   Colson, *White's* (1951), p. 40.

12   Potter, 'Confessions of a Clubman', *Holiday* (1956), p. 154.

13   Cited in Valerie Capdeville, 'Transferring the British Club Model to the American Colonies: Mapping Spaces and Networks of Power (1720-70)', *RSEAA*, XVII-XVIII, 74 (2017), 18. Also cited in Benjamin Mackie, draft Chapter 3 of forthcoming PhD thesis, University of California, Berkeley – I must entirely credit Mackie with bringing this comment to my attention.

ENDNOTES

14 Amy Milne-Smith interview, 'Should men-only private members' clubs still exist?', *Today in Focus Guardian* podcast, 25 September 2020, https://podcasts.apple.com/gb/podcast/should-men-only-private-members-clubs-still-exist/id1440133626?i=1000492445041.

15 *Feeney and Shannon v MacManus* [1937] IR 23, at 31 (Johnstone J), cited in David Ashton and Paul Reid, *Ashton & Reid on Clubs and Associations*, 3rd edn (London: Bloomsbury Professional, 2020), p. 8.

16 See R. C. Rome, *Union Club: An Historical and Descriptive Record* (London: B. T. Batsford, 1948), pp. 1-16.

17 Bernard Darwin, *British Clubs* (London: Collins, 1943), p. 11.

18 Thévoz, *Club Government* (2018), p. 28.

19 Henry S. Eeles and Earl Spencer, *Brooks's, 1764-1964* (London: Country Life, 1964), p. 121; Colson, *White's* (1951), p. 121; Fulford, *Boodle's* (1962), pp. 37, 41.

20 Jackson, *United Service Club* (1931), p. 14.

21 Quoted in ibid., p. 16.

22 Ibid., p. 4.

23 Tom Girtin, *The Abominable Clubman* (London: Hutchinson, 1964), p. 136.

24 An examination of the Gladstone personal papers for the 1840s and 1850s, held by Gladstone's Library, Hawarden, Flintshire, bears this out.

25 P. G. Wodehouse, *Leave It to Psmith* (London: Everyman, 2003 [first pub. 1923]), p. 75.

Chapter 3

1 See the pioneering study of masculinity in London clubs, Amy Milne-Smith, *London Clubland: A Cultural History of Gender and Class in Late-Victorian Britain* (Basingstoke: Palgrave Macmillan, 2011).

2 Boulton, *History of White's*, Vol. I (1892), p. 14.

3 Peter Mandler, 'From Almack's to Willis's: Aristocratic Women and Politics, 1815-1867', in Amanda Vickery (ed.), *Women, Privilege and Power: British Politics, 1750 to the Present* (Stanford, California: Stanford University Press, 2001), p. 159.

4 John Vincent, *The Formation of the Liberal Party 1857-1868* (London: Constable, 1966), p. 19.

5 Daniella Ben-Arie, 'A Ladies' Boodle's in the Eighteenth Century', in Binney and Mann (eds), *Boodle's* (2012), p. 177.

6 Ibid., p. 177.

7 F. H. W. Sheppard (ed.), *Survey of London*: Vols 29 and 30, *St James Westminster*, Part 1 (London, 1960), p. 333

8 Ben-Arie, 'A Ladies' Boodle's', in Binney and Mann (eds), *Boodle's* (London: Libanus Press, 2012), p. 178.

9 T. H. S. Escott, *Club Makers and Club Members* (London: T. F. Unwin, 1914), p. 317.

10 See Daniella Ben-Arie, 'Masquerades and Fetes, in Binney and Mann (eds), *Boodle's* (2012), pp. 65-73.

11 Binns, Massingberd and Markham, *A House of the First Class* (2003), p. 43.

12 Ibid., p. 43.

13 Flora Tristan, *Promenades dans Londres* (Paris: H.-L. Delloye, 1840), pp. 388-90. [Author's own translation.]

14 Edwin A. Ward, *Recollections of a Savage* (London: Herbert Jenkins, 1923), pp. 10-11.

15 George Augustus Sala, *Twice Round the Clock; or, The Hours of the Day and the Night in London* (London: Houlston and Wright, 1859), p. 213.

Chapter 4

1 Jules Verne, *Around the World in 80 Days* (London: Reader's Digest, 2001, first pub. in French, 1873), p. 12.

2   See J. Mordaunt Crook, *The Rise of the Nouveau Riches: Style and Status in Victorian and Edwardian Architecture* (London: John Murray, 1999).

3   Strong, *Feast* (2002), p. 273.

4   Matthew Sweet, *Inventing the Victorians* (London: Faber and Faber, 2001), p. 106.

5   See, for instance, Alexis Soyer, *The Pantropheon; or A History of Food and its Preparation in Ancient Times* (London: Paddington Press, 1977, first pub. 1853).

6   Tristan, *Promenades dans Londres* (1840), pp. 387. [Author's own translation.]

7   The only exceptions are Lord Palmerston's mansion, Cambridge House on Piccadilly, which was the Naval and Military Club for 134 years, but has lain derelict since 1999; and the rear half of the Marquess of Lansdowne's Lansdowne House, chopped in half by the decision to build an additional road into Berkeley Square in 1935, with the surviving half converted into the Lansdowne Club.

8   Michael Wheeler, *The Athenaeum: More Than Just Another London Club* (New Haven, Connecticut: Yale University Press), p. 56.

9   Peter Marsh, 'The Reform Club: Architecture and the Birth of Popular Government', Gresham College lecture, 25 September 2007.

10   Anita O'Brien and Chris Miles, *A Rep into Clubland. Cartoons from Private London Clubs* (London: Cartoon Museum, 2009), p. 7.

11   Quoted in Angus Hawkins, *The Forgotten Prime Minister: The 14th Earl of Derby*, Volume II – *Achievement, 1851–1869* (Oxford: Oxford University Press, 2008), p. 313.

12   Angus Hawkins and John Powell (eds), *The Journal of John Wodehouse, First Earl of Kimberley for 1862–1902* (London: Royal Historical Society, 1997), p. 196.

13   Milne-Smith, *Clubland* (2011), pp. 181–95.

14   Tim Newark, *The In & Out: A History of the Naval and Military Club* (London: Osprey Publishing, 2015), p. 162.

15   David Addison Harsha, *The Most Eminent Orators and Statesmen of Ancient and Modern Times; Containing Sketches of their Lives, Specimens of their Eloquence, and an Estimate of their Genius* (Philadelphia: Porter and Coates, 1857), p. 302.

16   See Angus Hawkins, *Parliament, Party and the Art of Politics in Britain, 1855–59* (Stanford, California: Stanford University Press, 1987); Angus Hawkins, *British Party Politics, 1852–1886* (London: Macmillan, 1998).

17   Joseph Coohill, *Ideas of the Liberal Party: Perceptions, Agendas and Liberal Politics in the House of Commons, 1832–52* (Oxford: Wiley-Blackwell/Parliamentary History Yearbook Trust, 2011), pp. 19–45, 61–76.

18   Thévoz, *Club Government* (2018), pp. 52–4.

19   Charles R. Dodd [later Dod] (ed.) (1842), Autobiography of Five Hundred Members of Parliament; Being a Collection of Letters and Returned Schedules Received by Charles R. Dodd During the First Four Reformed Parliament, viz., from 1832 to December 1842, and Constituting Materials for Compiling the Successive Editions of the Parliamentary Pocket Companion [microfilm] (New Haven, Connecticut: Yale University, James Marshall and Marie-Louise Osborn Collection [copy held at London: History of Parliament Trust]), MS 'Benjamin Disraeli'; Robert Blake, *Disraeli* (London: Eyre & Spottiswoode, 1966), pp. 81–2, 435; A. L. Humphreys, *Crockford's* (London: Hutchinson, 1953), p. 105.

20   Thévoz, *Club Government* (2018), pp. 175–208.

21   See Boyd Hilton, *A Mad, Bad, and Dangerous People? England 1783–1846* (Oxford: Oxford University Press, 2006).

22   Richard Usborne, *Clubland Heroes: A Nostalgic Study of Some Recurrent Characters in the Romantic Fiction of Dornford Yates, John Buchan and Sapper*, rev. 2nd edn (London: Barrie & Jenkins, 1974).

23   MS 'Carlton Club Minute Book, Vol. 3, 1839–1843', 24 May 1842, Carlton Club archive, London Metropolitan Archives, London.

Chapter 5

1   B. T. Hall, *Our Sixty Years* (London: Working Men's Club and Institute Union, 1922), p. 16.
2   David Doughan and Peter Gordon, *Women, Clubs and Associations in Britain* (Abingdon: Routledge, 2006), p. 25.
3   *Club and Institute Union Annual Report, 1874–5* (London: Working Men's Club and Institute Union, 1875), p. 19.
4   John Taylor, *From Self-Help to Glamour: The Working Man's Club, 1860–1972 – History Workshop Pamphlet Number 7* (London: History Workshop Journal, 1973), p. 5.
5   Ibid., p. 35.
6   Ibid., p. 21.
7   See Benedict Anderson, *Imagined Communities: Reflections on the Origin and Spread of Nationalism,* rev. 2nd edn (London: Verso, 2006, first pub. 1983).
8   Doughan and Gordon, *Women, Clubs and Associations* (2006), p. 25.
9   Barry Phelps, *Power and the Party: A History of the Carlton Club, 1832–1892* (London: Macmillan, 1983), p. 52.
10   I am grateful to Luke Blaxill for some pioneering statistical work undertaken in this area, for an academic article we have begun, looking at electoral performance of political parties in constituencies with political clubs in the late Victorian and Edwardian eras.
11   Quoted in Taylor, *Self-Help* (1973), p. 24.
12   See William Haslam Mills, *The Manchester Reform Club 1871–1921* (Manchester: Charles Hobson, 1922).
13   H. J. Hanham, *Elections and Party Management: Politics in the Time of Disraeli and Gladstone* (London: Longmans, 1959), pp. 100–102.
14   'Shaw has evicted the New Reformers', *New York Times*, 24 March 1912, p. 5.
15   Jackson, *United Service Club* (1931), p. 23.
16   George Tremlett, *Clubmen: The History of the Working Men's Club and Institute Union* (London: Secker & Warburg, 1987), pp. 296–7.
17   Rupert Morris, *Tories: From Village Hall to Westminster – A Political Sketch* (Edinburgh: Mainstream, 1991), p. 95.
18   'Swingers Club at Tory HQ', *Evening Chronicle*, 18 March 2007.

Chapter 6

1   I first started using the term 'Clubonomics' when promoting my first book, *Club Government,* and it was the subject of my November 2019 paper to the North American Conference on British Studies in Vancouver.
2   Girtin, *The Abominable Clubman* (1964), p. 102.
3   Potter, 'Confessions of a Clubman', *Holiday* (1956), p. 154.
4   See Gary W. Cox, *The Efficient Secret: The Cabinet and the Development of Political Parties in Victorian England* (Cambridge: Cambridge University Press, 1987).
5   *Hansard, HC Deb 14 June 1853 vol. 128 cc187–188.*
6   Milne-Smith, *London Clubland* (2011), pp. 35–57.
7   Cited in Milne-Smith, *London Clubland* (2011), p. 54.
8   Griffiths, *Clubs and Clubmen* (1907), p. 256.
9   Milne-Smith, *London Clubland* (2011), pp. 52–3.
10   Thévoz, *Club Government* (2018), p. 88; sourced from a study of Reform Club ballot books vols 1–2 (1836–78), Reform Club archive, London.
11   Thévoz, *Club Government* (2018), pp. 37–40; Westminster Reform Club minute book, Reform Club archive, London.
12   Thévoz, *Club Government* (2018), pp. 82–99.
13   Carlton Club candidates' books vols 1–12 (1834–69), London Metropolitan Archive, London; Athenaeum ballot books, Athenaeum Club archive, London.

14 Stephen Potter, *One-Upmanship* (London: Rupert Hart-Davis, 1952), p. 124. I have long followed this advice; and in addition to my 'main' club, belong to a basement speakeasy in Soho charging £5 a year.

15 Potter, 'Confessions of a Clubman', *Holiday* (1956), p. 158.

16 Sir Francis Burnand, *Records and Reminiscences, Personal and General*, Vol. 1 (London: Methuen, 1904), p. 385.

17 Griffiths, *Clubs and Clubmen* (1907), p. 194.

18 I must credit Jonathan Orr-Ewing, former Secretary of the Carlton Club, with this observation.

19 Ian Fleming, *Moonraker* (London: Penguin, 2002 [first pub. 1955]), p. 35.

20 Quoted in Boulton, *History of White's*, Vol. I (1892), p. 33.

21 Lee Jackson, *Palaces of Pleasure: From Music Halls to the Seaside to Football, How the Victorians Invented Mass Entertainment* (New Haven, Connecticut: Yale University Press, 2019), p. 139.

22 Flora Russell, *The University Women's Club: Extracts from Fifty Years of Minute Books, 1886–1936* (Eastbourne: Sumter & Day, 1985), p. 15.

23 Griffiths, *Clubs and Clubmen* (1907), p. 176.

24 O'Connor, *Clubland* (1976), p. 37.

25 Griffiths, *Clubs and Clubmen* (1907), pp. 165–7.

26 O'Connor, *Clubland* (1976), p. 36.

27 Griffiths, *Clubs and Clubmen* (1907), p. 174.

28 Ibid., pp. 89–90.

29 Ibid., p. 126.

30 See Robert D. Putnam, *Bowling Alone: The Collapse and Revival of American Community* (New York: Simon & Schuster, 2000).

31 A phrase used by Gladstone to describe London clubs. G. W. E. Russell, *Fifteen Chapters of Autobiography* (London: Thomas Nelson, 1910), p. 78.

32 See Jonathan Clarke, *Early Structural Steel in London Buildings: A Discreet Revolution* (London: English Heritage, 2014).

33 Binns, Massingberd and Markham, *A House of the First Class* (2003), p. 38.

34 Griffiths, *Clubs and Clubmen* (1907), p. 189.

35 Conversation with Brian Staley, 21 April 2015.

36 Marrisa Joseph, 'Members Only: The Victorian Gentlemen's Club as a Space for Doing Business 1843-1900', *Management & Organizational History*, 14:2 (2019), pp. 123–47.

37 See David McKie, *Jabez: The Rise and Fall of a Victorian Scoundrel* (London: Atlantic Books, 2004).

Chapter 7

1 Anthony Sampson, 'Clubs', in Anthony Sampson, *Anatomy of Britain* (London: Hodder & Stoughton, 1962), p. 66.

2 I am indebted to Mr Malhotra, as much for his gracious hospitality in India as for outlining this argument, based on his research for Purshottam Bhageria and Pavan Malhotra, *Elite Clubs of India* (New Delhi: Bhageria Foundation, 2005).

3 Dalrymple, *The Anarchy* (2019), p. xxxi.

4 See W. G. C. Frith, *The Royal Calcutta Turf Club* (Calcutta: Royal Calcutta Turf Club, 1976); R. I. MacAlpine and H. R. Panckridge, *The Bengal Club, 1827–1970* (Calcutta: Bengal Club, 1970); Malabika Sarkar, *The Bengal Club in History* (Kolkata: Bengal Club, 2006); Bhageria and Malhotra, *Elite Clubs of India* (2005), pp. 11–58.

5 J. Humphrey, Azhar Karim and Shuja Baig, *Sind Club, 1871–2016* (Karachi: Sind Club, 2016).

6 See Anonymous, *The Trees of Tollygunge Club* (Calcutta: Tollygunge Club, 1946); Pradip Das, *The Tollygunge Club Since 1895* (Kolkata: Tollygunge Club, 2008); Narendra Kumar Nayak (ed.), *Calcutta 200 Years: A Tollygunge Club Perspective* (Calcutta: Tollygunge Club, 1981).

7 See S. Muthiah, *The Spirit of Chepauk: The MCC Story – A 150-Year Sporting Tradition* (Chennai: Eastwest Books (Madras) Pvt. Ltd., 1998); S. Muthiah, *The Ace of Clubs: The Story of the Madras Club* (Chennai: Madras Club, 2002); S. Muthiah, *Down By the Adyar: The Story of the Madras Boat Club* (Chennai: Madras Boat Club, 2010); Bhageria and Malhotra, *Elite Clubs of India* (2005), pp. 99–126.

8 Bhageria and Malhotra, *Elite Clubs of India* (2005), pp. 127–54.

9 Ibid., pp. 267–302.

10 See Gulshan Rai, *The History of the Royal Bombay Yacht Club: From the Founding of the Empire's Most Majestic Club in the East in 1846 to the Present Day* (Mumbai: Royal Bombay Yacht Club, 2010).

11 See Bhageria and Malhotra, *Elite Clubs of India* (2005), pp. 335–58; Mushirul Hasan and Dinyar Patel (eds), *From Ghalib's Dilli to Lutyens' New Delhi* (Oxford: Oxford University Press, 2013).

12 Ashwajit Singh (ed.), *Delhi Gymkhana Club Ltd.: Centenary Souvenir* (New Delhi: Delhi Gymkhana Club, 2015), p. 6.

13 I am grateful to the Amateur Dramatic Club of Simla for access to their archive.

14 See Dilip Kumar Bose et al., *One Hundred Years of Calcutta Club, 1907–2007*, 2 vols (Kolkata: Calcutta Club, 2007); Dilip Kumar Saha et al., *The Centenary Elite: A Special Number to Mark the Centenary of the Calcutta Club* (Kolkata: Calcutta Club, 2007); Bhageria and Malhotra, *Elite Clubs of India* (2005), pp. 115–18, 139–42.

15 I am grateful to Dorab Sopariwala for making this point while hosting me at his own club in Mumbai.

16 See Vaudine England, *Kindred Spirits: A History of the Hong Kong Club* (Hong Kong: Hong Kong Club, 2016); Nigel Dunne, *Club: The Story of the Hong Kong Football Club, 1886–1986* (Hong Kong: Hong Kong Football Club, 1985).

17 See Jeff Nicholas, *Behind the Streets of Adelaide*, 3 vols (Adelaide: Torrens Press, 2016).

18 See Paul de Serville, *The Australian Club, Melbourne, 1878–1998* (Melbourne: Australian Club, 1998); Paul de Serville, *Athenaeum Club, Melbourne: A New History of the Early Years, 1868–1918* (Melbourne: Athenaeum Club, 2013); Paul de Serville, *Melbourne Club: A Social History, 1838–1918* (Melbourne: Melbourne Club, 2017); David M. Dow, *Melbourne Savages: A History of the First Fifty Years of the Melbourne Savage Club* (Melbourne: Melbourne Savage Club, 1947); Joseph Johnson, *Laughter and the Love of Friends: A History of the Melbourne Savage Club 1894–1994 and a History of the Yorick Club 1868–1966* (Melbourne: Melbourne Savage Club, 1994); F. F. Knight, *History of the Australian Club, Melbourne*, Vol. II: *1932–1965* (Melbourne: Australian Club, 1978); Ronald McNicoll, *Number 36 Collins Street: Melbourne Club, 1838–1988* (Sydney: Allen & Unwin/Haynes, 1988); John Pacini, *Windows on Collins Street: A History of the Athenaeum Club, Melbourne* (Melbourne: Athenaeum Club, 1991).

19 See Colin Black, *Sable: The Story of the Salisbury Club* (Salisbury: Salisbury Club, 1980); C. G. Botha, *The Civil Service Club, 1858–1938* (Cape Town: Civil Service Club, 1939); Louis Changuion, *The Club with a Capacity for Survival: A Centenary Album of the Highlights in the History of the Pietersburg Club, 1902–2002* (Pietersburg: Pietersburg Club, 2002); René de Villiers and S. Brooke-Norris, *The Story of the Rand Club* (Johannesburg: Rand Club, 1976); Peter Gibbs, *The Bulawayo Club* (Bulawayo: Bulawayo Club, 1970); A. I. Little, *History of the City Club, Cape Town, 1878–1938* (Cape Town: City Club, 1938); J. M. Osborne et al., *The Rand Club, 1887–1957* (Cape Town: Cape Times Ltd, 1957); W. E. Ranby, *The City Club, Cape Town: A Supplementary History to 1955* (Cape Town: Galvin & Sales, 1955); I. F. Sander, *Rand Club: Centenary Album, 1887–1987* (Johannesburg: Rand Club, 1987).

20 'History' handout collected from the Clube Tennis de Gaspar Dias, Goa, India.

21 Barry Millington, *Wagner* (London: J. M. Dent, 1985), p. 69.

22   See Yves de Clercq, *Cercle Royal La Concorde, 1809-2009* (Paris: Cercle Royal La Concorde, 2009); Christiane de Nicolay-Maery, *The Travellers Club: A Private Visit of the Hôtel Païva* (Paris: Travellers Club, 2012); Maria Felix Frazao (ed.), *Le Cercle de l'Union Interalliée: Un siècle dans l'histoire* (Paris: Cherche Midi, 2017).

Chapter 8

1   Rome, *Union Club* (1948), pp. 9–12.
2   Michael Jolles, *Jews and the Carlton Club; with Notes on Benjamin Disraeli, Henri Louis Bischoffsheim and Saul Isaac* (London: Jolles Publications, 2002), pp. 8–20.
3   Boulton, *History of White's*, Vol. 1 (1892), pp. 165–6.
4   Denys Forrest, *Foursome in St. James's: The Story of the East India, Devonshire, Sports and Public Schools Club* (London: East India Club, 1982), p. 57.
5   Mira Matikkala, 'William Dibgy and the Indian Question', *Journal of Liberal History*, 58 (Spring 2008), pp. 12–21.
6   Quoted in Antoinette Burton, 'Tongues Untied: Lord Salisbury's "Black Man" and the Boundaries of Imperial Democracy', *Comparative Studies in Society and History* 18.3 (July 2000), p. 634. See also Anonymous, *Lord Salisbury's 'Black Man'* (Lucknow: G. P. Varma, 1889); Dinyar Patel, *Naoroji: Pioneer of Indian Nationalism* (Cambridge, Massachusetts: Harvard University Press, 2020), pp. 123–89.
7   Anonymous, *Lord Salisbury's 'Black Man'* (1889), pp. 52–71.
8   Andrew Halliday (ed.), *The Savage Club Papers*, First Series (London: Tinsley Brothers, 1867), p. x.
9   A full account of the aborted 1911 Johnson–Wells fight can be found in Neil Carter, 'British Boxing's Colour Bar, 1911–48', n.d., https://www.academia.edu/3190661/British_Boxing_s_Colour_Bar_1911_48
10   National Liberal Club archive, London.
11   'The Amateur Championship: A Potted History', *English Amateur Billiards Association*, 14 April 2013, https://www.eaba.co.uk/?p=5885

Chapter 9

1   Erika Diane Rappaport, *Shopping for Pleasure: Women in the Making of London's West End* (Princeton, New Jersey: Princeton University Press, 2000), p. 76.
2   Sam Aldred. *Clubland's Hidden Treasures* (London: privately published, 2020), p. 133.
3   Griffiths, *Clubs and Clubmen* (1907), p. 153.
4   Elizabeth Crawford, *The Women's Suffrage Movement: A Reference Guide, 1866–1928* (London: Routledge, 2000), p. 123.
5   Doughan and Gordon, *Women, Clubs and Associations* (2006), p. 61.
6   Griffiths, *Clubs and Clubmen* (1907), p. 153.
7   A. G. E. Carthew (ed.), *The University Women's Club: Extracts from Fifty Years of Minute Books, 1886–1936* (Eastbourne: Sumfield and Day, 1936, repr. 1985), p. 1.
8   Rappaport, *Shopping for Pleasure* (2000), p. 90; see also Carthew (ed.), *University Women's Club* (1936).
9   See C. J. Schüler, *Writers, Lovers, Soldiers, Spies: A History of the Authors' Club of London, 1891–2016* (London: Authors' Club, 2016).
10   Darwin, *British Clubs* (1943), p. 33.
11   Doughan and Gordon, *Women, Clubs and Associations* (2006), p. 61.
12   Milne-Smith, *Clubland* (2011), p. 163.
13   Griffiths, *Clubs and Clubmen* (1907), pp. 154–5.
14   Doughan and Gordon, *Women, Clubs and Associations* (2006), p. 61.
15   Barbara Black, *A Room of His Own: A Literary-Cultural Study of Victorian Clubland* (Athens, Ohio: Ohio University Press, 2012), pp. 231–2; 'International Association of Lyceum Clubs' website, https://www.lyceumclubs.org/

16 Rappaport, *Shopping for Pleasure* (2000), p. 75.
17 Quoted in ibid., p. 102.
18 *Pall Mall Gazette*, 17 May 1909, p. 10, cited in Rappaport, *Shopping for Pleasure*, p. 102.
19 Rappaport, *Shopping for Pleasure* (2000), p. 105.
20 Hulda Friederichs, 'A Peep at the Pioneer Club', *Young Woman*, 45 (June 1896) p. 302; cited in Black, *A Room of His Own* (2012), p. 229.
21 Griffiths, *Clubs and Clubmen* (1907), p. 154.
22 Rappaport, *Shopping for Pleasure* (2000), p. 98.
23 Anthony Lejeune, *The Gentlemen's Clubs of London* (London: Macdonald and Jane's, 1979), p. 14.
24 Stephen Hoare, *Palaces of Power: The Birth and Evolution of London's Clubland* (Stroud: History Press, 2019), p. 247.
25 Ibid., pp. 160, 244.
26 See Rappaport, *Shopping for Pleasure* (2000).
27 Doughan and Gordon, *Women, Clubs and Associations* (2006); Black, *A Room of His Own* (2012), pp. 219–37.

Chapter 10

1 Tristan, *Promenades dans Londres* (1840), p. 391. [Author's own translation.]
2 Matt Houlbrook, *Queer London: Perils and Pleasures of the Sexual Metropolis, 1918-1957* (Chicago: University of Chicago Press, 2005), p.133.
3 Richard Ellman, *Oscar Wilde* (London: Hamish Hamilton, 1987), pp. 411–12.
4 Milne-Smith, *London Clubland* (2011), p. 71.
5 Peter Ackroyd, *Queer City: Gay London from the Romans to the Present Day* (New York: Abrams Press, 2018), p. 199.
6 Milne-Smith, *London Clubland* (2011), p. 71.
7 Interview with Gifford Skinner, *Gay Life*, 'Being Gay in the Thirties' episode (1981).
8 Ibid.
9 See Tom Driberg. *Ruling Passions: The Autobiography of Tom Driberg* (London: Jonathan Cape, 1977).
10 Rob Baker, 'The Turkish Baths in Jermyn Street, St James', http://www.nickelinthemachine.com/2011/04/the-turkish-baths-in-jermyn-street/
11 Malcolm Shifrin, *Victorian Turkish Baths* (Swindon: Historic England, 2015), p. 293.
12 Houlbrook, *Queer London* (2005), p. 95.
13 Ibid., p. 104.
14 Shifrin, *Victorian Turkish Baths* (2015), p. 287.
15 Houlbrook, *Queer London* (2005), p. 93.
16 Matt Cook, *London and the Culture of Homosexuality, 1885-1914* (Cambridge: Cambridge University Press, 2003), p. 46.
17 George Ives diary, cited in Cook, *Homosexuality* (2003), p. 32.
18 Interview with Gifford Skinner, *Gay Life*, 'Being Gay in the Thirties' episode (1981).
19 Laud Humphries, *Tearoom Trade: Impersonal Sex in Public Places*, 3rd edn (New Brunswick, New Jersey: Aldine Transaction, 1970, 2008). Humphries put the figures at 38 per cent of the men married to women who simultaneously engaged in gay sex.
20 O'Connor, *Clubland* (1976), p. 9.
21 Griffiths, *Clubs and Clubmen* (1907), p. 188; Seth Alexander Thévoz, 'The Diogenes Club: The Case for the Junior Carlton Club', *Baker Street Journal*, 69:3 (Autumn 2019), pp. 6–24.
22 Cook, *London and the Culture of Homosexuality* (2003), p. 30.
23 Rappaport, *Shopping for Pleasure* (2000), p. 105.
24 Dan Wootton, 'Causing a Stir: Women Complain They're Being Flashed by Men at Private Members' Club with the Queen as its Patron', *Sun*, 19 July 2019.

25 Paul Baker, *Fabulosa! The Story of Polari, Britain's Secret Gay Language* (London: Reaktion Books, 2019), pp. 38–72.
26 Ibid., p. 89.
27 'Testimony of Oscar Wilde; The Trials of Oscar Wilde (1895)', *Famous Trials*, n.d. https://famous-trials.com/wilde/342-wildetestimony
28 'Jack Saul', *The Sins of the Cities of the Plain or, The Recollections of a Mary-Ann, with Short Essays on Sodomy and Tribadis*, Vol. 1 (London: privately published, n.d.), pp. 80–81.
29 Ibid., Vol. 1, p. 81.
30 Ibid., Vol. 2, pp. 51–2.
31 Thévoz, *Club Government* (2018), p. 48.
32 Ibid., pp. 175–208.

Chapter 11

1   Dudley Noble (ed.), *R.A.C. Jubilee Year Book, 1897–1947* (London: Royal Automobile Club, 1947), p. 134.
2   Robert J. D. Harding (ed.), *The Savile Club 1914–18 War Memorial* (London: Savile Club, 2018), p. 232.
3   Sir Charles Petrie and Alistair Cooke [Lord Lexden], *The Carlton Club, 1832–2007* (London: Carlton Club, 2007), p. 150.
4   Lejeune, *Gentlemen's Clubs* (1979), p. 201.
5   Ibid.
6   Noble (ed.), *R.A.C. Jubilee* (1947), p. 133.
7   See Erskine Childers, *The Riddle of the Sands* (London: Smith, Elder & Co., 1903).
8   Piers Brendon, *The Motoring Century: The Story of the Royal Automobile Club* (London: Bloomsbury, 1997), p. 180.
9   Ibid., pp. 180–81.
10 Robinson, *Travellers Club* (2018), p. 214.
11 James Wilson, *Noble Savages: The Savage Club and the Great War, 1914–1918* (Folkestone: JH Productions, 2018), p. 14.
12 Arnold White, *The Hidden Hand* (London: G. Richards, 1917), p. 109.
13 Brendon, *Motoring Century* (1997), p. 186.
14 Ibid., p. 188.
15 Noble (ed.), *R.A.C. Jubilee* (1947), p. 134.
16 Strong, *Feast* (2002), p. 285.
17 Ibid., p. 284.
18 Sir Alan Frederick Lascelles to his father, 6 March 1918, quoted in David Mann, 'Boodle's Food', in Marcus Binney and David Mann (eds), *Boodle's: Celebrating 250 Years, 1762–2012* (Marlborough: Libanus Press-Boodle's, 2012), p. 160.
19 Charles Petrie, *Chapters of Life: Intimate Recollections and Reflections on Life, Literature, Politics and Diplomacy* (London: Eyre and Spottiswoode, 1950), p. 198.
20 Ibid., p. 199.
21 Doughan and Gordon, *Women, Clubs and Associations* (2006), p. 19.
22 'Lewis Harcourt', in Matthew Parris, *Great Parliamentary Scandals: Four Centuries of Calumny, Smear and Innuendo* (London: Robson Books, 1995), p. 83–5. Parris attributes the Savile connection to Savile Club member and former Labour MP Leo Abse.
23 Norman Makenzie (ed.), *The Letters of Sidney and Beatrice Webb*: Volume 3, *Pilgrimage 1912–1947* (Cambridge: Cambridge University Press, 1978), p. 363.
24 Nicholas Owen, 'MacDonald's Parties: The Labour Party and the "Aristocratic Embrace"', 1922–31', *Twentieth Century British History*, 18:1 (2007), pp. 1–53.
25 Rappaport, *Shopping for Pleasure*, p. 106.
26 O'Connor, *Clubland* (1976), pp. 9–10.

27 See Usborne, *Clubland Heroes* (1953, rev. 1974).
28 'Bingo Bans the Bomb', in P. G. Wodehouse, *Plum Pie* (London: Everyman, 2007, first pub. 1966), pp. 133–57.
29 William S. Baring-Gould (ed.), *The Annotated Sherlock Holmes*, Vol. I (New York: Clarkson N. Potter, 1967), p. 287n.
30 See, for instance, P. G. Wodehouse, *Heavy Weather* (London: Everyman, 2001, first pub. 1933).
31 The Junior Ganymede Club appears in P. G. Wodehouse, *The Code of the Woosters* (London: Everyman, 2000, first pub. 1938); P. G. Wodehouse, *Much Obliged, Jeeves* (London: Everyman, 2004, first pub. 1971).
32 Wodehouse, *Code of the Woosters* (2000), p. 124.
33 P. G. Wodehouse, *Psmith in the City* (London: Everyman, 2000; first pub. 1909), p. 65.

Chapter 12

1 Niven, *Moon's a Balloon* (1971), pp. 207–8.
2 Ibid., p. 208.
3 David Cannadine, 'Fantasy: Ian Fleming and the Realities of Escapism', in David Cannadine, *In Churchill's Shadow: Confronting the Past in Modern Britain* (Oxford: Oxford University Press, 2003), p. 289.
4 Ibid., p. 290; Gertrude Himmelfarb, *Victorian Minds: A Study of Intellectuals in Crisis* (New York: Alfred A. Knopf, 1968), pp. 271–2.
5 Randolph S. Churchill, *The Fight for the Tory Leadership: A Contemporary Chronicle* (London: Heinemann, 1964), p. 114.
6 Noble (ed.), *R.A.C. Jubilee* (1947), p. 137.
7 Anthony Dixon, *The Army & Navy Club, 1837–2008* (London: Army & Navy Club, 2009), p. 97.
8 Ibid., p. 88.
9 O'Connor, *Clubland* (1976), p. 34.
10 Niven, *Moon's a Balloon* (1971), p. 207.
11 David Mann, 'Boodle's Food', in Binney and Mann (eds), *Boodle's* (2012), p. 161.
12 Niven, *Moon's a Balloon* (1971), p. 229.
13 Victor Ceserani, quoted in Mann, 'Boodle's Food', in Binney and Mann (eds), *Boodle's* (2012), p. 161.
14 O'Connor, *Clubland* (1976), p. 35.
15 Noble (ed.), *R.A.C. Jubilee* (1947), p. 140.
16 Phelps, *Power and the Party* (1983), pp. 73–6.
17 John Boyd-Carpenter letter to Barry Phelps, quoted in ibid., p. 74.
18 The most detailed account was that of Lord Clanwilliam, reproduced in full in Petrie Alistair Cooke, *Carlton Club* (2007), pp. 161–5.
19 Winston S. Churchill, 'The Dream' [short story from 1947, unpublished in Churchill's lifetime], reproduced online at *The Churchill Project: Hillsdale College*, https://winstonchurchill. hillsdale.edu/winston-churchills-dream-1947/
20 Robinson, *Travellers Club* (2018), pp. 258–61.
21 Percy V. Bradshaw, *'Brother Savages and Guests': A History of the Savage Club, 1857–1957* (London: W. H. Allen, 1958), pp. 115–20.
22 Graves, *Leather Armchairs* (1963), p. 140.
23 Dixon, *Army & Navy Club* (2009), pp. 89, 93–4.
24 Noble (ed.), *R.A.C. Jubilee* (1947), pp. 137, 140–41.

Chapter 13

1 William Clarke and Peter Urbach, *History of the Austerity Club* (London: Reform Club, 2004), pp. 1–5.

2 Sean Rayment, *Tales from the Special Forces Club* (London: Collins, 2013), pp. 11–37.
3 See George James Ivey, *The Club Directory: A General Guide or Index to the London & County Clubs, and Those of Scotland, Ireland & British Colonial Possessions, Together with the English Clubs in Europe, the United States & Elsewhere throughout the World* (London: Harrison, 1879).
4 Dixon, *Army & Navy Club* (2009), pp. 115–68.
5 National Liberal Club archive, London.
6 O'Connor, *Clubland* (1976), pp. 10–11.
7 Ibid., p. 12.
8 Sampson, 'Clubs', in Sampson, *Anatomy of Britain* (1962), p. 67.
9 O'Connor, *Clubland* (1976), p. 48.
10 Ibid., pp. 40–42.
11 Graves, *Leather Armchairs* (1963), p. 140.
12 Ibid., p. 9.
13 Lejeune, *White's* (1993), pp. 200–202.
14 See Lejeune, *Gentlemen's Clubs* (1979).
15 Ibid., p. 14.
16 See Anthony Lejeune, *The Gentlemen's Clubs of London* (London: Stacey International, 2012).
17 Sampson, 'Clubs', in Sampson, *Anatomy of Britain* (1962), pp. 66–75.
18 Paul Willetts, *Members Only: The Life and Times of Paul Raymond* (London: Serpent's Tail, 2010), p. 90.
19 Darren Coffield, *Tales from the Colony Room: Soho's Lost Bohemia* (London: Unbound, 2020), p. 6.
20 Ibid., p. 6.
21 Barry Humphries, 'Foreword', in ibid., p. ix.
22 Ibid., p. 8.
23 Barry Humphries, 'Foreword', in ibid., p. xi.
24 Tom Baker, 'A Life in the Day of Tom Baker', *The Times*, colour supplement, 19 March 1978.
25 Coffield, *Tales from the Colony Room* (2020), p. xxv.
26 Ibid., p. xxvii.
27 Willetts, *Members Only* (2010), pp. 96–9.
28 Ibid., p. 96.
29 Ibid., p. 431.

Chapter 14
1 Peter Cook interview, *Saturday Night Clive*, episode 4.8 (1991), dir. Dominic Brigstocke.
2 Ibid.
3 Ibid.
4 See Richard Davenport-Hines, *An English Affair: Sex, Class and Power in the Age of Profumo* (London: HarperCollins, 2013).
5 Peter Cook, *Saturday Night Clive* (1991).
6 *Heroes of Comedy: Peter Cook* (1998), dir. Tom Atkinson.
7 Ronald Bergan, *Beyond the Fringe...And Beyond: A Critical Biography of Alan Bennett, Peter Cook, Jonathan Miller and Dudley Moore* (London: Virgin Books, 1989), p. 42.
8 Dominic Sandbrook, *Never Had It So Good: A History of Britain from Suez to the Beatles* (London: Little, Brown, 2005), p. 542.
9 Humphrey Carpenter, *That Was the Satire That Was: The Satire Boom of the 1960s* (London: Victor Gollancz, 2000), p. 148.
10 Peter Cook, *Saturday Night Clive* (1991).
11 Kenneth Tynan, 'Introduction', in Lenny Bruce, *How to Talk Dirty and Influence People* (London: Peter Owen, 1966), p. 10.
12 Peter Cook, *Saturday Night Clive* (1991).

13 Ibid.
14 Tamsin Blanchard, 'The Photo That Launched a Thousand Poses: Photographing Christine Keeler', *Guardian*, 10 February 2002.
15 Quoted in Carpenter, *That Was the Satire That Was* (2000), p. 179.
16 Ibid., p. 264.
17 Tim Adams, 'The Lady's Not a Tramp', *Guardian*, 18 February 2001.
18 Peter Cook, *Saturday Night Clive* (1991).
19 Bergan, *Beyond the Fringe...* (1989), p. 248.
20 Quoted in Carpenter, *That Was the Satire That Was* (2000), p. 265.
21 Bergan, *Beyond the Fringe...* (1989), p. 246.
22 *A Very Social Democrat: A Portrait of Roy Jenkins* (1996), dir. Michael Cockerell.
23 See John Campbell, *Roy Jenkins: A Well-Rounded Life* (London: Jonathan Cape, 2014).
24 Sampson, 'Clubs', in Sampson, *Anatomy of Britain* (1962), p. 67.
25 Alan Clark, *Tories: Conservatives and the Nation State, 1922–1997* (London: Weidenfeld & Nicolson, 1997), illus. 2 facing p. 334.
26 Derek Marks, 'How Will They Choose Mac's Successor?', *Evening Standard*, 18 June 1963.
27 Sampson, 'Clubs', in Sampson, *Anatomy of Britain* (1962), p. 70.
28 Phelps, *Power and the Party* (1983), p. 84.
29 See Richard Hall, *My Life with Tiny: A Biography of Tiny Rowland* (London: Faber and Faber, 1987); Tom Bower, *Tiny Rowland: A Rebel Tycoon* (London: Heinemann, 1993), pp. 50, 62, 64.
30 Graves, *Leather Armchairs* (1963), pp. 180–81; *The Mayfair Set* (1998), dir. Adam Curtis; Damian Whitworth, 'Annabel's Nightclub: The World's Most Exclusive Basement', *The Times*, 21 October 2014.

Chapter 15

1 Phelps, *Power and the Party* (1983), p. 79.
2 *The Mayfair Set*, episode 3, 'Destroy the Technostructure', (1999), dir. Adam Curtis.
3 Terry Lazarus, dealer specialising in vintage gambling chips, explanation of Curzon House Club's fate, 'Curzon House Club Plaques Available', *The Chip Board*, 17 October 1999, archived at http://www.thechipboard.com/archives/archives.pl/bid/302/md/read/id/39441/sbj/curzon-house-club-plaques-available-london-70-s/
4 *American Playboy: The Hugh Hefner Story*, episode 10, 'My Way' (2017), dir. Richard Lopez.
5 O'Connor, *Clubland* (1976), p. 9.
6 *The Mayfair Set*, episode 2, 'Entrepreneur Spelt S.P.I.V.' (1999), dir. Adam Curtis.
7 Private information.
8 Paul Foot, 'National Buggerall Club', *Private Eye*, 438, 29 September 1978, pp. 17–18.
9 'Taken for a Ride', *Panorama* (18 February 1980), dir. Martin Young.
10 Foot, 'National Buggerall Club', *Private Eye* (1978), pp. 17–18.
11 Ibid.
12 Lewis Chester, Magnus Linklater and David May, *Jeremy Thorpe: A Secret Life* (London: Fontana, 1979), pp. 277–80.
13 Alice Patten, *The Groucho Club – Our First Thirty Years* (London: Preface Publishing, 2015), p. 8.
14 Michael Bloch, *Jeremy Thorpe* (London: Little, Brown, 2014), p. 142.
15 James Rattue, *Kissing Your Sister: A History of the Oxford University Liberal Club, 1913–1993* (Umbra 1993), p. 24.
16 See Staley, *My Road from Saigon* (2020).
17 'Taken for a Ride', *Panorama* (1980).
18 'Colour Section', *Private Eye*, 439, 13 October 1978, p. 3.
19 Ibid.
20 'Taken for a Ride', *Panorama* (1980).

21   National Liberal Club archive, National Liberal Club, London.
22   'Taken for a Ride', *Panorama* (1980).
23   Ibid.
24   Chester, Linklater and May, *Jeremy Thorpe* (1979), pp. 277–80.
25   National Liberal Club archive, National Liberal Club, London; 'Taken for a Ride', *Panorama* (1980).
26   Private information.
27   Conversation with Brian Staley, 21 April 2015.
28   Christina Baron, 'Obituary: Philip Watkins', *Liberal Democrat News*, 23 June 1995, p. 6.
29   Foot, 'National Buggerall Club', *Private Eye* (1978), pp. 17–18.
30   Ibid.
31   Conversation with Brian Staley, 21 April 2015; Staley, *My Road from Saigon* (2020).
32   Conversation with Brian Staley, 21 April 2015.
33   Chester, Linklater and May, *Jeremy Thorpe* (1979), p. 280.
34   Jack Wales, *Charlton Park, Bishopsbourne: History of the House, the Land and the People* (Bishopsbourne: privately published, 2016), p. 8.
35   Martin Young, *Opposable Truths* (London: Matador, 2013), pp. 131–4.
36   'Taken for a Ride', *Panorama* (1980).

Chapter 16

1   Phelps, *Power and the Party* (1983), p. 83.
2   'Londoner's Diary: Irish Pomp Fades in Eaton Square', *Evening Standard*, 20 September 1988, p. 6.
3   'Private Worship', *Evening Standard*, 27 March 1984.
4   'Obituary: Colin Merton', *Daily Telegraph*, 16 February 2008.
5   Patten, *Groucho Club* (2015), p. 8.
6   Stephen Fry, *More Fool Me: A Memoir* (London: Penguin/Michael Joseph, 2014), pp. 162–3.
7   See Robert H. Dedman and Debbie DeLoach, *King of Clubs: Grow Rich in More Than Money* (Dallas: Taylor Publishing, 1999), the memoir of the founder and Chairman of ClubCorp.
8   Joy Lo Dico, 'How 5 Hertford Street became the most influential members' club in London', *Evening Standard*, 12 December 2019.
9   Gabriel Pogrund, 'Liz Truss Wants to Lunch, and Only a Tory Donor's Place Will Do', *The Times*, 2 January 2022.
10   Robinson, *Travellers Club* (2018), p. 318.
11   Stephen Fry, *The Fry Chronicles* (London: Penguin/Michael Joseph, 2010), p. 379.
12   Ibid., p. 380.
13   Ibid.
14   Ibid., pp. 381–2.
15   See Catherine Belton, *Putin's People: How the KGB Took Back Russia and Then Took on the West* (London: William Collins, 2020); Luke Harding, *Shadow State: Murder, Mayhem and Russia's Remaking of the West* (London: Guardian Faber, 2020).
16   Doughan and Gordon, *Women, Clubs and Associations* (2006), p. 20.
17   *The Times*, 11 January 1995.
18   *The Times*, 25 January 1995, quoted in Michael Crick, *Sultan of Swing: The Life of David Butler* (London: Biteback, 2018), pp. 321–2.
19   Crick, *Sultan of Swing* (2018), p. 321–2.
20   Seth Thévoz, 'Inside the Elite Tory Fundraising Machine', *openDemocracy*, 9 December 2019, https://www.opendemocracy.net/en/dark-money-investigations/inside-elite-tory-fundraising-machine/
21   Doughan and Gordon, *Women, Clubs and Associations* (2006), p. 21.

ENDNOTES

22 'Carlton Club Votes Against Women', *BBC News*, 30 November 2000, http://news.bbc. co.uk/1/hi/uk_politics/1048081.stm
23 Andrew Mcbride, 'Division Two Club', *Daily Telegraph*, 29 December 2001.
24 Gemma Perlin, Jess-Luisa Flynn and Nimrod Kamer, 'Women in White's – Penetrating an All-Male Safe Space', *YouTube*, 27 January 2018, https://www.youtube.com/watch?v=olPstpyHZt4
25 Patrick Kidd, 'Diary: Club Searches for Its Soul', *The Times*, 16 November 2021; Robbie Smith, 'Diary: East India Club's Behind the Times', *Evening Standard*, 24 November 2021.
26 Layden's report to Travellers Club members was subsequently leaked. Anthony Layden, 'Chairman Anthony Layden's Report to Travellers Club Members', *Evening Standard*, 9 April 2014.
27 Doughan and Gordon, *Women, Clubs and Associations in Britain* (2006), p. 17.
28 When the NLC eventually put its dress code to a vote in 2019, members voted by 80 votes to 19 for permanent relaxation.
29 Amelia Gentleman, 'Garrick Club Votes to Continue with Ban on Female Members', *Guardian*, 6 July 2015.
30 'The Garrick is No Match for Joanna Lumley', *Evening Standard*, 25 July 2011.
31 Gabriella Swerling, 'Garrick Club Faces Legal Fight from Female Lingerie Tycoon Over 'Sexist' Male-Only Policy', *Telegraph*, 8 September 2020.
32 Amelia Gentleman, 'Over 100 QCs Sign Petition for the Garrick Club to Admit Women', *Guardian*, 1 December 2020.
33 Conversation with Emily Bendell, 30 September 2020.
34 Abe Hawken, 'Mayfair's Savile Club Bends 150-Year-Old "Men Only" Rule to Allow a Transgender Member to Stay on After a Sex Change to a Woman (But Don't Get Your Hopes Up Ladies, it is a One Off Only)', *Daily Mail*, 5 September 2017.
35 Glynda Alves, 'Gender Bender! When London's Savile Club Bent its 150-Year-Old Rule', *Economic Times of India*, 12 December 2017.
36 O'Connor, *Clubland* (1976), p. 9.
37 Quoted in Doughan and Gordon, *Women, Clubs and Associations* (2006), p. 19.
38 'The Daily Telegraph: The Complete Expenses Files' supplement, *Daily Telegraph*, 20 June 2009, p. 43.
39 Simon Walter, 'Cabinet Minister in Sex Blackmail Plot: Politician confesses to affair after Cameron aide is accused of scheme to film trysts', *Daily Mail*, 15 November 2015; Kate Allen, 'The key figures in the Conservative youth party scandal', *Financial Times*, 29 November 2015.
40 Rashid Razaq, 'Worker "Stole £500,000 from East India Club"', *Evening Standard*, 24 February 2014.
41 Robinson, *Travellers Club* (2018), pp. 326-7.

Epilogue
1 Thévoz, *Club Government* (2018), pp. 1-2.

Bibliography

More so than most topics, the discretion around clubs lends some ambiguity around which print sources are primary, and which are secondary.

Primary sources

Manuscript collections

Athenaeum Club, London
Athenaeum Club archive.

Bodleian Library, Oxford, Oxon
National Club MSS.

Gladstone's Library, Hawarden, Flintshire
Glynne-Gladstone MSS.

History of Parliament Trust, London
Charles R. Dodd [later Dod] (ed.) (1842), *Autobiography of Five Hundred Members of Parliament; Being a Collection of Letters and Returned Schedules Received by Charles R. Dodd During the First Four Reformed Parliament, viz., from 1832 to December 1842, and Constituting Materials for Compiling the Successive Editions of the Parliamentary Pocket Companion* [microfilm] (New Haven, Connecticut: Yale University, James Marshall and Marie-Louise Osborn Collection [copy held at London: History of Parliament Trust]).

London Metropolitan Archive, London
Brooks's archive.
Carlton Club archive.
Junior Carlton Club archive.

National Archives, Kew, London
CREST St James's planning records.

National Liberal Club, London
National Liberal Club archive.

Reform Club, London
Parthenon Club minute book.
Reform Club archive.
Westminster Reform Club minute book.

Amateur Dramatic Club, Shimla, India
Amateur Dramatic Club archive.

Newspapers and journals
Age.
Blackwood's Magazine.
Club and Institute Union Annual Reports.
Daily Mail.
Daily Telegraph.
Economic Times of India.
Evening Chronicle.
Evening Standard.
Figaro in London.
Financial Times.
Hansard, House of Commons debates.
Hansard, House of Lords debates.
John Bull.
Judy.
Liberal Democrat News.
Liverpool Mercury.

Illustrated London News.
Morning Chronicle.
Morning Post.
News and Sunday Herald.
New York Times.
Pall Mall Gazette.
Penny Illustrated Paper.
Private Eye.
Punch.
Satirist, and the Censor of the Time.
Saturday Review.
Sunday Times.
Sun.
The Times.
Vanity Fair.
Young Woman.

Memoirs, diaries and autobiography
Anonymous, *Lord Salisbury's 'Black Man'* (Lucknow: G. P. Varma, 1889).
David Addison Harsha, *The Most Eminent Orators and Statesmen of Ancient and Modern Times; Containing Sketches of their Lives, Specimens of their Eloquence, and an Estimate of their Genius* (Philadelphia: Porter and Coates, 1857).
Sir Francis Burnand, *Records and Reminiscences, Personal and General*, 2 vols (London: Methuen, 1904).
Robert H. Dedman and Debbie DeLoach, *King of Clubs: Grow Rich in More Than Money* (Dallas: Taylor Publishing, 1999).
Tom Driberg. *Ruling Passions: The Autobiography of Tom Driberg* (London: Jonathan Cape, 1977).
Stephen Fry, *The Fry Chronicles* (London: Penguin/Michael Joseph, 2010).
—, *More Fool Me: A Memoir* (London: Penguin/Michael Joseph, 2014).
David Niven, *The Moon's a Balloon* (London: Hamish Hamilton, 1971).
Charles Petrie, *Chapters of Life: Intimate Recollections and Reflections on Life, Literature, Politics and Diplomacy* (London: Eyre and Spottiswoode, 1950).

Bernard Pool (ed.), *The Croker Papers, 1808–1857* (London: B. T. Batsford, 1967).

G. W. E. Russell, *Fifteen Chapters of Autobiography* (London: Thomas Nelson, 1910).

George Augustus Sala, *Twice Round the Clock; or, The Hours of the Day and the Night in London* (London: Houlston and Wright, 1859).

Alexis Soyer, *The Pantropheon; or A History of Food and its Preparation in Ancient Times* (London: Paddington Press, 1977, first pub. 1853).

Brian Staley, *My Road to Saigon* (Canterbury: Conrad Press, 2020).

Lytton Strachey and Roger Fulford (eds), *The Greville Memoirs*, 8 vols (London: Macmillan, 1938).

Flora Tristan, *Promenades dans Londres* (Paris: H. L. Delloye, 1040).

Fiction

William S. Baring-Gould (ed.), Arthur Conan Doyle, *The Annotated Sherlock Holmes*, 2 vols (New York: Clarkson N. Potter, 1967).

Erskine Childers, *The Riddle of the Sands* (London: Smith, Elder & Co., 1903).

Ian Fleming, *Moonraker* (London: Penguin, 2002 [first pub. 1955]).

'Jack Saul', *The Sins of the Cities of the Plain or, The Recollections of a Mary-Ann, with Short Essays on Sodomy and Tribadis* (London: privately published, n.d.).

Jules Verne, *Around the World in 80 Days* (London: Reader's Digest, 2001, first pub. in French, 1873).

P. G. Wodehouse, *Psmith in the City* (London: Everyman, 2000; first pub. 1909).

—, *Leave It to Psmith* (London: Everyman, 2003 [first pub. 1923]).

—, *Heavy Weather* (London: Everyman, 2001, first pub. 1933).

—, *The Code of the Woosters* (London: Everyman, 2000, first pub. 1938).

—, *Plum Pie* (London: Everyman, 2007, first pub. 1966).

—, *Much Obliged, Jeeves* (London: Everyman, 2004, first pub. 1971).

Secondary sources

General club histories

Robert J. Allen, *The Clubs of Augustan London* (Cambridge, Massachusetts: Harvard University Press, 1933).

Sam Aldred, *Clubland's Hidden Treasures* (London: privately published, 2020).

Anonymous, *Echoes from the Clubs: A Record of Political Topics and Social Amenities* – Vol. I, *May–October 1867* (London: privately published, 1867).

—, *Echoes from the Clubs: A Record of Political Topics and Social Amenities* – Vol. II, *November 1867–April 1868* (London: privately published, 1868).

—, *Echoes from the Clubs: A Record of Political Topics and Social Amenities* – Vol. III, *May–December 1868* (London: privately published, 1868).

Anonymous, *Your Club* (London: Whitbread, 1950).

P. Gordon Bamber (ed.), *Clubland* (London: W. Speaight and Sons, 1910).

Barbara Black, *A Room of His Own: A Literary-Cultural Study of Victorian Clubland* (Athens, Ohio: Ohio University Press, 2012).

Valérie Capdeville, *L'Âge d'Or des Clubs Londiniens (1730–1784)* (Paris: Editions Champion, 2008).

Valérie Capdeville and Eric Francalanza (eds), *La sociabilité en France et en Grande-Bretagne au Siècle des Lumières: l'émergence d'un nouveau modèle de société*, Tome III: *Les Espaces de sociabilité* (Paris: Editions Le Manuscrit, 2014).

Peter Clark, *British Clubs and Societies, 1580–1800: The Origins of an Associational World* (Oxford: Oxford University Press, 2000).

Bernard Darwin, *British Clubs* (London: Collins, 1943).

David Doughan and Peter Gordon, *Women, Clubs and Associations in Britain* (London: Routledge, 2006).

T. H. S. Escott, *Club Makers and Club Members* (London: T. F. Unwin, 1914).

Tom Girtin, *The Abominable Clubman* (London: Hutchinson, 1964).

Charles Graves, *Leather Armchairs: The Chivas Regal Book of London Clubs* (London: Cassell, 1963).

Arthur Griffiths, *Clubs and Clubmen* (London: Hutchinson, 1907).

Joseph Hatton, *Club-Land, London and Provincial* (London: J. S. Virtue, 1890).

Stephen Hoare, *Palaces of Power: The Birth and Evolution of London's Clubland* (Stroud: The History Press, 2019).

George James Ivey, *The Club Directory: A General Guide or Index to the London & County Clubs, and Those of Scotland, Ireland & British Colonial Possessions, Together with the English Clubs in Europe, the United States & Elsewhere throughout the World* (London: Harrison, 1879).

—, *Clubs of the World: A General Guide or Index to the London & County Clubs, and Those of Scotland, Wales, Ireland, United Kingdom Yacht Clubs, and British Colonial Possessions, Together with the English & Other Clubs in Europe, the United States & Elsewhere throughout the World*, 2nd edn (London: Harrison, 1880).

Louis Clark Jones, *The Clubs of the Georgian Rakes* (New York: Columbia University Press, 1942).

Diana Kendall, *Members Only: Elite Clubs and the Process of Exclusion* (Lanham, Maryland: Rowland & Littlefield, 2008).

Anthony Lejeune, *The Gentlemen's Clubs of London* (London: Macdonald and Jane's, 1979).

—, *The Gentlemen's Clubs of London* (London: Stacey International, 2012).

Robert Machray, 'Club Life', in Robert Machray, *The Night Side of London* (Philadelphia: J. B. Lippincott, 1902), pp. 60–73.

Charles Marsh and Colin Mackenzie, *The Clubs of London*, 2 vols (London: H. Colburn, 1828).

Robin McDouall, *Clubland Cooking* (London: Phaidon, 1974).

Amy Milne-Smith, *London Clubland: A Cultural History of Gender and Class in Late Victorian Britain* (London: Palgrave Macmillan, 2011).

K. Mervin More, *Despatches from Ladies' Clubland* (London: privately published, 1908).

Ralph Nevill, *London Clubs* (London: Chatto & Windus, 1912).

Anita O'Brien and Chris Miles, *A Peep into Clubland: Cartoons from Private London Clubs* (London: Cartoon Museum, 2009).

Anthony O'Connor, *Clubland: The Wrong Side of the Right People* (London: Martin Brian & O'Keefe, 1976).

David Palfreyman, *London's Pall Mall Clubs* (Oxford: privately published, 2019).

Henry C. Shelley, *Inns and Taverns of Old London: Setting Forth the Historical and Literary Associations of Those Ancient Hostelries, Together with an Account of the Most Notable Coffee-Houses, Clubs, and Pleasure Gardens of the British Metropolis* (Boston: L. C. Page, 1866, 1908 edn).

F. H. W. Sheppard (ed.), *Survey of London*: Vols 29 and 30, *St. James's and Westminster*, Parts 1 & 2 (London: HMSO, 1960).

Seth Alexander Thévoz, *Club Government: How the Early Victorian World Was Ruled from London Clubs* (London: I. B. Tauris, 2018).

John Timbs, *Clubs and Club Life in London, with Anecdotes of its Famous Coffee Houses, Hostelries, and Taverns from the Seventeenth Century to the Present Time* (London: Chatto & Windus, 1866).

Richard Usborne, *Clubland Heroes: A Nostalgic Study of Some Recurrent Characters in the Romantic Fiction of Dornford Yates, John Buchan and Sapper* (London: Barrie & Jenkins, 1953, rev. 1974).

Histories of individual London clubs

Army & Navy Club (1837–)

Anthony Keith Dixon, *The Army & Navy Club 1837–2008* (London: Army & Navy Club, 2009).

C. W. Firebrace, *The Army & Navy Club 1837–1933* (London: John Murray, 1934).

Arts Club (1864–)

Bernard Denvir, *A Most Agreeable Society: A Hundred and Twenty-Five Years of the Arts Club* (London: Arts Club/Studio Editions, 1989).

G. A. F. Rogers, *The Arts Club and its Members* (London: Truslove and Hanson, 1920).

The Athenaeum (1824–)

Anonymous, *A Catalogue of the Library of the Athenaeum* (London: Athenaeum Club, 1845).

Frank Richard Cowell, *The Athenaeum: Club and Social Life in London 1824–1974* (London: Heinemann, 1975).

Felipe Fernández-Armesto, *Armchair Athenians: Essays from the
Athenaeum* (London: Athenaeum, 2001).
Hugh Tait and Richard Walker, *The Athenaeum Collection* (London:
Athenaeum, 2000).
Humphry Ward, *History of the Athenaeum, 1824–1925* (London:
Athenaeum, 1926).
Francis G. Waugh, *The Athenaeum and its Associations*, Vol. I (London:
Athenaeum, 1895).
—, *Members of the Athenaeum Club from its Foundation* (London:
Athenaeum, 1900).
Michael Wheeler, *The Athenaeum: 'More Than Just Another London Club'*
(New Haven: Yale University Press, 2020).

Authors' Club (1891–)
C. J. Schuler, *Writers, Lovers, Soldiers, Spies: A History of the Authors' Club
of London, 1891–2016* (London: Authors' Club, 2016).

Beefsteak Club (1876–)
John Julius Norwich, *Beefsteak Lives, 1876–1997* (London: Beefsteak
Club, 2006).

Boodle's (1762–)
Marcus Binney and David Mann (eds), *Boodle's: Celebrating 250 Years,
1762–2012* (Marlborough: Libanus Press-Boodle's, 2012).
Roger Fulford, *Boodle's, 1762–1962: A Short History* (London: Boodle's,
1962).
Stephen R. Hill, *Boodle's Apocrypha: A Story of Men and their Club in
London* (London: Duck Editions, 2009).

Brooks's (1764–)
Henry S. Eeles and Earl Spencer, *Brooks's, 1764–1964* (London:
Country Life, 1964).
J. Mordaunt Crook and Charles Sebag-Montefiore (eds), *Brooks's
1764–2014: The Story of a Whig Club* (London: Brooks's, 2013).
Charles Sebag-Montefiore, *Charles James Fox – Brooks's and Whiggery –
The Fox Club* (London: Brooks's, 2006).

J. F. Wegg-Prosser (ed.), *Memorials of Brooks's, from the Foundation of the Club, 1764, to the Close of the Nineteenth Century, Compiled from the Records of the Club* (London: Ballantyne, 1907).
Philip Ziegler and Desmond Seward (eds), *Brooks's: A Social History* (London: Constable, 1991).

Buck's (1919–)
Henry Buckmaster, *Buck's Book: Ventures – Adventures and Misadventures* (London: Grayson & Grayson, 1933).

Caledonian Club (1890–)
Jan Coughtrie, *The Caledonian Club, Belgravia, London: A History of the Club and its Collection of Art and Artefacts* (London: Caledonian Club, 2014).

Carlton Club (1832–)
Lord Boyd-Carpenter and Eric Koops (eds), *Great Men of Our Time: Macmillan, Home and Hailsham – Carlton Lectures 1986 & 1987 / Earl of Stockton Memorial Address 1987* (London: Carlton Club Political Committee, 1987).
H. T. Cox (ed.), *Carlton Club Library Catalogue* (London: Carlton Club, 1901).
Michael Jolles, *Jews and the Carlton Club; with Notes on Benjamin Disraeli, Henri Louis Bischoffsheim and Saul Isaac* (London: Jolles Publications, 2002).
John Major, *Conservatism in the 1990s: Our Common Purpose – the Fifth Carlton Lecture* (London: Carlton Club Political Committee/ Conservative Political Centre, 1993).
Sir Charles Petrie, *The Carlton Club* (London: Eyre and Spottiswoode, 1955).
Sir Charles Petrie and Alistair Cooke [Lord Lexden], *The Carlton Club, 1832–2007* (London: Carlton Club, 2007).
Barry Phelps, *Power and the Party: A History of the Carlton Club, 1832–1982* (London: Macmillan, 1983).

Cavalry and Guards Club (1810–)
Val Horsler, *Cavalry & Guards: A London Home* (London: Third Millennium, 2009).

Chelsea Arts Club (1891-)
Tom Cross, *Artists and Bohemians: 100 Years with the Chelsea Arts Club* (London: Quiller, 1991).
Don Grant, *Private Parts: The Secret History of the Chelsea Arts Club* (London: Unicorn, 2020).

City Liberal Club (1874–1928)
Hyde Clarke (ed.), *Catalogue of the Library of the City Liberal Club* (London: Unwin Brothers, 1887).

City of London Club (1832-)
J. Owen Unwin, *The City of London Club. Centenary Notes on its History and Traditions, 1832–1932* (London: City of London Club, 1932).

Civil Service Club (1953-)
Mark Quinlan, *A Brief History of the Civil Service Club, Great Scotland Yard, Whitehall* (London: Civil Service Club, 2020).
Norman Seymour, *The Story of 13–15 Great Scotland Yard, compiled for the Civil Service Club* (London: Civil Service Club, 1992).

The Club (1764–1969)
Leo Damrosch, *The Club: Johnson, Boswell, and the Friends who Shaped an Age* (New Havem: Yale University Press, 2019).
Sir Mountstuart E. Grant Duff, *The Club, 1764–1905* (London: privately published, 1905).

Cobden Club (1866–1979)
C. J. L. Brock and G. H. B. Jackson, *The Cobden Club* (London: Cobden-Sanderson, 1939).

Colony Room Club (1948–2008)
Darren Coffield, *Tales from the Colony Room: London's Lost Bohemia* (London: Unbound, 2020).
Sophie Parkin, *The Colony Room Club: A History of Bohemian Soho* (London: Palmtree, 2nd edn 2008).

Constitutional Club (1883–1979)
The Constitutional Club, R. W. Edis, F.S.A., Architect – Founded 1883
(London: The British Architect, 1890).
Philip G. Cambray, *Club Days and Ways: The Story of the Constitutional Club, London, 1883–1962* (London: Constitutional Club, 1963).

Crockford's (1823–1846)
A. L. Humphreys, *Crockford's; or, The Goddess of Chance in St. James's Street, 1828–1844* (London: Hutchinson, 1953).
Henry Turner Waddy, *The Devonshire Club and 'Crockford's'* (London: Eveleigh Nash, 1919).

East India Club (1849–); including the Devonshire Club (1874–1976), Public Schools Club (1909–1915, 1919–1972), and Sports Club (1893–1938)
Tom Clarke, *The Devonshire Club* (London: Devonshire Club, 1943).
Denys Forrest, *Foursome in St. James's: The Story of the East India, Devonshire, Sports and Public Schools Club* (London: East India Club, 1982).
Henry Turner Waddy, *The Devonshire Club and 'Crockford's'* (London: Eveleigh Nash, 1919).
Charlie Jacoby, *The East India Club: A History* (London: East India Club, 2009).
W. W. Marsh, *The Sports Club, 1893–1938* (London: Sports Club, 1938).

Farmers' Club (1842–)
The Farmers Club, 1842–2017 (London: Farmers' Club, 2018).
Kevin Fitzgerald, *Ahead of Their Time: A Short History of the Farmers' Club, 1842–1967* (London: Heinemann, 1968).
Paul Hogben, *Food at the Farmers' Club* (London: Farmers' Club, 2019).

Flyfishers' Club (1884–)
Anonymous, *The Book of the Flyfishers' Club, 1884–1934* (Croydon: Croydon Advertiser Printing Works, 1934).
Jack Chance and Julian Paget (eds), *The Flyfishers': An Anthology to Mark the Centenary of the Flyfishers' Club, 1884–1984* (London: Flyfishers' Club, 1984).

Andrew Herd, *The Flyfishers: A History of the Flyfishers' Club* (London: Flyfishers' Club/Medlar Press, 2019).

Ken Robson (ed.), *Flyfishers' Progress: An Anthology* (London: Flyfishers' Club, 2000).

Garrick Club (1831–)

C. K. Adams, *A Catalogue of Pictures in the Garrick Club* (London: Garrick Club, 1936).

Geoffrey Ashton, *Pictures in the Garrick Club: A Catalogue of the Paintings, Drawings, Watercolours and Sculpture* (London: Garrick Club, 1997 [rev. edn 2002]).

R. H. Barham, *The Garrick Club. Notes of 133 of its Former Members* (London: Garrick Club, 1896).

John Baskett, *Brief Lives: Biographies of Sitters and Artists in the Garrick Club Collection* (London: Unicorn, 2005).

Kalman A. Burnim and Andrew Wilton, *The Richard Bebb Collection in the Garrick: A Catalogue of Figures, Sculptors and Paintings* (London: Unicorn, 2001).

Guy Boas, *The Garrick Club, 1831–1964* (London: Garrick Club, 1948 [rev. 1964]).

Percy Fitzgerald, *The Garrick Club* (London: Elliot Stock, 1904).

Richard Hough, *The Ace of Clubs: A History of the Garrick* (London: Andre Deutsch, 1986).

Desmond Shawe-Taylor, *Dramatic Art: Theatrical Paintings from the Garrick Club* (London: Dulwich Picture Gallery, 1997).

Thomas St Vincent Wallace-Troubridge, *A Guide to the Pictures in the Garrick Club* (London: Garrick Club, 1951).

Robert Walters (ed.), *Catalogue of the Pictures and Miniatures in the Possession of the Garrick Club* (London: Eyre & Spottiswoode, 1909).

Geoffrey Wansell, *The Garrick Club: A History* (London: Unicorn, 2004).

Grillion's (1812–2013)

'P. G. E.', *Annals of Grillion's Club; from its Origin in 1812, to its Fiftieth Anniversary* (London: Chiswick Press, 1880).

Groucho Club (1985–)
Alice Patten, *The Groucho Club – 30th Anniversary* (London: Preface Publishing, 2015).

Hell-Fire Club (1718–1766)
Geoffrey Ashe, *The Hell-Fire Clubs: A History of Anti-Morality* (Stroud: History Press, 2005 [rev. edn]).
Louis Clark Jones, *The Clubs of the Georgian Rakes* (New York: Columbia University Press, 1942).
Evelyn Lord, *The Hell-Fire Clubs: Sex, Satanism and Secret Societies* (New Haven: Yale University Press, 2008).

Hurlingham Club (1869–)
Taprell Dorling, *The Hurlingham Club, 1869–1953* (London: Hurlingham Club, 1953).
Nigel Miskin, *Pigeons, Polo, and Other Pastimes: A History of the Hurlingham Club* (London: Hurlingham Club, 2000).

Junior United Service Club (1827–1967)
R. H. Firth, *The Junior: A History of the Junior United Service Club, from its formation in 1827, to 1929* (London: Junior United Service Club, 1929).

Kit-Cat Club (1700–1817)
Ophelia Field, *The Kit-Cat Club: Friends Who Imagined a Nation* (New York: HarperPress, 2008).

Lansdowne Club (1935–)
Maria Perry, *The House in Berkeley Square: A History of the Lansdowne Club* (London: Lansdowne Club, 2003).

London Sketch Club (1898–)
David Cuppleditch, *The London Sketch Club* (London: Sutton Publishing, 1994).

National Liberal Club (1882–)

Anonymous, *The National Liberal Club* (London: National Liberal Club, 1905).

Anonymous, *The National Liberal Club* (London: National Liberal Club, 1933).

Coss Bilson (ed.), *The National Liberal Club, 1882–1982* (London: National Liberal Club, 1982).

Veronica Herrington, *Works of Art, National Liberal Club* (London: National Liberal Club, 1997).

Michael Meadowcroft, *A Guide to the Works of Art of the National Liberal Club, London*, 2nd edn (London: National Liberal Club, 2011).

Gerhart Raichle (ed.), *National Liberal Club, London – Ausstellung Galerie im Margarethenhof der Friedrich-Naumann-Stiftung Königswinter-Ittenbach, 6. September–28. Oktober 1984* (Königswinter: Friedrich-Naumann-Stiftung, 1984).

Robert Steven, *The National Liberal Club: Politics and Persons* (London: Robert Houghton, 1925).

Naval and Military Club ('In & Out' Club) (1862–)

Tim Newark, *The In & Out: A History of the Naval and Military Club* (London: Osprey Publishing, 2015).

Den Norske Klub (1887–)

John Birch, *Vikings in London: Den Norske Klub – 100 Years* (London: Den Norske Klub, 1988).

G. Conradi, *Den Norske Klub i London, 17 Mai 1887–17 Mai 1937* (London: Den Norske Klub, 1937).

Oriental Club (1824–)

Alexander F. Baillie, *The Oriental Club and Hanover Square* (London: Longmans, 1901).

Denys Forrest, *The Oriental: Life Story of a West End Club* (London: B. T. Batsford, 1968 [rev. edn 1979]).

Hugh Riches, *History of the Oriental Club* (London: Oriental Club, 1998).

John Walters, *Paintings at the Oriental* (London: Oriental Club, 2002).

Stephen Wheeler (ed.), *Annals of the Oriental Club, 1824–1858* (London: The Arden Press, 1925).

Oxford and Cambridge Club (1830–); including the United University Club (1821–1971) and the New University Club (1864–1938)
Anonymous, *Catalogue of the Library of the Oxford and Cambridge Club* (London: Oxford and Cambridge Club, 1887).
—, *Catalogue of the Library of the Oxford and Cambridge Club: Supplement, Containing the Additions from 1887–1908* (London: Oxford and Cambridge Club, 1909).
Francesca Herrick, *A Guide to the Art Collections of the Oxford and Cambridge Club* (London: Oxford and Cambridge Club, 2012).
Richard Price et al. (eds), *Oxford and Cambridge Club Membership List 2013: Published to Commemorate the 175th Anniversary of the Opening of the Club House* (London: Oxford and Cambridge Club, 2013).
John Thole, *The Oxford and Cambridge Clubs in London* (Henley-on-Thames: Alfred Waller-United Oxford and Cambridge University Club, 1992).

Queen's Club (1886–)
Roy McKelvie, *The Queen's Club Story, 1886–1986* (London: Stanley Paul, 1986).

Reform Club (1836–)
The Reform Club Library: A Retrospect, 1841–1991 (London: Reform Club, 1991).
Russell Burlingham and Roger Billis (eds), *Reformed Characters: The Reform Club in History and Literature, an Anthology with Commentary* (London: Reform Club, 2005).
William Clarke and Peter Urbach, *History of the Austerity Club* (London: Reform Club, 2004).
Louis Fagan, *The Reform Club: Its Founders and Architect* (London: B. Quaritch, 1887).
Craig McDonald Marshall, Alex Fulluck and Amy Crangle, *Recipes from the Reform: A Selection of Recipes from the Reform Club, London* (London: Reform Club, 2014).

J. Mordaunt Crook, *The Reform Club* (London: Reform Club, 1973).
Jeff Nicholas, *Behind the Streets of Adelaide*, Vol. I: *Born of Reform –
A Pantheon of Dissent* (Adelaide: Torrens Press, 2016).
—, *Behind the Streets of Adelaide*, Vol. II: *From Rundle to Morphett*
(Adelaide: Torrens Press, 2016).
—, *Behind the Streets of Adelaide*, Vol. III: *From Wellington to Mann*
(Adelaide: Torrens Press, 2016).
Michael Sharpe, *The Political Committee of the Reform Club* (London:
Reform Club, 1996).
Peter Urbach, *The Reform Club: Some Twentieth Century Members –
A Photographic Collection* (London: Reform Club, 1999).
Charles W. Vincent and W. Fraser Rae (eds), *Catalogue of the Library of
the Reform Club, with Historical Introduction* (London: Reform Club,
1883).
—, *Catalogue of the Library of the Reform Club, with Revised Historical
Introduction: Second and Enlarged Edition* (London: Reform Club,
1894).
George Woodbridge, *The Reform Club, 1836–1978: A History from the
Club's Records* (New York: Clearwater, 1978).

Roehampton Club (1901–)
Elizabeth Hennessy, *A History of the Roehampton Club, 1901 to 2001*
(London: Roehampton Club, 2001).

Royal Air Force Club (1918–)
Henry Probert and Michael Gilbert, *'128': The Story of the Royal Air
Force Club* (London: Royal Air Force Club, 2004).

Royal Automobile Club (1897–)
Piers Brendon, *The Motoring Century: The Story of the Royal Automobile
Club* (London: Bloomsbury, 1997).
Dudley Noble (ed.), *The Jubilee Book of the Royal Automobile Club,
1897–1947: The Record of a Historic 50 years, during which the R.A.C.
has fostered the Development and Progress of Automobilism in all its many
and varied aspects* (London: Royal Automobile Club, 1947).

Royal Ocean Racing Club (1925–)
Ian Dear, *The Royal Ocean Club: The First 75 Years* (London: Adlard Coles Nautical, 2000).

Royal Overseas League (1910–)
Adele Smith, *The Royal Overseas League: From Empire to Commonwealth, a History of the First 100 Years* (London: I. B. Tauris, 2009).

Royal Thames Yacht Club (1775–)
A. R. Ward, *The Chronicles of the Royal Yacht Club* (Oxford: John Wiley, 1999).

Savage Club (1857–)
Percy V. Bradshaw, *'Brother Savages and Guests': A History of the Savage Club, 1857– 1957* (London: W. H. Allen, 1958).
Thomas Catling and Walter Jerrold, *A Savage Club Souvenir* (London: Savage Club, 1916).
Andrew Halliday (ed.), *The Savage Club Papers, First Series* (London: Tinsley Brothers, 1867).
—, *The Savage Club Papers for 1868* (London: Tinsley Brothers, 1868).
Mark Hambourg, *The Eighth Octave: Tones and Semi-Tones Concerning Piano-Playing, the Savage Club and Myself* (London: Williams & Norgate, 1951).
J. E. Muddock (ed.), *The Savage Club Papers* (London: Hutchinson, 1897).
Matthew Norgate and Alan Wykes, *Not So Savage* (London: Jupiter Books, 1976).
William Bernard Tegetmeier, *Reminiscences of the Savage Club* (London: privately published, 1900).
Edwin A. Ward, *Recollections of a Savage, i.e. a Member of the Savage Club* (London: Frederick A. Stokes, 1923).
John Wade, *Dining with Savages: A New Savage Miscellany* (Northam: Roundhouse, 2000).
Aaron Watson and Mark Twain, *The Savage Club: A Medley of History, Anecdote and Reminiscence* (London: T. Fisher Unwin, 1907).
James Wilson, *Noble Savages: The Savage Club and the Great War, 1914–1918* (London: J. H. Productions, 2018).

Savile Club (1868–)

Anonymous, *The Savile Club, 1868 to 1923* (London: Savile Club, 1923).

Anonymous, *The Savile Club, 1868–1958* (London: Savile Club, 1957).

Garrett Anderson, *Hang Your Halo in the Hall: A History of the Savile Club* (London: Savile Club, 1993).

Monja Danischewsky, *The Savile Club, 1868–1968* (London: Savile Club, 1968).

Robert J. D. Harding (ed.), *Suggestions' Books: A Selection of Entries, 1869–1969 – Savile Club 1868–2018* (London: Savile Club, 2018).

—, *The Savile Club 1914–1918 War Memorial – Savile Club 1868–2018* (London: Savile Club, 2018).

Smithfield Club (1798–)

Sir B. T. Brandreth Gibbs, *The Smithfield Club: A Condensed History of its Origin and Progress, from its Formation in 1798, up to the year 1880* (London: Smithfield Club, 1881).

E. J. Powell, *History of the Smithfield Club: from 1798 to 1900* (London: Smithfield Club, 1902).

Soho House (1995–)

Anonymous, *Eat, Drink, Nap: Bringing the House Home* (London: Preface Publishing, 2014).

Anonymous, *Morning, Noon, Night: A Way of Living* (London: Preface Publishing, 2016).

Special Forces Club (1946–)

Sean Rayment, *Tales from the Special Forces Club* (London: Collins, 2013).

Travellers Club (1819–)

Graham Binns, Hugh Massingberd and Sheila Markham, *A House of the First Class: The Travellers Club and its Members* (London: Travellers Club, 2003).

Almeric Fitzroy, *History of the Travellers Club* (London: George Allen & Unwin, 1927).

Frank Herrmann and Michael Allen (eds), *Travellers' Tales: By Members of the Travellers Club* (London: Castlereagh, 1999).
—, *More Tales from the Travellers: A Further Collection of Tales by Members of the Travellers Club, London* (London: Michal Tomkinson, 2005.)
John Martin Robinson, *The Travellers Club: A Bicentennial History, 1819–2019* (Marlborough: Libanus Press-Travellers Club, 2018).

Union Club (1799–1949)
R. C. Rome, *Union Club: An Illustrated Descriptive Record of the Oldest Members' Club in London, founded circa 1799* (London: B. T. Batsford-Union Club, 1948).

United Service Club (1815–1977)
Louis C. Jackson, *The United Service Club and its Founder* (London: Sanders Phillips, 1931).
—, *History of the United Service Club* (London: United Service Club, 1937).

University Women's Club (1886–)
A. G. E. Carthew (ed.), *The University Women's Club: Extracts from Fifty Years of Minute Books, 1886–1936* (Eastbourne: Sumfield and Day, 1936, repr. 1985).

White's (1693–)
W. B. Boulton, *The History of White's, with the Betting Book from 1743 to 1878 and a List of Members from 1736 to 1892*, 2 vols (London: Algernon Bourke, 1892).
Percy Colson, *White's: 1693–1950* (London: Heinemann, 1951).
Anthony Lejeune, *White's: The First Three Hundred Years* (London: A&C Black, 1993).

Working men's clubs
Ruth Cherrington, *Not Just Beer and Bingo! A Social History of Working Men's Clubs* (London: AuthorHouse, 2012).
Henry Clarke, *Working Men's Clubs: Hints for their Formation, with Rules, etc.* (London: Working Men's Club and Institute Union, 1865).

B. T. Hall, *Working Men's Clubs: Why and How to Establish and Manage Them* (London: Working Men's Club and Institute Union, 1920).
Stan Shipley, *Club Life and Socialism in Mid-Victorian London – History Workshop Pamphlets Number Five* (London: History Workshop Journal, 1971).
Henry Solly, *Working Men's Social Clubs and Educational Institutes* (London: Working Men's Club and Institute Union, 1858).
John Taylor, *From Self-Help to Glamour: The Working Man's 1860-1972 – History Workshop Pamphlets Number Seven* (London: History Workshop Journal, 1972).
George Tremlett, *Clubmen: The History of the Working Men's Club and Institute Union* (London: Secker & Warburg, 1987).

Histories of select clubs of Australia
Adrian Akhurst, *History of the Australian Club, Melbourne, 1878-1932* (Melbourne: Australian Club, 1943).
J. R. Angel, *The Australian Club, 1838-1988: The First 150 Years* (Sydney: John Ferguson, 1988).
David Clements Jackson, *Queensland Club, 1959-1989* (Brisbane: Queensland Club, 1989).
Caroline de Mori, *A Club for All Seasons: A History of the Western Australian Club Inc.* (Perth: Western Australian Club, 1990).
Paul de Serville, *The Australian Club, Melbourne, 1878-1998* (Melbourne: Australian Club, 1998).
—, *3 Barrack Street: The Weld Club, 1871-2001* (Wahroonga: Helicon Press, 2003).
—, *Athenaeum Club, Melbourne: A New History of the Early Years, 1868-1918* (Melbourne: Athenaeum Club, 2013).
—, *Melbourne Club: A Social History, 1838-1918* (Melbourne: Melbourne Club, 2017).
David M. Dow, *Melbourne Savages: A History of the First Fifty Years of the Melbourne Savage Club* (Melbourne: Melbourne Savage Club, 1947).
Kenneth R. Dutton, *Splendid Companions: 125 Years of the Newcastle Club, 1885-2010* (Newcastle, Newcastle Club, 2010).
Gordon Forth, *'We Are Not All Gentlemen Here': The Hamilton Club, 1875 to 2011* (Hamilton: Halstead Press, 2021).

Joseph Johnson, *Laughter and the Love of Friends: A History of the Melbourne Savage Club 1894–1994 and a History of the Yorick Club 1868–1966* (Melbourne: Melbourne Savage Club, 1994).

F. F. Knight, *History of the Australian Club, Melbourne*, Vol. II: *1932–1965* (Melbourne: Australian Club, 1978).

Rob Linn, *The Adelaide Club, 1863–2013* (Adelaide: Adelaide Club, 2013).

T. S. Louch, *A History of the Weld Club (1871–1950)* (Perth: Weld Club, 1950).

Ronald McNicoll, *Number 36 Collins Street: Melbourne Club, 1838–1988* (Sydney: Allen & Unwin/Haynes, 1988).

John Pacini, *Windows on Collins Street: A History of the Athenaeum Club, Melbourne* (Melbourne: Athenaeum Club, 1991).

Mark Reid, James J. Auchmuty and Geoffrey Tanner, *Newcastle Club Centenary 1985* (Newcastle, Newcastle Club, 1985).

Robert Whitelaw and Paul Deprat, *Stories from the Archives: The Union, University & Schools Club of Sydney* (Sydney: Union, University & Schools Club, 2017)

Histories of select clubs of Canada

Paul S. Besley, *The History of the Vancouver Club* (Vancouver: Vancouver Club, 1971).

D. F. Hawkes, *The National Century: A History of the National Club, 1874 to 1974* (Toronto: National Club, 1974).

Reginald H. Roy, *The Vancouver Club; First Century, 1889–1989* (Vancouver: Vancouver Club, 1989).

David Ricardo Williams, *Yesterday, Today and Tomorrow: A History of Vancouver's Terminal City Club* (Vancouver: Terminal City Club, 1992).

Histories of select clubs of France

Yves de Clercq, *Cercle Royal La Concorde, 1809–2009* (Paris: Cercle Royal La Concorde, 2009).

Christiane de Nicolay-Maery, *The Travellers Club: A Private Visit of the Hôtel Païva* (Paris: Travellers Club, 2012).

Maria Felix Frazao (ed.), *Le Cercle de l'Union Interalliée: Un siècle dans l'histoire* (Paris: Cherche Midi, 2017).

Joseph-Antoine Roy, *Histoire du Jockey Club de Paris* (Paris: M. Rivière, 1958).

Histories of select clubs of India
Anonymous, *The Trees of Tollygunge Club* (Calcutta: Tollygunge Club, 1946).
Naval J. Ardeshir, Minoo P. Azifdaar and Sylvester de Cunha (eds), *Willingdon Sports Club, 1917–1977* (Bombay: Willingdon Sports Club, 1977).
Purshottam Bhageria and Pavan Malhotra, *Elite Clubs of India* (New Delhi: Bhageria Foundation, 2005).
M. Bhaktavatsala, *The Club World: Bangalore Club 1868–1993 – Successors to the Bangalore United Services (BUS) Club* (Bangalore: Bangalore Club, 1993).
Dilip Kumar Bose et al., *One Hundred Years of Calcutta Club, 1907–2007*, 2 vols (Kolkata: Calcutta Club, 2007).
Benjamin B. Cohen, *In the Club: Associational Life in Colonial South Asia* (Hyderabad: Orient Black Swan, 2015).
Pradip Das, *The Tollygunge Club Since 1895* (Kolkata: Tollygunge Club, 2008).
Monish Datta (ed.), *Wellington Gymkhana Club, Est. 1873: Courtesy, Care, Comfort* (Wellington: Wellington Gymkhana Club, 2013).
W. G. C. Frith, *The Royal Calcutta Turf Club* (Calcutta: Royal Calcutta Turf Club, 1976).
R. I. MacAlpine and H. R. Panckridge, *The Bengal Club, 1827–1970* (Calcutta: Bengal Club, 1970).
S. Muthiah, *The Spirit of Chepauk: The MCC Story – A 150-Year Sporting Tradition* (Chennai: Eastwest Books (Madras) Pvt. Ltd, 1998).
—, *The Ace of Clubs: The Story of the Madras Club* (Chennai: Madras Club, 2002).
—, *Down By the Adyar: The Story of the Madras Boat Club* (Chennai: Madras Boat Club, 2010).
Sumil Anant Naik, *Clube Tennis de Gaspar Dias, Est. 1926* (Panaji, Goa: Clube Tennis de Gaspar Dias, 2018).
Narendra Kumar Nayak (ed.), *Calcutta 200 Years: A Tollygunge Club Perspective* (Calcutta: Tollygunge Club, 1981).

Gulshan Rai, *The History of the Royal Bombay Yacht Club: From the Founding of the Empire's Most Majestic Club in the East in 1846 to the Present Day* (Mumbai: Royal Bombay Yacht Club, 2010).

Aliyeh Rizvi, *Another World: Bangalore Club (Bangalore United Service Club), 1868–2018* (Bangalore: Bangalore Club, 2018).

Malabika Sarkar, *The Bengal Club in History* (Kolkata: Bengal Club, 2006).

Dilip Kumar Saha et al., *The Centenary Elite: A Special Number to Mark the Centenary of the Calcutta Club* (Kolkata: Calcutta Club, 2007).

Ashwajit Singh (ed.), *Delhi Gymkhana Club Ltd.: Centenary Souvenir* (New Delhi: Delhi Gymkhana Club, 2015).

Histories of select clubs of New Zealand

A. W. Beasley, *The Club on the Terrace: The Wellington Club, 1841–1996* (Wellington: Wellington Club, 1996).

Arthur Manning, *The Wellesley Club, 1891–1991* (Wellington: Wellesley Club, 1991).

John Stacpoole, *Beyond the Ivy Curtain: The Story of the Northern Club, 1869–2009* (Auckland: Northern Club, 2009).

Histories of select clubs of Portugal

Henrique Almeida, *O Clube Feinianos Portuenses: Na Oposição ao Facismo na Década de 40* (Porto: Clube Feinianos Portuenses, 1982)

D. Theodora Andresen de Abreu, *Biblioteca do Clube Poreuense: Catálogo* (Porto: Club Poretuense, 1965).

Conde de Campo Bello et al., *O Primeiro Centenário do Club Portuense* (Porto: Club Poretuense, 1957).

A. de Magalhâes Basto, *O Club Portuense: Breve Monografia Histórica* (Porto: Club Poretuense, 2004).

José de Meireles, *Pelo Pôrto: O 'Clube Feinanos Portuenses' desde a sua Fundaçâo* (Porto: Fernando Machado, 1941).

John Delaforce, *The Factory House at Oporto: Its Historic Role in the Port Wine Trade* (London: Christie's, 1990).

Acácio Tavares, *O Clube Feinianos Portuenses a a sua Obra* (Porto: Clube Feinianos Portuenses, 1970)

Histories of select clubs of South Africa

C. G. Botha, *The Civil Service Club, 1858–1938* (Cape Town: Civil Service Club, 1939).

Louis Changuion, *The Club with a Capacity for Survival: A Centenary Album of the Highlights in the History of the Pietersburg Club, 1902–2002* (Pietersburg: Pietersburg Club, 2002).

René de Villiers and S. Brooke-Norris, *The Story of the Rand Club* (Johannesburg: Rand Club, 1976).

A. I. Little, *History of the City Club, Cape Town, 1878–1938* (Cape Town: City Club, 1938).

J. M. Osborne et al., *The Rand Club, 1887–1957* (Cape Town: Cape Times Ltd, 1957).

W. E. Ranby, *The City Club, Cape Town: A Supplementary History to 1955* (Cape Town: Galvin & Sales, 1955).

I. F. Sander, *Rand Club: Centenary Album, 1887–1987* (Johannesburg: Rand Club, 1987).

Histories of select clubs of the United States

Sarah Blaskey, Nicholas Nehamas, Caitlin Ostroff and Jay Weaver, *The Grifter's Club: Trump, Mar-a-Lago, and the Selling of the Presidency* (New York: PublicAffairs, 2020).

Emmett Dedmon, *A History of the Chicago Club* (Chicago: Chicago Club, 1960).

William C. Edgar, Loring M. Staples and Henry Doerr, *Minneapolis Club: A Review of its History* (Minneapolis: Minneapolis Club, 1974).

Laurence Leamer, *Mar-a-Lago: Inside the Gates of Power at Donald Trump's Presidential Palace* (New York: Flatiron Books, 2019).

Arnold S. Lott and Raymond J. McHugh, *A New Century Beckons: A History of the Army and Navy Club* (Washington, DC: Army and Navy Club, 1988).

Geoffrey H. Movius and James M. Fitzgibbons, *The Book of the Harvard Club of Boston, 75th Anniversary, 1908-1983* (Boston, Massachusetts: Harvard Club of Boston, 1983).

Troupe Noonan, *A Youthful Hundred; The History of the Racquet Club, St. Louis, 1906–2006* (Chapel Hill, North Carolina: Heritage Histories, 2007).

Nat B. Read, *The Jonathan Club Story* (Los Angeles: Balcony Press, 2005).

Frank Vos, *The Lotos Experience: The Tradition Continues – A Celebration of the 125th Anniversary* (New York: Lotos Club, 1995).

Oscar Whitelaw Rexford, *The History of the University Club of St Louis, 1872–1978* (St Louis, Missouri: University Club of St Louis, 1979).

Jim Zebora (ed.), *The Metropolitan Club of New York: Celebrating 125 Years*, 2 vols (New York: Harper, 2015).

Histories of select clubs worldwide
Colin Black, *Sable: The Story of the Salisbury Club* (Salisbury: Salisbury Club, 1980).

Deloraine Brohier, *The Saga of the Colombo Club* (Colombo: Colombo Club, 2001).

Nigel Dunne, *Club: The Story of the Hong Kong Football Club, 1886–1986* (Hong Kong: Hong Kong Football Club, 1985).

Vaudine England, *Kindred Spirits: A History of the Hong Kong Club* (Hong Kong: Hong Kong Club, 2016).

Peter Gibbs, *The Bulawayo Club* (Bulawayo: Bulawayo Club, 1970).

William Haslam Mills, *The Manchester Reform Club 1871–1921* (Manchester: Charles Hobson, 1922).

J. Humphrey, Azhar Karim and Shuja Baig, *Sind Club, 1871–2016* (Karachi: Sind Club, 2016).

Andrew Hutchinson et al., *The Barbados Yacht Club: Celebrating Ninety Years, 1924–2014* (Bridgetown: Barbados Yacht Club, 2014).

S. G. Simmons, *Club Class in Asia Pacific: The Insiders' Guide to Private Members' Clubs* (Singapore: Editions Didier Millet, 2007).

Barbara Ann Walsh, *Forty Good Men: The Story of the Tanglin Club in the Island of Singapore, 1865–1990* (Singapore: Tanglin Club, 1991).

Richard Wilson, Anthony Howe and Michael Sayer, *The Norfolk Club: A History, 1770–2020* (Norwich: The Norfolk Club, 2022).

Legal textbooks on clubs
David Ashton and Paul Reid, *Ashton & Reid on Clubs and Associations*, 3rd edn (London: Bloomsbury Professional, 2020).

Kerry Barker and Henry Stephens, *Club Law Manual*, 2nd edn

(London: Wildy, Simmonds and Hill, 2011).

Arthur F. Leach, *Club Cases: Being Considerations on the Formation, Management and Dissolution of Clubs, with Especial Reference to the Liabilities and Expulsion of Members* (London: Harrison, 1879).

Philip R. Smith, *Club Law and Management* (London: Association of Conservative Clubs, 2008).

Philip R. Smith and Charles Littlewood, *Club Law and Management: Questions and Answers* (London: Association of Conservative Clubs, 2017).

Nicholas Stewart QC, Natalie Campbell and Simon Baughen, *The Law of Unincorporated Associations* (Oxford: Oxford University Press, 2008).

Books

Peter Ackroyd, *Queer City: Gay London from the Romans to the Present Day* (New York: Abrams Press, 2018).

Benedict Anderson, *Imagined Communities: Reflections on the Origin and Spread of Nationalism,* rev. 2nd edn (London: Verso, 2006, first pub. 1983).

Ann Arnold, *The Adventurous Chef: Alexis Soyer* (London: Reform Club, 2002).

Rosemary Ashton, *142 Strand: A Radical Address in Victorian London* (London: Chatto & Windus, 2006).

—, *Victorian Bloomsbury* (New Haven, Connecticut: Yale University Press, 2012).

Peter Bailey, *Leisure and Class in Victorian England: Rational Recreation and the Contest for Control, 1830–1885* (London: Methuen, 1978 [rev. 1987 edn]).

—, *Music Hall: The Business of Pleasure* (Milton Keynes: Open University Press, 1986).

Paul Baker, *Fabulosa! The Story of Polari, Britain's Secret Gay Language* (London: Reaktion Books, 2019).

Catherine Belton, *Putin's People: How the KGB Took Back Russia and Then Took on the West* (London: William Collins, 2020).

Ronald Bergan, *Beyond the Fringe…And Beyond: A Critical Biography of Alan Bennett, Peter Cook, Jonathan Miller and Dudley Moore* (London: Virgin Books, 1989).

Robert Blake, *Disraeli* (London: Eyre & Spottiswoode, 1966).

Michael Bloch, *Jeremy Thorpe* (London: Little, Brown, 2014).

Tom Bower, *Tiny Rowland: A Rebel Tycoon* (London: Heinemann, 1993).

John Campbell, *Roy Jenkins: A Well-Rounded Life* (London: Jonathan Cape, 2014).

David Cannadine, *The Decline and Fall of the British Aristocracy* (New Haven, Connecticut: Yale University Press, 1990).

—, *In Churchill's Shadow: Confronting the Past in Modern Britain* (Oxford: Oxford University Press, 2003).

Valérie Capdeville, *L'Âge d'Or des Clubs Londoniens (1730–1784)* (Paris: Editions Champion, 2008).

Valérie Capdeville and Alain Kerhervé (eds), *British Sociability in the Long Eighteenth Century: Challenging the Anglo-French Connection* (Woodbridge: Boydell Press 2019).

Humphrey Carpenter, *That Was the Satire That Was: The Satire Boom of the 1960s* (London: Victor Gollancz, 2000).

Kellow Chesney, *The Victorian Underworld* (London: Temple Smith, 1970).

Lewis Chester, Magnus Linklater and David May, *Jeremy Thorpe: A Secret Life* (London: Fontana, 1979).

Randolph S. Churchill, *The Fight for the Tory Leadership: A Contemporary Chronicle* (London: Heinemann, 1964).

Alan Clark, *Tories: Conservatives and the Nation State, 1922–1997* (London: Weidenfeld & Nicolson, 1997).

Jonathan Clarke, *Early Structural Steel in London Buildings: A Discreet Revolution* (London: English Heritage, 2014).

Joseph Coohill, *Ideas of the Liberal Party: Perceptions, Agendas and Liberal Politics in the House of Commons, 1832–1852* (Oxford: Wiley-Blackwell, 2011).

Matt Cook, *London and the Culture of Homosexuality, 1885–1914* (Cambridge: Cambridge University Press, 2003).

Penelope J. Corfield, *Power and the Professions in Britain, 1700–1850* (London: Routledge, 1995).

Gary W. Cox, *The Efficient Secret: The Cabinet and the Development of Political Parties in Victorian England* (Cambridge: Cambridge University Press, 1987).

Elizabeth Crawford, *The Women's Suffrage Movement: A Reference Guide, 1866–1928* (London: Routledge, 2000).

Michael Crick, *Sultan of Swing: The Life of David Butler* (London: Biteback, 2018).

William Dalrymple, *The Anarchy: The Relentless Rise of the East India Company* (London: Bloomsbury, 2019).

Arthur Irwin Dasent, *The History of St. James's Square and the Foundation of the West End of London, with a Glimpse of Whitehall in the Reign of Charles the Second* (London: Macmillan, 1895).

Richard Davenport-Hines, *An English Affair: Sex, Class and Power in the Age of Profumo* (London: HarperCollins, 2013).

Leonore Davidoff and Catherine Hall, *Family Fortunes: Men and Women of the English Middle Class, 1780–1850* (London: Hutchinson, 1987).

Richard Ellman, *Oscar Wilde* (London: Hamish Hamilton, 1987).

Norman Gash, *Politics in the Age of Peel: A Study in the Technique of Parliamentary Representation, 1830–1850* (London: Longman, 1953).

Vic Gatrell, *City of Laughter: Sex and Satire in Eighteenth Century London* (New York: Walker and Company, 2006).

Kathryn Gleadle, *Borderline Citizens: Women, Gender, and Political Culture in Britain, 1815–1867* (Oxford: Oxford University Press, 2009).

Eleanor Gordon and Gwyneth Nair, *Public Lives: Women, Family and Society in Victorian Britain* (New Haven, Connecticut: Yale University Press, 2003).

Richard Hall, *My Life with Tiny: A Biography of Tiny Rowland* (London: Faber and Faber, 1987).

H. J. Hanham, *Elections and Party Management: Politics in the Time of Disraeli and Gladstone* (London: Longmans, 1959).

Luke Harding, *Shadow State: Murder, Mayhem and Russia's Remaking of the West* (London: Guardian Faber, 2020).

Adrian Harvey, *The Beginnings of a Commercial Sporting Culture in Britain, 1793–1850* (Aldershot: Ashgate, 2004).

Mushirul Hasan and Dinyar Patel (eds), *From Ghalib's Dilli to Lutyens' New Delhi* (Oxford: Oxford University Press, 2013).

Angus Hawkins, *Parliament, Party and the Art of Politics in Britain, 1855–59* (Stanford, California: Stanford University Press, 1987).

—, *British Party Politics, 1852–1886* (London: Macmillan, 1998).

—, *The Forgotten Prime Minister: The 14th Earl of Derby*, Vol. I – *Ascent, 1799–1851* (Oxford: Oxford University Press, 2007).

—, *The Forgotten Prime Minister: The 14th Earl of Derby*, Vol. II – *Achievement, 1851–1869* (Oxford: Oxford University Press, 2008).

Angus Hawkins and John Powell (eds), *The Journal of John Wodehouse, First Earl of Kimberley for 1862–1902* (London: Royal Historical Society, 1997).

Boyd Hilton, *A Mad, Bad, and Dangerous People? England 1783–1846* (Oxford: Oxford University Press, 2006).

Gertude Himmelfarb, *Victorian Minds: A Study of Intellectuals in Crisis* (New York: Alfred A. Knopf, 1968).

Pamela Horn, *Pleasures and Pastimes in Victorian Britain* (Stroud: Sutton Publishing, 1999).

Matt Houlbrook, *Queer London: Perils and Pleasures in the Sexual Metropolis, 1918–1957* (Chicago: University of Chicago Press, 2005).

Laud Humphries, *Tearoom Trade: Impersonal Sex in Public Places*, 3rd edn (New Brunswick, New Jersey: Aldine Transaction, 1970, 2008).

Tristram Hunt, *Building Jerusalem: The Rise and Fall of the Victorian City* (London: Weidenfeld & Nicolson, 2004).

Lucy Inglis, *Georgian London: Into the Streets* (London: Viking, 2013).

Lee Jackson, *Palaces of Pleasure: From Music Halls to the Seaside to Football, How the Victorians Invented Mass Entertainment* (New Haven, Connecticut: Yale University Press, 2019).

Nimrod Kamer, *The Social Climber's Handbook: A Shameless Guide* (Amsterdam: BIS, 2018).

Stephen Koss, *The Rise and Fall of the Political Press in Britain*: Vol. 1 – *The Nineteenth Century* (London: Hamish Hamilton, 1981).

—, *The Rise and Fall of the Political Press in Britain*: Vol. 2 – *The Twentieth Century* (London: Hamish Hamilton, 1985).

David Kynaston, *The City of London*, Vol. I: *A World of its Own, 1815–1890* (London: Chatto & Windus, 1994).

—, *The City of London*, Vol. II: *Golden Years, 1815–1890–1914* (London: Chatto & Windus, 1995).

Henri Lefebvre [trans. Gerald Moore, Neil Brenner and Stuart Elden, ed. Neil Brenner and Stuart Elden], *State, Space, World: Selected Essays* (Minneapolis, Minnesota: University of Minnesota Press, 2009).

Nancy D. LoPatin [subsequently LoPatin-Lummis], *Political Unions, Popular Politics and the Great Reform Act of 1832* (London: Macmillan, 1999).

William C. Lubenow, *Liberal Intellectuals and Public Culture in Modern Britain, 1815–1914: Making Words Flesh* (Woodbridge: Boydell and Brewer, 2010).

—, *'Only Connect': Learned Societies in Nineteenth Century Britain* (Woodbridge: Boydell Press, 2015).

—, *Learned Lives in England, 1900–1950: Institutions, Ideas and Intellectual Experience* (Woodbridge: Boydell Press, 2020).

David McKie, *Jabez: The Rise and Fall of a Victorian Scoundrel* (London: Atlantic Books, 2004).

Rohan McWilliam, *London's West End: Creating the Pleasure District, 1800–1914* (Oxford: Oxford University Press, 2020).

Norman Makenzie (ed.), *The Letters of Sidney and Beatrice Webb*: Volume 3, *Pilgrimage 1912–1947* (Cambridge: Cambridge University Press, 1978).

Peter Mandler, *Aristocratic Government in the Age of Reform: Whigs and Liberals, 1830–1852* (Oxford: Clarendon Press, 1990).

Richard Mayson, *Port and the Douro* (Oxford: Infinite Ideas, 2013).

Barry Millington, *Wagner* (London: J. M. Dent, 1985),

Ellen Moers, *The Dandy: Brummell to Beerbohm* (New York: Viking Press, 1960).

J. Mordaunt Crook, *The Rise of the* Nouveaux Riches: *Style and Status in Victorian and Edwardian Architecture* (London: John Murray, 1999).

Marjorie Morgan, *Manners, Morals and Class in England, 1774–1858* (New York: St Martin's Press, 1994).

Rupert Morris, *Tories: From Village Hall to Westminster – A Political Sketch* (Edinburgh: Mainstream, 1991).

Frank O'Gorman, *Voters, Patrons, and Parties: The Unreformed Electoral System of Hanoverian England, 1734–1832* (Oxford: Clarendon Press, 1989).

Moisei Ostrogorski, *Democracy and the Organisation of Political Parties*, 2 vols (reprint, New York: Macmillan, 1970, of orig. edn, London: Macmillan, 1902).

Christina Parolin, *Radical Spaces: Venues of Popular Politics in London, 1790–c.1845* (Canberra, Australia: Australian National University E Press, 2012).

Matthew Parris, *Great Parliamentary Scandals: Four Centuries of Calumny, Smear and Innuendo* (London: Robson Books, 1995).

Jonathan Parry, *The Rise and Fall of Liberal Government in Britain* (New Haven, Connecticut: Yale University Press, 1993).

—, *The Politics of Patriotism: English Liberalism, National Identity and Europe, 1830–1886* (Cambridge: Cambridge University Press, 2009).

Dinyar Patel, *Naoroji: Pioneer of Indian Nationalism* (Cambridge, Massachusetts: Harvard University Press, 2020).

Robert D. Putnam, *Bowling Alone: The Collapse and Revival of American Community* (New York: Simon & Schuster, 2000).

Nirmal Puwar, *Space Invaders: Race, Gender and Bodies Out of Place* (Oxford: Berg, 1985).

James Rattue, *Kissing Your Sister: A History of the Oxford University Liberal Club, 1913–1993* (Umbra, 1993).

K. D. Reynolds, *Aristocratic Women and Political Society in Victorian Britain* (Oxford: Clarendon Press, 1998).

Fern Riddell, *Sex Lessons from History* (London: Hodder & Stoughton, 2021).

Anthony Sampson, *The Anatomy of Britain* (London: Hodder & Stoughton, 1962).

—, *The Anatomy of Britain Today* (London: Hodder & Stoughton, 1965).

Dominic Sandbrook, *Never Had It So Good: A History of Britain from Suez to the Beatles* (London: Little, Brown, 2005).

Malcolm Shifrin, *Victorian Turkish Baths* (Swindon: Historic England, 2015).

Godfrey Spence, *The Port Companion: A Connoisseur's Guide* (Hove: Apple, 1997).

Roy Strong, *Feast: A History of Grand Eating* (London: Jonathan Cape, 2002).

Matthew Sweet, *Inventing the Victorians* (London: Faber and Faber, 2001).
—, *The West End Front: The Wartime Secrets of London's Grand Hotels* (London: Faber and Faber, 2011).
John Tosh, *Manliness and Masculinities in Nineteenth-Century Britain: Essays on Gender, Family and Empire* (London: Longman, 2005).
Amanda Vickery (ed.), *Women, Privilege and Power: British Politics, 1750 to the Present* (Stanford, California: Stanford University Press, 2001).
John Vincent, *The Formation of the Liberal Party 1857–1868* (London: Constable, 1966).
Jack Wales, *Charlton Park, Bishopsbourne: History of the House, the Land and the People* (Bishopsbourne: privately published, 2016).
Arnold White, *The Hidden Hand* (London: G. Richards, 1917).
Paul Willetts, *Members Only: The Life and Times of Paul Raymond* (London: Serpent's Tail, 2010).
Martin Young, *Opposable Truths* (London: Matador, 2015).

Chapters
T. G. Ashplant, 'London Working Men's Clubs, 18751914', in Eileen Yeo and Stephen Yeo (eds), *Popular Culture and Class Conflict, 1590–1914: Explorations in the History of Labour and Leisure* (Sussex: Harvester Press, 1981).
Valérie Capdeville, 'Taste as the ultimate refinement of London club culture and sociability', in Frédéric Ogée & Peter Wagner (eds), *Taste and the Senses in the Eighteenth Century* (Trier: Wissenschaftlicher Verlag Trier, 'LAPASEC', Vol. 3, 2011), pp. 285–97.
Valerie Capdeville 'Transferring the British Club Model to the American Colonies: Mapping Spaces and Networks of Power (1720–70)', *RSEAA*, XVII–XVIII, 74 (2017).
Brian Cowan, 'Pasqua Rosée', *Dictionary of National Biography* (2006).
Hunter Davies (ed.), *The New London Spy: An Intimate Guide to the City's Pleasures* (London: Anthony Blond, 1966), pp. 190–203.
John Davis, 'Radical Clubs and London Politics, 1870–1900', in David Feldman and Gareth Stedman-Jones (eds), *Metropolis London: Histories and Representations since 1800* (London: Routledge, 1989).

Elizabeth F. Evans, 'Women's Clubs and Clubwomen: "Neutral Territory," Feminist Heterotopia, and Failed "Diplomacy"', in *Threshold Modernism: New Public Women and the Literary Spaces of Imperial London* (Cambridge: Cambridge University Press, 2019).

Henry Leach, 'In London's Lesser Club-Land', in George R. Sims (ed.), *Living London*, Vol. III (London: Cassell, 1902), pp. 159–65.

Robert Machray, 'A Saturday Night with the "Savages"', in Robert Machray, *The Night Side of London* (Philadelphia: J. B. Lippincott, 1902), pp. 74–90.

—, 'La Vie de Bohème', in Robert Machray, *The Night Side of London* (Philadelphia: J. B. Lippincott, 1902), pp. 199–216.

Stephen Potter, 'Clubmanship', *One-Upmanship* (London: Rupert Hart-Davis, 1952), pp. 123–8.

Sir Wemys Reid, 'In London Club-Land', in George R. Syms (ed.), *Living London*, Vol. I (London: Cassell, 1902), pp. 74–80.

Kenneth Tynan, 'Introduction', in Lenny Bruce, *How to Talk Dirty and Influence People* (London: Peter Owen, 1966), pp. 8–11.

Articles

Mike Aherne, 'A Dangerous Obsession? Gambling and Social Stability', Judith Rowbotham and Kim Stevenson (eds), *Behaving Badly: Social Panic and Moral Outrage – Victorian and Modern Parallels* (Aldershot: Ashgate, 2003), pp. 127–41.

William Aytoun, 'Clubs and Clubbists', *Blackwood's Edinburgh Magazine*, 73 (March 1853), pp. 265–77.

Antoinette Burton, 'Tongues Untied: Lord Salisbury's "Black Man" and the Boundaries of Imperial Democracy', *Comparative Studies in Society and History*, 42:3 (July 2000), pp. 632–61.

Valérie Capdeville, 'Gender at Stake: the Role of Eighteenth-century London Clubs in Shaping a New Model of English Masculinity', *Culture, Society & Masculinities*, 4:1 (Spring 2012), pp. 13–32.

—, 'Convivialité et sociabilité : le club londonien, un modèle unique en son genre?', *Revue Lumières*, 21 (June 2013).

—, 'The Ambivalent Identity of Eighteenth-Century London Clubs as a Prelude to Victorian Clublife', *Cahiers victoriens et édouardiens,* 81 (Spring 2015).

—, 'Noise and Sound Reconciled: How London Clubs Shaped Conversation into a Social Art', *Études Épistémè*, 29 (2016).

—, '"Clubability": A Revolution in London Sociability?', *Lumen*, 35 (2016), pp. 63–80.

—, 'Transferring the British Club Model to the American Colonies: Mapping Spaces and Networks of Power (1720–70)', *Révue de la Société d'Études Anglo-Américaines*, XVII–XVIII:74 (2017).

Benjamin B. Cohen, 'Social Clubs in a Princely State: The Case from Hyderabad, Deccan', *Indian Historical Review* (2022), forthcoming in print at time of writing; first pub. online, 17 October 2021.

Peter Harris, 'A Meeting Place for Liberals', *Journal of Liberal History*, 51 (Summer 2006), pp. 18–23.

Abraham Hayward, 'Clubs', *Fraser's Magazine*, 73 (March 1866), pp. 342, 362–7.

Alfred Kinnear, 'London Clubs', *Munsey's Magazine* (February 1902).

Marrisa Joseph, 'Members Only: The Victorian Gentlemen's Club as a Space for Doing Business 1843–1900', *Management & Organizational History*, 14:2 (2019), pp. 123–47.

Sol Pérez Martínez, 'Club Architecture: A Vessel of Behavior, Language and Politics', *ARQ*, 92 (Santiago, Chile, abr. 2016), pp. 104–13.

Mira Matikkala, 'William Dibgy and the Indian Question', *Journal of Liberal History*, 58 (Spring 2008), pp. 12–21.

Amy Milne-Smith, 'A Flight to Domesticity? Making a Home in the Gentlemen's Clubs of London, 1880–1914', *Journal of British Studies*, 45 (2006), pp. 796–818.

—, 'Club Talk: Gossip, Masculinity, and the Importance of Oral Communities in Late Nineteenth-Century London', *Gender and History*, 21 (2009), pp. 86–109.

Nicholas Owen, 'MacDonald's Parties: The Labour Party and the "Aristocratic Embrace", 1922–31', *Twentieth Century British History*, 18:1 (2007), pp. 1–53.

Stephen Potter, 'Confessions of a Clubman', *Holiday*, Vol. 19, No. 4, April 1956, pp. 114, 154–8.

Richard Price, 'The Working Men's Club Movement, and Victorian Social Reform Ideology', *Victorian Studies*, 15 (1971), pp. 117–47.

W. Fraser Rae, 'Political Clubs and Party Organisation', *Nineteenth Century*, 3 (1878), pp. 908–32.

Jane Rendell, 'The Clubs of St. James's: Places of Public Patriarchy – Exclusivity, Domesticity and Secrecy', *Journal of Architecture*, 4 (1999), pp. 167–89.
Henry Solly, 'Working Men's Clubs and Institutes', *Fraser's Magazine*, 71 (March 1865), pp. 383–95.
Seth Alexander Thévoz, 'Club Government', *History Today*, 63:2 (February 2013), pp. 58–9.
—, 'The Diogenes Club: The Case for the Junior Carlton Club', *Baker Street Journal*, 69:3 (Autumn 2019), pp. 6–24.
—, 'The Mystery of Doctor Watson's Club', *Sherlock Holmes Journal*, 35:1 (Winter 2019), pp. 110–16.

Academic papers
Neil Carter, 'British Boxing's Colour Bar, 1911–48', n.d., https://www.academia.edu/3190661/British_Boxing_s_Colour_Bar_1911_48
Peter Marsh, 'The Reform Club: Architecture and the Birth of Popular Government', Gresham College lecture, 25 September 2007.
Antonia Taddei, 'London Clubs in the Late Nineteenth Century', University of Oxford Discussion Papers in Economic and Social History, No. 28 (April 1999).
Seth Alexander Thévoz, 'Clubonomics', North American Conference on British Studies, Vancouver, November 2019.

Theses
Genevieve Arblaster-Hulley, 'The National Liberal Club: A late nineteenth century clubhouse in context', MSt thesis, Cambridge University, 2019.
Brendan Mackie, draft chapter from a forthcoming PhD thesis on eighteenth-century English clubs, University of California, Berkeley.
Seth Alexander Thévoz, 'The Political Impact of London Clubs, 1832–68', PhD thesis, Warwick University, 2014.

Film and TV
A Very Social Democrat: A Portrait of Roy Jenkins (1996), dir. Michael Cockerell.
American Playboy: The Hugh Hefner Story, episode 10, 'My Way' (2017), dir. Richard Lopez.

Gay Life, 'Being Gay in the Thirties' episode (1981), dir. John Oven.
Heroes of Comedy: Peter Cook (1998), dir. Tom Atkinson.
The Mayfair Set (1998), dir. Adam Curtis.
Panorama, 'Taken for a Ride' episode (1981), dir. Martin Young.
Saturday Night Clive, episode 4.8 (1991), dir. Dominic Brigstocke.
Unnatural Causes, 'Ladies' Night' episode (1986), dir. Herbert Wise, w. Nigel Kneale.
Yes, Minister, TV series (1980–84), dir. various, w. Jonathan Lynn and Antony Jay.

Websites consulted

'The Amateur Championship: A Potted History', *English Amateur Billiards Association*, 14 April 2013, https://www.eaba.co.uk/?p=5885
'Carlton Club Votes Against Women', *BBC News*, 30 November 2000, http://news.bbc.co.uk/1/hi/uk_politics/1048081.stm.
'International Association of Lyceum Clubs' website, https://www.lyceumclubs.org/
'Should men-only private members' clubs still exist?', *Today in Focus Guardian* podcast, 25 September 2020, https://podcasts.apple.com/gb/podcast/should-men-only-private-members-clubs-still-exist/id1440133626?i=1000492445041
Winston S. Churchill, 'The Dream' [short story, c.1947, unpublished in Churchill's lifetime], reproduced online at *The Churchill Project: Hillsdale College*, https://winstonchurchill.hillsdale.edu/winston-churchills-dream-1947/
Terry Lazarus, 'Curzon House Club Plaques Available', *The Chip Board*, 17 October 1999, archived at http://www.thechipboard.com/archives/archives.pl/bid/302/md/read/id/39441/sbj/curzon-house-club-plaques-available-london-70-s/
Gemma Perlin, Jess-Luisa Flynn and Nimrod Kamer, 'Women in White's – Penetrating an All-Male Safe Space', *YouTube*, 27 January 2018, https://www.youtube.com/watch?v=olPstpyHZt4
Seth Thévoz, 'Inside the Elite Tory Fundraising Machine', *openDemocracy*, 9 December 2019, https://www.opendemocracy.net/en/dark-money-investigations/inside-elite-tory-fundraising-machine/

INDEX